KARAKALPAKSTAN

T0272549

SOPHIE IBBOTSON & STEPHANIE ADAMS

www.bradtguides.com

Bradt Guides Ltd, UK
The Globe Pequot Press Inc, USA

Bradt GUIDES

TRAVEL TAKEN SERIOUSLY

First edition published June 2023
Bradt Guides Ltd
31a High Street, Chesham, Buckinghamshire, HP5 1BW, England
www.bradtguides.com
Print edition published in the USA by The Globe Pequot Press Inc,
PO Box 480, Guilford, Connecticut 06437-0480

Text copyright © 2023 Bradt Guides
Maps copyright © 2023 Bradt Guides Ltd; includes map data ©
OpenStreetMap contributors
Photographs copyright © 2023 Individual photographers (see below)
Project Manager: Anna Moores
Cover research: Ian Spick, Bradt Guides

ISBN: 9781804690819

British Library Cataloguing in Publication Data
A catalogue record for this book is available from the British Library

Photographs © individual photographers credited beside images and also those
from picture libraries credited as follows: Alamy (A); Shutterstock.com (S)

Front cover View over the Aral Sea from the cliffs on the Ustyurt Plateau (Azamat
Matkarimov)
Back cover Clockwise from top left: Savitsky Museum, Nukus (monticello/S);
Mizdakhan (MehmetO/S); Saiga antelope (Yakov Oskanov/S); Festival goer at
Stihia (Rakhim Kalibaev/Stihia Festival)
Title page Clockwise from top left: Camel in a yurt camp (Anya Newrcha/S);
Mizdakhan (monticello/S); Handicrafts on sale (Nicole Haeusler)

Maps David McCutcheon FBCart.S

Typeset by Ian Spick, Bradt Guides
Production managed by Page Bros; printed in UK
Digital conversion by www.dataworks.co.in

AUTHORS

Sophie Ibbotson is the founder of Maximum Exposure Ltd, a tourism and culture development consultancy focused on emerging destinations. She has a particular interest in Afghanistan and Central Asia, where she has worked since 2008 for national and regional governments and for the World Bank. Sophie is Chairman of the Royal Society for Asian Affairs, which was founded in 1901 as the Central Asia Society; Uzbekistan's Ambassador for Tourism; and the author of Bradt Guides' *Uzbekistan*. Her writing about Central Asia is widely published, including in *The Telegraph*, *The Economist* and *The Independent*.

Stephanie Adams is a bilingual (English and Russian) writer and researcher who has lived and studied in England, Russia, Tunisia, Kyrgyzstan and Georgia. She recently graduated from the University of Plymouth with a degree in English and Publishing, and is currently studying an MA in Fashion Journalism at the University of the Arts London. Her travel writing has been published in outlets including *Asian Geographic*, *TNT Magazine* and *The Travel Magazine*, and she also contributed to Bradt's *Uzbekistan* and *Tajikistan* guidebooks.

FEEDBACK REQUEST

At Bradt Guides we're aware that guidebooks start to go out of date on the day they're published – and that you, our readers, are out there in the field doing research of your own. You'll find out before us when a fine new family-run hotel opens or a favourite restaurant changes hands and goes downhill. So why not tell us about your experiences? Contact us on ☎ 01753 893444 e info@bradtguides.com. We will forward emails to the author who may post updates on the Bradt website at w bradtguides.com/updates. Alternatively, you can add a review of the book to Amazon, or share your adventures with us on social:

f BradtGuides
🐦 BradtGuides & UZAmbassador
📷 BradtGuides & uzambassador

Acknowledgements

SOPHIE IBBOTSON The idea for this guidebook germinated during the Covid pandemic, and it is a tribute to so many people's persistence that it survived and finally made it to print. From the very beginning, Gulbahor Izentaeva, Culture and Tourism Advisor to the Government of Karakalpakstan, was its greatest cheerleader, and without her determination, enthusiasm, knowledge and contacts, you wouldn't be holding this book in your hands today. We also received ideas and practical help from Karakalpakstan's Ministry of Tourism and the Department of Cultural Heritage, the Mayor of Nukus, and Uzbektourism and the National PR Centre in Tashkent.

Finding people who share your passion for a place is vital, especially when they provide their insights and recommendations and become friends. I'm immensely grateful to Tigran Mkrtychev, Julian Felten and Nora Heinonen for many conversations, email exchanges and cups of tea; and to Azamat Matkarimov, whose extraordinary photo adorns the cover. Joe Bull and Elena Bykova contributed a great deal to this guide's coverage of natural history and protected areas, and I discovered Karakalpak literature, in particular its poets, thanks to Andrew Staniland. Otabek Suleimanov and Sanjar Halmuradov welcomed me (and my dad) to the Stihia Festival with open arms, and Sanjar rose to yet another challenge when he and Farrukh Rakhmanov of Peopletravel organised my ground logistics for the book's final research trip. Farrukh: thank you for being the most patient and committed of travel buddies. Adrian Phillips, Claire Strange and Laura Osborne at Bradt Guides all seemed to have unshakeable faith in the guide and in readers' curiosity about the destination. As always, you've been hugely supportive and produced a brilliant book.

My parents, Sharon and John, travelled with me not once but twice to Karakalpakstan, throwing themselves into everything from desert fortresses to sandstorms, a children's holiday camp to electronic music, and providing plenty of valuable feedback. And last but most importantly of all, Ed. I love you more than anything and after every adventure you make it worth coming home.

STEPHANIE ADAMS When Sophie told me about the idea for this travel guide, I knew it would be such an amazing experience. Karakalpakstan isn't well known, and hopefully this guide will help people learn more about this beautiful republic. The people I met on my travels showed what it means to be Karakalpak, what it means to be proud of their heritage, culture, and way of life. Everyone wanted to tell me their stories, and see them printed in this guide. I'm so honoured to have been involved in the research and writing of this guide, and will never forget the people I met on the way.

First, I would like to thank Bakhitjar Utemuratov, my trusted driver during my research trip to Karakalpakstan, and Islambek Seytbaev from the Department of

Cultural Heritage. They were my companions throughout the journey, showing me their beautiful republic, making my trip so comfortable, and teaching me a lot. I wouldn't have been able to do it without them both. Thank you also to Elshad from the Ministry of Tourism, to Gulbahor Izentaeva, and to every single person I met on the trip.

The biggest thank you is to Sophie Ibbotson, for being a long-time friend, colleague, and the best mentor anyone could wish for. I owe so much to you, and will never stop thanking you for everything you have helped me do. Lastly, thank you to my mum Irina Adams, my dad Mark Adams, and my sister Anna Kopach, for being the biggest supporters and always celebrating my wins with me.

AUTHORS' STORY

Karakalpakstan is not just the Aral Sea; it is not just a disaster tourism destination. It was the desire to challenge this limited view and show the destination in all its complicated, fascinating glory which made us want to write this book, the very first guidebook to Karakalpakstan. After all, if potential tourists aren't inspired by a place and what it can offer, and they struggle to find the practical information required to make a trip idea into a reality, they are highly unlikely to visit. And that would be a huge loss to both the would-be visitors and to the people of Karakalpakstan.

Over the course of 2021/22, just as the world was reopening after Covid-19, we undertook four research trips to Karakalpakstan. We wanted to travel as far as possible within the autonomous republic, but also to dig deep, which is why we returned to places such as Nukus, Muynak, and the desert fortresses time and again. It was the Aral Sea which had the most magnetic appeal however, whichever side we looked at it from.

Seeing the Aral Sea for the first time comes with a whole gamut of emotions which will take some time to process. First, the sea is a shimmer in the distance, which could well be a desert mirage. Then, it is a strip of greyish blue along the horizon. Navigating the way down the track from the top of the Ustyurt cliffs to the seabed, between crumbling pillars and stacks and chinks, takes impressive driving skills. We drove past the abandoned, derelict buildings which once formed the old military port, and stopped on the jetty where a depth marker confirms that the water level is still dropping. Stripping off socks and shoes, dangling our legs off the edge and then plunging knee-deep into the water for a paddle brought with it childlike excitement. I can't describe it as hope, because the Aral Sea's future prospects are bleak, but for a few moments there was relief: the sea is still here, albeit as a shadow of its former self.

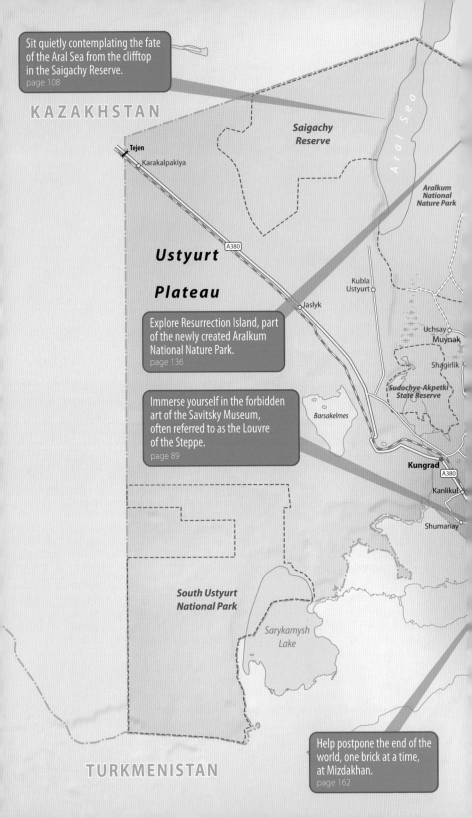

Sit quietly contemplating the fate of the Aral Sea from the clifftop in the Saigachy Reserve.
page 108

KAZAKHSTAN

Saigachy Reserve

Tejen

Karakalpakiya

Aralkum National Nature Park

Aral Sea

Ustyurt

A380

Plateau

Kubla Ustyurt

Jaslyk

Uchsay

Muynak

Shģirlik

Explore Resurrection Island, part of the newly created Aralkum National Nature Park.
page 136

Sudochye-Akpetki State Reserve

Barsakelmes

Immerse yourself in the forbidden art of the Savitsky Museum, often referred to as the Louvre of the Steppe.
page 89

Kungrad

A380

Kanlikul

Shumanay

South Ustyurt National Park

Sarykamysh Lake

Help postpone the end of the world, one brick at a time, at Mizdakhan.
page 162

TURKMENISTAN

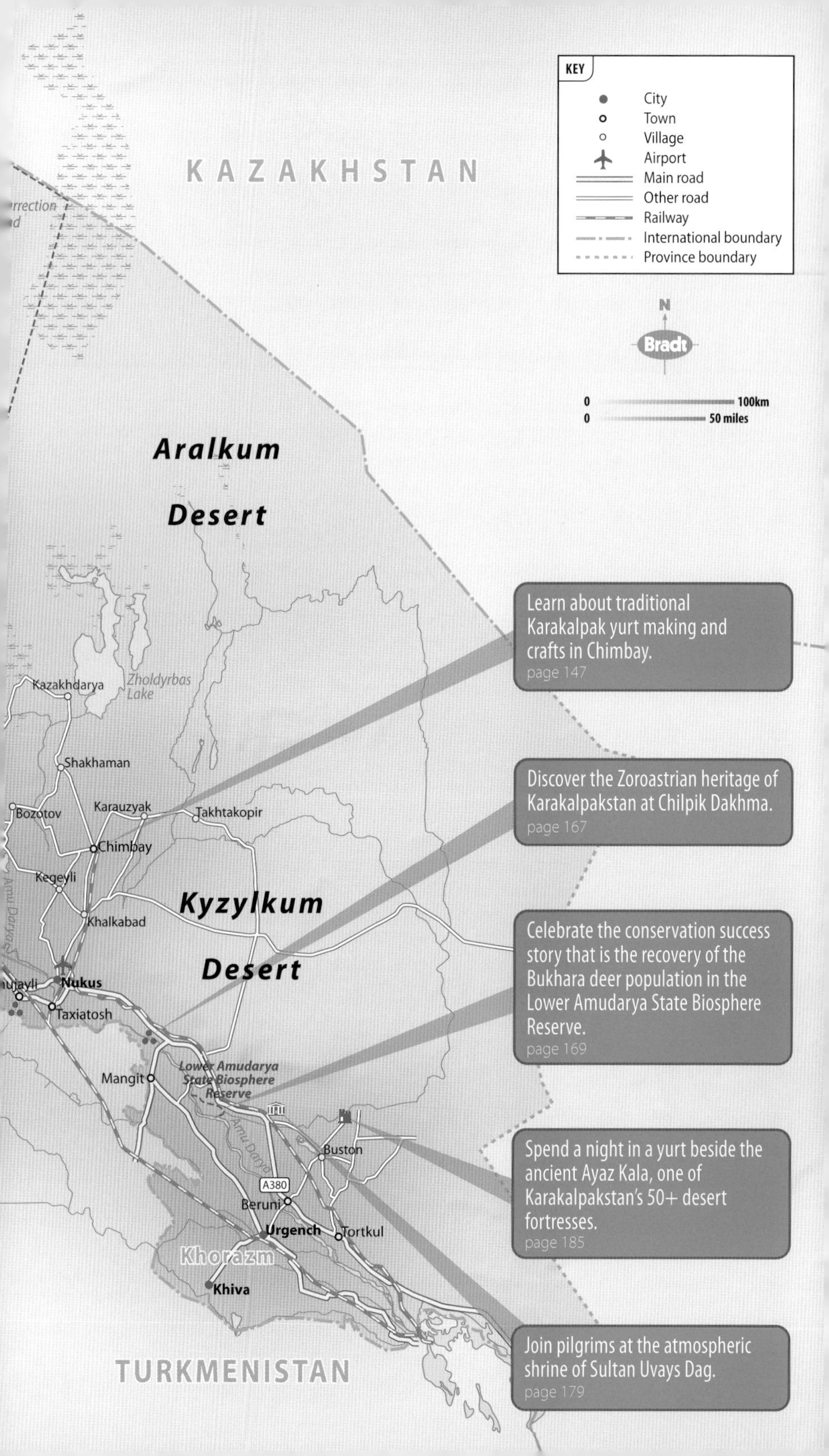

KAZAKHSTAN
KEY
City
Town
Village
Airport
Main road
Other road
Railway
International boundary
Province boundary
N
Bradt
0 100km
0 50 miles
Aralkum
Desert
Kazakhdarya
Zholdyrbas
Lake
Shakhaman
Bozotov
Karauzyak
Takhtakopir
Chimbay
Kegeyli
Kyzylkum
Khalkabad
Desert
Amu Darya
Nukus
Taxiatosh
Mangit
Lower Amudarya
State Biosphere
Reserve
Amu Darya
Buston
A380
Beruni
Urgench
Tortkul
Khorazm
Khiva
TURKMENISTAN
Learn about traditional Karakalpak yurt making and crafts in Chimbay.
page 147
Discover the Zoroastrian heritage of Karakalpakstan at Chilpik Dakhma.
page 167
Celebrate the conservation success story that is the recovery of the Bukhara deer population in the Lower Amudarya State Biosphere Reserve.
page 169
Spend a night in a yurt beside the ancient Ayaz Kala, one of Karakalpakstan's 50+ desert fortresses.
page 185
Join pilgrims at the atmospheric shrine of Sultan Uvays Dag.
page 179

Contents

LIST OF MAPS

Introduction

'How can you write a guidebook about Karakalpakstan? There's nothing for tourists here!' This wasn't a reassuring start to one of the first conversations we had with a local on arrival in Nukus. It was a message we'd heard time and again in Uzbekistan, but even that was one up from 'Karakalpak-what?', which was the usual response abroad. If you are seeking adventure in an under-the-radar destination in already out-of-the-way Central Asia, Karakalpakstan is the place to go. It is such a well-kept secret, in fact, that even the most well-travelled of tourists is unlikely to have heard about it, let alone have been there.

This book, the first ever guidebook to the Autonomous Republic of Karakalpakstan, is our challenge to all those who have a black hole in their knowledge of geography, lack imagination or curiosity, or simply won't make the effort to see what to us is now blindingly obvious: Karakalpakstan is an extraordinary place. Just over twice the size of Scotland, with a similar land area to Tunisia, and with human history dating back to the Palaeolithic period, it's a destination that deserves not only more attention but also more respect.

The tragic thing is that even if people haven't heard of Karakalpakstan, they may well know about the Aral Sea. The shrinking of what was within living memory the world's fourth largest lake is one of the most serious – if not the most serious – manmade environmental disasters of the 20th century. And in Karakalpakstan the water level is now so low, and the end of the river so far from the shore, that the Aral Sea has passed the point of no return. It is no longer a case of wondering if the sea will disappear completely, but simply a question of when. If you do want the privilege of looking out at the last of the sea, watching the sunset shimmering on its waters, and perhaps even paddling in its waters, you had better get your skates on.

On a much happier note, the Aral Sea disaster has cast a spotlight on Karakalpakstan's fragile ecosystems and directed much needed funding and expertise to conservation issues. There are now two national parks, both created since 2020, plus the Lower Amudarya State Biosphere Reserve, Saigachy Reserve and Sudochye-Akpetki State Reserve. Bukhara deer were on the brink of extinction in the 1970s but thanks to a reintroduction and breeding programme they are now thriving; and the Saiga Conservation Alliance is actively monitoring, managing and educating local people about the importance of saiga antelope, stabilising their populations, too. The stargazing in these protected areas is second to none, and thanks to a growing number of yurt camps in the deserts and on the shores of the Aral Sea you can spend a comfortable night out in the wild.

Turning now to its history, Karakalpakstan has long been on the frontier of Central Asian and Persian empires, all of which built substantial fortifications,

---

1 Sudochye Lakes (page 132). 2 Aral Sea Monument (page 126). 3 Toprak Kala (page 182).
4 Stihia Festival (page 128). ▶

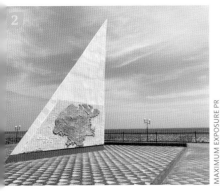

and so you would be hard pushed to find anywhere in the world with a higher concentration of archaeological sites. You can see Neolithic petroglyphs made by a sophisticated ancient culture. There are more than 50 desert fortresses, many of which date back to the 1st millennium BC and are remarkably well preserved thanks to Karakalpakstan's dry climate. Necropolises, shrines and even a Zoroastrian tower of silence teach about the beliefs and burial practices of people who lived hundreds and sometimes thousands of years ago. And if you want to find out how to delay Armageddon, you need to visit Mizdakhan.

The intangible cultural heritage of the Karakalpaks and other communities living in Karakalpakstan is no less fascinating. Museums give a hint of the richness of the region's applied arts, but to really understand and appreciate Karakalpakstan's folk traditions it is best to visit Chimbay with its workshops of yurt makers, reed weavers, sculptors, jewellers and more. You can lose yourself in music and dance, and in the epic stories that have been transmitted in song from one generation to the next. Then, of course, there's the food, with its mouthwatering, multicultural tastes of the Silk Roads, with flavours reminiscent of Turkey, Iran, China, and India, all combined with a local twist.

Karakalpakstan's history and traditions are strong, but they are a foundation for development rather than tying people down to the past. Russian collector Igor Savitksy showed remarkable bravery and foresight in challenging Soviet authorities when he amassed his vast and controversial avant garde art collection in the 1960s and 1970s and preserved it for the world in Nukus, Karakalpakstan's capital; and the founders of Stihia Festival recognised the potential of Muynak, a former fishing port now miles from the Aral Sea to host what has unpredictably become Central Asia's foremost electronic music event. What you will find time

KEY TO SYMBOLS

— ·— ·	International boundary	⸠	Mosque
═══	Main road	Ⓒ	Cemetery
═══	Minor road	⌂	Yurt camp
══════	Track	🏛	Tomb/mausoleum
═══	Railway	☆	Soviet mosaic
☐	Railway station	⁚⁚	Archaeological/historic site
✈	Airport	⤛	Birdwatching
🚁	Heliport	❄	Viewpoint
🚌	Bus station	⤙	Border crossing
🚕	Taxis	•	Other place of interest
🯄	Museum/art gallery	🖈	Sports stadium
🎭	Theatre		National park/reserve/protected area
🏰	Castle/fort		Urban park
✉	Post office	⬨	Urban market/square
$	Bank		Marsh/wetlands
✚	Hospital/clinic		Salt lake/pan
✚	Pharmacy		

and again in Karakalpakstan is that people surprise you in wonderful ways, and whatever challenges they face, natural or manmade, they respond with creativity, determination and resilience.

Part One

GENERAL INFORMATION

Location Northwestern Uzbekistan, landlocked in Central Asia
Neighbouring countries Kazakhstan, Turkmenistan, Uzbekistan
Size/area 166,590km²
Climate Extreme continental climate with low rainfall
Status Autonomous Republic
Population 1.97 million (2022)
Life expectancy 71.7 years (men), 75.8 years (women)
Capital Nukus, population 329,100 (2022)
Other main towns Beruni, Chimbay, Khujayli, Kungrad, Muynak, Taxiatosh
Economy Agriculture, in particular cotton; natural resources, with large gas reserves; some manufacturing
GDP US$2.37 billion (2021)
Languages Karakalpak, Uzbek, Russian
Religion Sunni Islam
Currency Uzbek som (UZS)
Exchange rate £1 = UZS14,400; US$1 = UZS11,450; €1 = UZS12,530 (May 2023)
National airline/airport Uzbekistan Airways, Nukus International Airport
International telephone code +998
Time UTC +5
Electrical voltage 220AC (50Hz)
Weights and measures Metric
Flag Three horizontal bands of blue, yellow and green, separated from each other with thinner red and white lines. In the top left corner is a white crescent moon and five white stars.
National anthem 'Qaraqalpaqstan Respublikasınıń Mámleketlik Gimni'
National bird Kumai, a mythical bird which spends its whole life in flight
National sport Angalaq, a native game akin to hockey
Public holidays 14 January (Day of Defenders of the Fatherland); 8 March (International Women's Day); 21 March (Nowruz); 9 May (Remembrance Day); 1 September (Independence Day); 1 October (Teachers' Day); 8 December (Constitution Day); 31 December–4 January (New Year). The dates of Eid al Fitr and Eid al Adha change in the Gregorian calendar each year.

Background Information

GEOGRAPHY AND CLIMATE

Karakalpakstan lies in the heart of Central Asia, an autonomous republic within the already doubly landlocked Republic of Uzbekistan. To its east and southeast are Uzbekistan's Navoi, Bukhara and Khorezm regions; to the south is Turkmenistan; and to the west and north is the Republic of Kazakhstan. In total, Karakalpakstan covers an area of 166,590km² (64,320 square miles) and is roughly contiguous with the oasis known historically as Khwarazm or Khorezm. Most but not all of the territory is desert, covered with the transboundary Aralkum (Aral Desert), Kyzylkum (Red Desert) and Ustyurt Plateau.

Look closer, and you will appreciate the subtle differences in Karakalpakstan's landscapes. To the west, the seemingly endless flat and arid scrublands of the Ustyurt Plateau average a height just 150m above sea level. The plateau is remote, dry, and experiences extremely variable temperatures ranging from −30˚C in the winter to +50˚C in the summer. The annual rainfall here is as little as 120mm, most of which falls in the autumn and winter.

From Ustyurt, short picturesque 'chink' cliffs descend to the now partially vegetated desert left behind by the almost complete disappearance of the Aral Sea (page 4). The remnant Southern Aral Sea is strikingly beautiful against this backdrop, but what was once the world's fourth largest lake shrinks more and more every year. In the middle of the former sea basin is situated, among other islands, Vozrozhdeniya (Resurrection Island; page 136), though with the lack of water it is now more of a peninsula. Vozrozhdeniya is characterised by interesting sandstone geology (page 7), and otherwise covered in scrub and patches of low-lying saxaul (*Halyoxylon*) forests. Manmade climate change causes horrendous sand and dust storms here, which the World Bank estimates now carry as much as 75 million tonnes of sand, dust and salt across Central Asia every year, resulting in soil erosion, air pollution and consequently a negative impact on both the natural environment and human health.

To the south of the former sea lies the fertile agricultural lands of the Amu Darya river delta, stretching all the way to Karakalpakstan's capital, Nukus. The Amu Darya was known to the Ancient Greeks as the River Oxus, and from its source in the Pamir Mountains in Afghanistan's Wakhan Corridor it winds its way 2,540km to Karakalpakstan. The Amu Darya is the lifeblood of all Central Asia, but as so much water has been taken out for irrigation, or is lost to leakage and evaporation, that it no longer reaches the Aral Sea but rather peters out into the lakes and marshes of Sudochye and Kok Su.

To the east of the Aral Sea lies the Uzbek portion of the vast Kyzylkum, a place of red sand dunes and saline depressions that stretches across an area the size of Italy, reaching as far east as the Zarafshan Mountains on the border of Uzbekistan and

THE ARAL SEA

It is within living memory that the Aral Sea was the fourth largest lake in the world, equivalent to Georgia or Sri Lanka in size. Created in the late Neogene period (23 million to 2.6 million years ago) when water from the Syr Darya began flowing into a natural depression, the sea endured alternating wet and dry spells until the early Holocene Epoch (around 11,700 years ago) when the Amu Darya changed its course and the combined waters of Central Asia's two greatest rivers maintained consistently high water levels. In recent centuries there was never more than 6m fluctuation between the maximum and minimum water levels, and the annual variation didn't exceed 3m.

Clearly evident from the 1960s onwards, the Aral Sea began to shrink. More and more water was taken out of the river system to irrigate water-intensive crops such as cotton, reducing the two rivers' flow (page 144). The water level fell, the sea retreated from its former coastline, and by 1989 it had split into two separate parts, the Greater Sea and the Lesser Sea. The Aral Sea was also almost three times more saline than it had been in the mid 20th century, making the water unfit to drink and uninhabitable for many of the species of fish which had previously flourished here. With a shore now far away from the harbours, with boats stranded in the desert and dramatically decreasing volumes of fish, the once highly profitable Aral Sea fishing industry was all but destroyed. Towns such

as Muynak, which depended economically on catching and processing fish, were devastated and hope is ebbing that they can ever revive.

The shrinking of the Aral Sea is the epitome of a collapsed ecosystem, and is often cited as the worst manmade environmental disaster of the 20th century. Tragically, it was not ignorance that caused the problem: Soviet irrigation engineers knew the likely outcome of these politically and economically motivated schemes, and voiced their concerns about the predictable fate of the Aral Sea, but the Politburo pressed ahead with its five-year plans regardless, considering the disappearance of the lake a price worth paying for increased agricultural output.

Preserving what is left of the Aral Sea and stabilising the ecosystem has become a multi-billion dollar project, but one with no guarantee of success. The construction of a concrete dam in Kazakhstan's North Aral Sea, and at the same time repairs and improvements to the Syr Darya irrigation channels, have resulted in a notable rise in water levels and reduction in salinity, but sadly this option isn't viable for the Southern Aral Sea in Karakalpakstan. Here, the authorities seem to be resigned to the sea's fate and instead are focusing efforts on planting saxaul and other drought-resistant plants to reduce desertification, diversifying the agricultural sector to reduce dependence on cotton, and attempting to mitigate the economic damage and health problems wrought on local communities.

Tajikistan. The altitude here is a little higher than on the Ustyurt Plateau, and the continental climate is less extreme, but still one of cold winters and warm summers, with plenty of sunshine and little precipitation.

Karakalpakstan's natural spaces are punctuated with urban centres, though Nukus is the only city of any great size. Only a few of the district capitals, Chimbay and Khujayli among them, have more than 50,000 inhabitants, and half the population lives in rural areas.

NATURAL HISTORY AND CONSERVATION

GEOLOGY The easiest way to think about the geology of Karakalpakstan is to divide the republic into two separate zones. The Ustyurt Plateau in the northwest is composed primarily of Sarmatian limestone, which was formed sometime between 23.7 million and 5.3 million years ago. Sarmatian deposits typically contain the fossils of bryozoans, clams and gastropods (which gives them a chalky whitish colour), as well as ferromanganese nodules, marine sedimentary mineral deposits, evidence that this area was once beneath the Tethys Sea.

Steep escarpments divide the edge of the plateau from adjoining territories. This is where you will see the impressive 'chinks' – near vertical slopes – and also the pillars and cliffs which are collectively known as the Aral Sea Canyons, though they are not actually canyons at all. The best place to see these marvellous geological formations is on the eastern side of the Saigachy Reserve (page 108), an area UNESCO is considering developing as a Global Geopark.

In southern Karakalpakstan, within the flat alluvial plain of the Amu Darya, the geology is entirely different. The plain comprises sand, loam and clay deposits, interspersed with layers of silt and finer sand. Much of the soil is saline, and around lakes and in depressions it becomes very boggy due to the height of the water table.

Karakalpakstan is rich in raw materials, and mining is a critical component of the local economy. Sodium chloride (rock salt) collects naturally in the Aral Sea Basin and there are two major deposits, one at Barsakelmes (page 105) and the other at Qaraumbet Solonchak, a gulf in the Ustyurt chink. Visiting Barsakelmes on a tour you might well see artisanal salt harvesting; the other site is exploited on an industrial scale, with a plant big enough to produce more than 100,000 tonnes of soda ash every year.

It is estimated that the Dzheroy Phosphate Field in eastern Karakalpakstan has reserves of 300 million tonnes. What is more, the phosphate rock is no more than 50m beneath the surface, making it relatively easy to extract. Marble quarried on the Ustyurt Plateau is processed at Nukus Marble Plant and used in high-end construction projects; gravel and other crushed stones are extracted from the Sultan Uvays Dag Mountains in southeastern Karakalpakstan; and clay and iron are plentiful, too. In terms of higher-value minerals, Sultan Uvays Dag has been known as a source of turquoise since ancient times, and there are multiple large deposits of silver, gold and uranium in the Kyzylkum. Open-cast mining would be economically viable here, but significant investment would be required to begin operations.

FLORA The deserts and scrublands of Karakalpakstan contain more than 100 species of vascular plant but are particularly characterised by low-lying scrub vegetation communities (dominated by different species of Artemisia and Anabasis), with occasional patches of highly valuable saxaul (*Haloxylon ammodendron*) 'forest'. This critical plant (page 8) is widely used in attempts to halt desertification.

◀ 1 The arid scrublands of the Ustyurt Plateau. 2 The Amu Darya Delta stretches past Nukus.

Travelling across Karakalpakstan you will probably notice more saxaul (*Haloxylon ammodendron*) than any other plant. In dry desert climates it is most often a shrub, but when its nutritional and hydration needs are met it can grow into a tree up to 8m tall. It is a member of the Amaranthaceae family of flowering plants, which includes distant relatives such as spinach (*Spinacia oleracea*) and sugarbeet (*Beta vulgaris*). Saxaul is distributed across the lowlands of Central Asia, especially in desert and steppe ecosystems in Karakalpakstan, southern Kazakhstan and Turkmenistan.

The trunk of a saxaul bush is heavy, coarse and resinous. It makes good firewood and was traditionally used by nomads for heating and cooking, but during the 2008 energy crisis many saxaul forests were over-harvested in Karakalpakstan. The collection of saxaul for firewood is therefore discouraged.

By far the most important use of saxaul today, however, is in the fight against climate change. It is hoped that in Karakalpakstan afforestation – planting trees in a place where they did not previously exist – can improve the ecological situation in the dried-up seabed of the Aral Sea. The saxaul stores water, helps to stabilise the soil, and creates a physical barrier against wind and sandstorms. Between 2018 and 2020 alone, the UN and other international donors supported the State Forestry Committee with finance, equipment and technical assistance to plant saxaul on 35,100ha of land. Nurseries have been established in multiple locations to grow seedlings, as this is proven to increase the survival rate of the plants, compared to planting the seeds straight into the wild.

The ecosystems in the Amu Darya plain, including riparian woodland and reedbeds, have a greater variety of plant life. Within the Lower Amudarya State Biosphere Reserve (page 169), two species of poplar, *Populus diversifolia* and *Populus pruinosa*, form the base of the forest. They are endemic and are not found outside Central Asia. There are also smaller numbers of oleaster (commonly known as Russian olive, *Elaeagnus angustifolia*), varieties of tamarisk (*Tamarix*) and willow (*Salix*). Among the trees are plenty of flowering plants, such as oriental clematis (*Clematis orientalis*), pink and white bindweed (*Convolvulus arvensis*) and *Asparagus persicus*. Most of these species are tolerant to salt and their seeds sprout rapidly when they fall in wet silt.

The wetlands are dominated with reedbeds; the types of reeds are known by their local names, *shiy* and *jezshiy*. Here you will also find liquorice (*Glycyrrhiza glabra*), sword leaf dogbane (*Apocynum venetum*), ribwort plantain (*Plantago lanceolata*) and many other herbs and medicinal plants.

FAUNA Karakalpakstan is full of interesting wildlife, if one is patient and knows where to look. This includes endemic and rare species from the IUCN (International Union for the Conservation of Nature) Red List of threatened species.

Birds Historically Karakalpakstan was one of the richest areas in Central Asia for birding: the Russian artist Nikolay Karazin visited in the 1870s and described vividly in his account of the trip how:

1 Eastern imperial eagle. 2 Short-toed snake eagle. 3 Lesser flamingo. 4 Terek sandpipers. ▶

Thousands of birds tweet and twitter in these shady thickets… Large noisy pelicans fly out from the thicket and come down to swim in the open areas; graceful swans touch the bottom after extending their long neck, catching the air with their wings… Pale blue bee-eaters, like a turquoise dot, shake and sparkle in the air, swaying after landing on the tip of a stem only the thickness of a finger… Noisy clouds of rose-coloured starlings arrive, flying in from the coast to hunt the midges and mosquitoes.

The shrinking of the Aral Sea and depletion of water levels in the Amu Darya have severely impacted Karakalpakstan's birdlife, but thankfully there are still pockets of avian biodiversity, including the lakes, marshes and streams in the Aral Sea Basin and also the cliffs on the edge of the Ustyurt Plateau. Migrant species rest here while en route from Siberia to spend the winter in warmer climes (and follow the same route in reverse in the autumn), and in total 307 species of birds can still be sighted here.

The Ustyurt Plateau is fantastic for sightings of birds of prey. There are multiple species of eagles, including tawny (*Aquila rapax*), eastern imperial (*Aquila heliaca*), golden (*Aquila chrysaetos*), white-tailed (*Haliaeetus albicilla*), and short-toed snake eagles (*Circaetus gallicus*), and you can also see steppe kestrel (*Falco naumanni*). These birds particularly like the cliff zone of the Eastern Ustyurt, where the cracks, ledges and ravines provide plenty of places for nesting and resting, and from which to spot small mammals to snack on. You will also see them in large numbers on the cliffs above Old Urga, overlooking Sudochye Lakes.

The cliffs along the western edge of the Aral Sea act as a migration corridor in the spring and autumn, and water birds love the brackish pools and lakes in the Aral Sea Basin, in particular the Sudochye Lakes in the Sudochye-Akpetki State Reserve (page 130). There are plenty of common, purple, and Terek sandpipers (*Actitis hypoleucos*, *Calidris maritima* and *Xenus cinereus*), common and arctic tern (*Sterna hirundo* and *Sterna paradisaea*), oystercatchers (*Haematopus ostralegus*), glossy ibis (*Plegadis falcinellus*), little egret (*Egretta garzetta*) and grey herons (*Ardea cinerea*). Present in large numbers and gorgeous to see are the flamboyances of threatened lesser flamingo (*Phoeniconaias minor*). The flamingo is a migrant species, best seen in April and May on Sudochye and Sarykamysh lakes. The flamingos feast on artemia (page 13), which gives them their pretty pink colour – their feathers otherwise would be greyish white.

Some of the most common species you will see in desert areas of Karakalpakstan include saxaul jays (also known as a Turkestan ground jay, *Podoces panderi*), Zarudny's or Asian desert sparrows (*Passer zarudnyi*) and Eurasian magpies (*Pica pica*). Even in the driest parts of the Ustyurt Plateau there are tawny pipits (*Anthus campestris*) and Eurasian skylarks (*Alauda arvensis*).

There are, as yet, no specialist local bird guides working in Karakalpakstan, though there are very knowledgeable staff at the State Committee for Ecology and Environment Protection (w uznature.uz) and the Academy of Sciences, whose services local tour operators can sometimes hire. However, if you are keen on birding then the easiest thing is to take your own field guide. M Ametov's *Birds of Karakalpakia and their Conservation* (1981) has been published in Russian only and copies can be hard to come by, but M Schweizer, R Ayé and T Roth's *Birds of Central Asia* (2012), part of the Helm Field Guides series, is a fairly comprehensive English-language resource.

Mammals Of the 498 species of vertebrates recorded in Karakalpakstan, 68 of them are mammals. They vary from the small, cute and velvety piebald shrew

---

1 Honey badger. 2 Steppe agama. 3 Severtzov's jerboa. ▶

(*Diplomesodon pulchellum*) to the rather more impressive saiga antelope (*Saiga tatarica*). Saiga were widespread in this region during the Ice Age, but would surely have been poached to extinction had it not been for extensive conservation efforts (page 113) in recent years.

Many of Karakalpakstan's mammals have evolved interesting characteristics to be better suited to desert life. Have you ever seen a fast-moving hedgehog? In British gardens, hedgehogs aren't known for their turns of speed. But the long-eared and Brandt's hedgehogs (*Hemiechinus auritus* and *Paraechinus hypomelas*) living in Karakalpakstan have developed much longer legs than their European cousins. Rather than curling up in a ball when faced with a predator, they at least attempt to run away! Similarly well adapted, Severtzov's jerboa (*Allactaga severtzovi*) is a desert rodent which looks a little like a miniature kangaroo, has exceptional hearing, and jumps around so quickly and erratically that it has a fair chance of escaping the clutches of nocturnal predators. In the same arid desert ecosystems as these two creatures, you will also find Tolai hare (*Lepus tolai*) and long-clawed ground squirrel (*Spermophilopsis leptodactylus*).

Karakalpakstan also has a number of larger mammals. In the Lower Amudarya State Biosphere Reserve there are two types of ungulates, wild boar and Bukhara deer (page 170); and also golden jackal (*Canis aureus*), honey badger (*Mellivora capensis*) and steppe cats (*Otocolobus manul*). We were fortunate enough to see a Turkmenian fox (*Vulpes vulpes flavescens*) dashing across the road along the bottom of the cliffs alongside Sudochye Lakes.

In terms of very rare mammals, the Turkmen caracal (*Caracal caracal schmitzi*), Turkmen onager (*Equus hemionus kulan*) and Ustyurt mountain sheep (*Ovis vignei cycloceros*) are all on IUCN's list of critically endangered species. You are sadly very unlikely to see these animals in the wild, but with a guide who knows their ranges, a lot of patience, and a strong pair of binoculars, it is not impossible.

Reptiles and amphibians It is relatively common to see a snake slithering through the dust of an unmade road in Karakalpakstan. The desert is home to many reptiles including a diversity of lizards, turtles, such as the Central Asian turtle and steppe turtle, and multiple snake species including threatened and rare species like the four-lined snake (*Elaphe quatuorlineata*) and the desert sand boa (*Eryx miliaris*). There are plenty of geckos, including the Caspian bent-toed gecko (*Tenuidactylus caspius*) and the even-fingered gecko (*Alsophylax pipiens*), steppe agama (*Trapelus sanguinolentus*) and Lichtenstein's toadhead agama (*Phrynocephalus interscapularis*), and also the aptly named Central Asian racerunner (*Eremias vermiculata*). The Afghan, Russian or Central Asian tortoise (*Testudo horsfieldii*) – it seems everyone wants to claim this particular reptile – has threatened status but is quite regularly sighted by scientists in Karakalpakstan. Desert lidless skink (*Ablepharus deserti*) live in the thickets, hiding in piles of leaves.

Amphibian species are fewer and further between: there is a lot of desert in Karakalpakstan, after all. In the Lower Amudarya State Biosphere Reserve there are two kinds of amphibians, however, green toad (*Bufotes viridis*) and marsh frog (*Pelophylax ridibundus*), both of which are categorised as species of least concern.

Fish The remnant Southern Aral Sea has now almost entirely lost the rich marine ecosystem that used to allow fish to be supplied to much of the former Soviet Union; however, it still contains the much sought after and commercially harvested artemia (brine shrimp; page 13), which feeds the beautiful lesser flamingos.

There are more species of fish in the Amu Darya and Kok Darya (a smaller tributary of the Amu Darya) than in the sea. Both species of Amu Darya shovelnose

Whether or not you know it, you have probably seen artemia. In fact, you might even have kept some as pets: 'sea monkeys' were all the rage in the 1990s! That nickname, of course, is ludicrous: there is nothing monkey-like about this tiny pink crustacean, a primitive organism which grows to a maximum of 1cm long. They have been around since the time of the dinosaurs and are extremophiles: they can survive in extreme environments.

Artemia, sometimes also called brine shrimp, were first discovered in the Aral Sea in 1998. It is thought that they may have been introduced after migrating birds ate them somewhere else and pooped them out in the sea. By 2004 the artemia population had grown significantly, as the sea had become uninhabitable for most species of fish, so nothing was eating the shrimp.

The collection of artemia cysts (eggs) has become big business in Karakalpakstan. In the autumn months artisanal collectors gather on the seashore to harvest and dry the cysts, which are then shipped around the world to fish farms. Their life in their new homes is short: once they are hatched, they are eaten by the fish. It is estimated that as much as 4,000 tonnes of artemia cysts are consumed every year, and the trade has created around 5,000 new jobs in Muynak District alone.

Some of the artemia cysts will meet a rather more interesting fate, however. At the College of Life Sciences at Zhejiang University in China, scientists are researching whether the embryonic dormancy of artemia (which is one of the longest of any known species) might be relevant to the treatment of therapy-resistant, dormant cancer stem cells.

To learn more about this extraordinary species, see w bit.ly/3EEUnki.

Artemia harvesters on the shore of the South Aral Sea

SAXON BOSWORTH

Background Information   NATURAL HISTORY AND CONSERVATION

1

sturgeons, large and small (*Pseudoscaphirhynchus kaufmanni* and *Pseudoscaphirhynchus hermanni*), are included on the IUCN Red List as critically endangered. Rather more common are Amu Darya trout (*Salmo trutta oxianus*), asp and pike asp (*Leuciscus aspius* and *Aspiolucius esocinus*), grass carp and silver carp (*Ctenopharyngodon idella* and *Hypophthalmichthys molitrix*), Aral barbel (*Luciobarbus brachycephalus*), Wels catfish (*Silurus glanis*), bream (*Abramis brama*) and sablefish (*Anoplopoma fimbria*).

CONSERVATION As a region that has suffered devastating environmental trauma in recent memory, and continues to be adversely affected, environmental protection is a hot topic in Karakalpakstan. The government, with the support of international donors, scientists and civil society partners, has been proactive about designating protected areas, and although the plans and finances for managing them are not as comprehensive as is needed, they do at least give some hope for the future of these fragile ecosystems.

Two national parks were recently created in Karakalpakstan in quick succession. South Ustyurt National Park (page 119) was founded in 2020 in Kungrad District, on the western side of the Ustyurt Plateau; and the Aralkum National Nature Park (page 133), created in 2022, centres on Resurrection Island and the Southern Aral Sea. Arguably, at the moment both sites are national parks in name only, but it is expected that they will become more developed during the lifetime of this book, and will become important destinations for ecotourism.

More easily accessible due to their locations are Karakalpakstan's three nature reserves. Lower Amudarya State Biosphere Reserve (LABR; page 169), formerly known as Baday-Tugay National Reserve, covers 68,718ha of Amu Darya and Beruni Districts. There is more tourism infrastructure here than anywhere else, including a permanent park office with a small museum and information boards. The main reason for coming here is to see the Bukhara deer (page 170). The population was on the brink of extinction in the 1970s but has revived thanks to a successful breeding programme.

The Saiga Conservation Alliance (w saiga-conservation.org) focuses, as the name suggests, on the conservation of critically endangered saiga antelope. There are small numbers of saiga in the northern part of the Saigachy Reserve in Kungrad District, and on Resurrection Island in Muynak District. Their presence is a major motivation factor for the 'Resurrection Island: Enterprise, conservation and development around the Aral Sea' project (page 136). You can find out more about saiga conservation efforts in the box on page 113.

The third of Karakalpakstan's reserves, Sudochye-Akpetki State Reserve (page 130), is in Muynak District. Created in 2021, it covers 280,507ha of lakes, tugai forest, desert and Ustyurt chinks. The birding here is excellent, and the State Committee for Ecology and Environment Protection has recently set up a yurt camp (page 135) by Sudochye Lakes so that visitors can stay on site.

The State Committee of the Republic of Uzbekistan for Ecology and Environment Protection (w uznature.uz) is responsible for biodiversity and ecosystem management across the country, and there is a local committee in Karakalpakstan. The committee's activities include creating and implementing regulations, deciding on the inter-sectoral use of the environment and natural resources, monitoring soil, water, flora, fauna and natural hazards, and developing and delivering ecological educational programmes.

HISTORY AND ARCHAEOLOGY

There is often a tendency to conflate the history of a place and of a people, in particular when modern states have been created along ethnic or linguistic lines. In Karakalpakstan that would be a flawed approach though, as although this region has been inhabited since Palaeolithic times, those first inhabitants were not the community now known as Karakalpaks, and multiple waves of migration have shaped the ethnic, cultural and linguistic composition of the population in the intervening millennia (page 26).

PREHISTORY There is a hypothesis that the first humans arrived in Karakalpakstan in the Middle Palaeolithic period, about 250,000 to 30,000 years ago. At this time the water level in the Caspian Sea had fallen significantly and the northern part of the sea dried up entirely, making it possible for Stone Age humans to migrate on foot from the North Caucasus to Central Asia. These first arrivals would have been hunter-gatherers who made tools and weapons from stone, wood and bone. There is significant evidence of Palaeolithic habitation on the Ustyurt Plateau, including the settlements of Esen-2, Karakuduk and Shakhpakhty, which were discovered by archaeologists from the Karakalpak branch of the USSR Academy of Sciences in the 1960s and 1970s.

In these same expeditions the archaeologists also identified and surveyed Mesolithic and Neolithic sites, building upon previous excavations in the 1930s. By the 4th millennium BC there were already two distinctive, well-established areas of human habitation in Karakalpakstan, on the Ustyurt Plateau and in the Akchadarya Delta, which is the southern part of the Amu Darya Delta. This second area was a particularly fertile hunting ground, with plenty of fish as well as birds and animals, and it was the centre of the Kelteminar Culture (5500–3500BC).

The Kelteminar Culture covered the desert and semi-desert of the Karakum and Kyzylkum and the Amu Darya Delta. At first, this was a mobile population, but over time they became sedentary, still hunting and fishing but also stock breeding. They built and lived in large communal houses with space for up to 120 people, and made clay vessels for cooking. We know that they used dogs for hunting and shot animals with bows and arrows because hunting and fishing scenes are clearly depicted in the Prisarykamyshya petroglyphs (rock carvings) discovered in 1940 at Kara Tepe. Animals clearly identifiable in these ancient artworks include camels, goats, horses, saiga antelope and sheep. There are also drawings of astronomical symbols, suggesting that the sun and stars had some ritual importance.

ANCIENT HISTORY The term 'Scythian' is often used, lazily and inaccurately, as a catch-all name for all early Eurasian nomads. Although these eastern Iranic groups did have certain aspects of culture in common, including their horse culture and design elements of their weaponry, domestic vessels and ornaments, they belonged to distinct ethnic groups. Those who inhabited Karakalpakstan in the 1st millennia BC were Saka-Massagetae, whose arrival may have driven existing groups out of Central Asia towards the Caucasus.

The name Massagetae comes to us via Greek and Latin, but it was probably originally a Young Avestan word meaning 'fishermen'. This is corroborated by the Greek historian Herodotus, who reported that the Massagetae lived on livestock and fish. In Karakalpakstan a Massagetaen sub-group called the Apasiacae (Water Sakas) lived in the marshes on the eastern side of the Aral Sea and along the banks of the Amu Darya. They seem to have been subjugated by Darius the Great (r. 522–486BC), the Achaemenid king of kings, as 'Saka of the marshes and Saka of the plains' are listed as being among the 24 nations that were part of the Achaemenid Empire. The vassal state in which they lived was known as Khorezm (page 16).

Herodotus and the Greek historian and geographer Strabo both wrote about the culture of the Massagetae. From them we know that the Massagetae did not farm but herded and fished. Some bred sheep for their milk and wool, which they used for clothing. They worshipped a sun god and sacrificed horses to him; buried their dead; and were respected as warriors. They wore elaborate armour, and put bronze armour on their horses as well as wearing it themselves. In the later period their nomadic culture would have been influenced by Hellenistic and Indian cultures, too.

Khorezm is the name of an oasis and also the region of modern Uzbekistan that includes the cities of Khiva and Urgench and borders Karakalpakstan. It is somewhat confusing, however, because when we talk about Ancient Khorezm in a historical sense, it refers to a much larger area that incorporates not only these places but also contemporary Karakalpakstan and parts of Turkmenistan. The Arab geographer Yaqut al-Hamawi wrote that the name Khorezm, like Massagetae, was a reference to the abundance of fish in the local diet, but some later scholars have suggested that the etymology is different and it actually means 'the land from which the sun rises.'

Khorezm (also Khwarazm or Chorasmia) was a vassal state to the Achaemenid Empire, but became independent by the time of Darius III in the 4th century BC. We know that the King of Khorezm sent missives to Alexander the Great in 328BC, offering to lead Alexander's army against enemies in the Caucasus; and Khorezm remained largely independent until the time of Arab Conquests in the 8th century. The kings significantly expanded their territories in the late 1000s, establishing the last Turco-Persian Empire before the arrival of the Mongols.

The first fortified sites were built in this area in the 7th century BC, and once Khorezm broke away from Achaemenid control in the 4th century BC and became independent, the fortress builders went into overdrive: this was frontier territory and it needed ever bigger and stronger structures to defend it. Khorezm flourished, however, and although the Massagetae rebelled against Alexander the Great (r. 336–323BC), along with the Bactrians and Sogdians, and ultimately submitted to him, Khorezm was largely untouched. Alexander's focus was on territories further east, and although the Khorezmian king Pharasmenes offered him assistance, Alexander declined his help.

After the breakup of Alexander's empire following his death, a variety of successor states emerged but it is unclear what the exact nature of their relationship was with Khorezm. The most famous of these states, the Kushan Empire, incorporated much of Central Asia and northern India. Trade was certainly flourishing between the two, but we don't know if Khorezm was formally part of the empire. As the Kushan Empire declined, the Sassanian Empire expanded east from Persia into Central Asia, but this was to be the last significant period of Persian rule. The Huns – steppe nomads possibly related to the Xiongnu tribal confederation from the northwest of the Altai Mountains – conquered Khorezm in the 4th century AD, followed by Turks two centuries later.

The dominant dynasty in Khorezm from the arrival of the Huns through to the end of the 10th century was the Afrigids. They were a subordinate power to larger empires, but nevertheless managed – at least according to the medieval Khorezmian scholar al-Biruni (page 175) – to put 22 kings on the throne and keep control for 690 years. That's no mean feat, especially as this period coincided with the Arab Conquest.

We start to get reliable written sources about the Afrigids in the 8th century. The first Arab raids were poorly organised and ineffective, but in 712 Qutayba ibn Muslim, an Arab commander and Governor of Khurasan, was able to take advantage of fraternal conflict and killed the Afrigid shah Azkajwar II (r. ?–712). After this, the Afrigids' territory was divided; they kept control of the eastern bank of the Amu Darya only, and the short-lived Ma'munid family took the western bank.

The Afrigids spoke Old Khorezmian, a language with a script derived from Aramaic which had been imported at the time of the Achaemenid Empire. Their faith was an import from the west, too: Zoroastrianism, a monotheistic faith which developed in what is now Iran or Azerbaijan perhaps as early as the 2nd millennium BC (page 29), combined with the influence of local paganism. Their first capital was the fortress Toprak Kala (page 182), but it then moved to Kath, modern day Beruni (page 175).

The Afrigids and Ma'munid were replaced by a much larger Persianate dynasty of Turkic origin, the Anushteginids, also known as the Khorezmian dynasty. The dynasty's founder, Anushtegin Gharchai (r. 1077–97) had been a slave solider in the Seljuq army, but was appointed as Governor of Khorezm. He made the position hereditary, passing power to his son Qutb ad-Din Muhammad I, who used the title Shah of Khorezm. At first, this was a vassal state to the Seljuks and then the Kara Kitai, but it did become independent and expanded to the point that the Khorezmian Empire ultimately included not only most of Central Asia and Afghanistan, but also Iran and even Egypt. The empire would last until the Mongol invasion.

THE MONGOL INVASION Genghis Khan's invasion of Central Asia is generally regarded to have been one of the bloodiest wars in history, and Khorezm bore the brunt of the violence. The Khorezmshah (king of Khorezm) Muhammad II had come to power in 1200 and initially had a good relationship with the Mongols: they had both fought successfully against the Kara Kitai, and as a result of this, Muhammad II had acquired new territories in what today are Pakistan and Iran. Historians are generally in agreement that Genghis Khan had no intention of attacking Khorezm at this stage – he was too busy fighting against the Jin Dynasty in China – and instead viewed the empire as an attractive trading partner and potential ally.

And then it went horribly wrong. Possibly Muhammad II became too arrogant; perhaps he was paranoid. In 1218, the Mongols sent a valuable caravan to Khorezm. Inalchuq, Governor of Otrar (a Khorezmian city now in Kazakhstan) thought that the merchants were spies, executed them, and seized their goods. Rather than apologising, Muhammad II killed one of the ambassadors sent by Genghis Khan to establish what had happened, and humiliated the two other envoys. Understandably furious, Genghis Khan turned his forces away from China and headed to Khorezm. The exact size of the Mongol army is unknown, but the medieval chronicler Minhaj al-Siraj Juzjani estimated there were 800,000 men. This is probably a gross exaggeration, but what we do know is that they outnumbered Muhammad II's forces and they took in quick succession the cities of Otrar, Bukhara, Samarkand and Gurganj (Konye Urgench). In Gurganj, perhaps as many as 1.2 million people were massacred. The Mongols then broke the dams and flooded the city with water from the Aral Sea.

There were by this time already many different nomadic groups in Khorezm. These included the Pechenegs and Oghuz, who were recruited by the Kievan Rus (a confederation of slavic tribes) as frontier guards known as Chernye Klobuki (Black Hats); and also the Kipchak, immigrants from Siberia. In fact, the name 'Kipchak' was used for all the nomadic tribes, regardless of their ethnic origin, and the area to the north of Transoxiana (the land between the Amu Darya and Syr Darya) became known as the Kipchak Steppe. Some people have proposed that the Chernye Klobuki were the forefathers of the Karakalpaks, but as they were often settled agriculturalists and Christians, this seems unlikely.

In the wake of the Mongol invasion, the period of the Golden Horde, one of the smaller hordes (tribes) would prove particularly influential in Khorezm. They were called the Shaybanids, though increasingly they called their tribe Uzbeks. They came from the steppe east of the Ural River and moved south into Central Asia to occupy lands along the Syr Darya.

THE TIMURIDS AND SHAYBANIDS Khorezm bounced back from the Mongol invasion, but there was soon another warlord on the march: Amir Timur (1370–1405), the Turco-Mongol ruler who is now regarded as the national hero of Uzbekistan. From his capital in Samarkand he led five campaigns against Khorezm, ultimately subjugating the area. Although Timur established a mighty empire stretching from Ankara in the west to Delhi in the east, it fractured soon after his death and the centre of power shifted from Samarkand to Herat. Control of Khorezm was given to Shah Malik, the tutor of Timur's grandson Ulugbeg, and it became a tributary state.

As Timurid power declined, the Shaybanids grew in strength. The Shaybanid khan Abul Khayr (r. 1428–69) raised a formidable nomad army and marched on Khorezm in 1430, sacking Urgench and seizing town after fortified town. Many of the tribes who supported him would later migrate east and become known as the Kazakhs, but at the same time there was an influx of Uzbeks, causing tensions with the Turkmen who occupied much of Khorezm. Abul Khayr's grandson, Muhammad Shaybani (1451–1510), would go on to conquer Bukhara and Samarkand, consolidate the Uzbek tribes, and found the Shaybanid Dynasty. With his brother, Mahmud Sultan, he took back full control of Khorezm, and then neighbouring Khorasan, bringing his new Uzbek Empire into direct contact and conflict with the Safavids next door.

After Muhammad Shaybani's death the Persian Safavids were able to annex Khorezm and they installed city governors rather than a single ruler who might become a rallying figure for opposition. In principle this was a good idea, but it failed because there was no single point of authority. Ilbars Khan (r. 1511–17), whose ancestor Timur Shaikh had been made Khan of Khiva by Abul Khayr, led the resistance and then successfully ruled Khorezm from Urgench. Ilbars was the founder of a new Khorezmian dynasty, the Arabshahids, who would remain in power for almost 300 years.

Although his reign was short, Ilbars Khan was active: he raised the oases of Abiward, Merv and Nisa and incorporated them into the Khorezmian state; he subjugated the Turkmen; and oversaw another wave of inward Uzbek migration.

THE EMERGENCE OF THE KARAKALPAKS The first historical record of the Karakalpaks (page 27) dates from 1598 and it refers to one of a number of tribes living near Signaq in what is now Kazakhstan. It is likely that this specific tribal confederation emerged earlier in the 16th century and that along with the Kazakhs they led a succession of raids on Bukhara. Russian sources from the 17th century suggest they also raided cities in Siberia, and a Russian map made in 1696 shows Karakalpaks occupying two areas, along the Syr Darya and the land between the northern Aral Sea and the Caspian Sea. The earliest monuments that were definitely built by Karakalpaks in Karakalpakstan are the fortress-like burial structures at the Krantau Archaeological Complex in Nukus District (page 100).

In the 17th century the Kazakhs were threatened by Jungars, or Oirats (Mongol tribes), and together with the Karakalpaks they sought the support of Russia. The Russians did send an ambassador to negotiate in 1721 but without success; the Jungars continued to advance along the Syr Darya, causing the Kazakhstan and easternmost Karakalpaks to flee. A small number of Karakalpaks settled around

Tashkent and Samarkand, but most headed west to the Aral Sea, joining up with the existing Karakalpak population there. There were further diplomatic exchanges between the Karakalpaks and Russians as the Karakalpaks believed Russian citizenship would offer protection, and after naturalisation papers were issued to their leaders the Karakalpaks became part of Russia in the 1730s. The deal gave the Karakalpaks favourable trade terms, and stated that they would pay tribute to the Russians instead of the Kazakhs.

You don't need to be a genius to guess who wasn't happy with the new arrangement: the Kazakhs. They attacked the Karakalpaks, driving them south to the Aral Sea, and attacked the Russians' frontier settlements, too. The Karakalpaks remaining in the Syr Darya were forced out. The Russians offered them no protection and so the only recently signed deal fell apart.

One of the issues the Karakalpaks had was that they were not unified. Each clan had its own leader, a *biy*, and religious figures were also wealthy and influential. As the Kazakh attacks continued, many of the Karakalpak clans came together, building mud-brick fortresses to protect the community and their livestock. Collectively they also began developing sophisticated irrigation systems to support their way of life.

THE KHIVAN CONQUEST By the early 19th century, the Karakalpaks were also facing threats from the south. In Khiva, the Arabshahids had finally been replaced by the Qongirot Khans, who claimed descent from Genghis Khan. Muhammad Rahim Khan (r. 1806–25) was preoccupied with subduing Khorezm's rebels, who threatened the lucrative caravan trade, and this included the Karakalpaks. With the support of the Turkmen, he defeated the Karakalpaks on the western bank of the Amu Darya in 1810, and perhaps as many as 10,000 Karakalpak households were forced to move across the river to Khujayli in south–central Karakalpakstan.

The Khivan Conquest continued for the next two years and Muhammad Rahim Khan's troops gained more and more territory by force. Karakalpak leaders submitted to Khiva in exchange for land grants, and in many cases they sold out their peasants to labour in awful conditions building the new canals required to expand agriculture in the oasis. Other peasants scraped a living working in exchange for a share of the crops harvested, but even this meagre amount was taxed by the khan. The situation was desperate, and after Muhammad Rahim Khan's death the Karakalpaks took advantage of the crisis to rebel.

In 1856 the Karakalpaks unified behind Ernazar Alakoz (page 139) in what has become known as the Karakalpak Uprising. Kazakhs and Uzbeks from northern Khorezm joined their fight. There was a major battle close to Khujayli, followed by a three-month siege. The rebellion was crushed by Khiva's new khan, Sayyid Muhammad Khan (1823–64). The following year there was famine across the region, and then an outbreak of cholera. Barely clinging on to life, many Karakalpaks chose to leave Khorezm to seek sanctuary in Bukhara or Russia.

ARRIVAL OF THE RUSSIANS There had been a small Russian presence and influence in Khorezm for a couple of hundred years. In 1839, however, partly in response to British advances in Afghanistan, the Russians decided it was time to take direct control of Khiva, and by doing so control Khorezm. General Perovsky led a force of 5,000 men south from Orenburg but the harsh winter weather prevented him reaching his target and he was forced to turn back, losing 8,500 of his 10,000 camels on the way. The British sent envoys to Khiva with a message of friendship and intelligence about the Russian advance, but they could not or would not make a

1

solid offer of military assistance, so Allah Quli Khan (r. 1825–42) had little interest in what they had to say.

The Russian envoys who arrived in 1841 and 1842 received a warmer welcome and were able to sign an admittedly unenforceable treaty stating that Khiva would not engage in hostilities with Russia, nor commit acts of robbery. There was no such commitment from the Russians to the Khivans, however, and the Russians built a chain of forts between the Caspian and Aral seas. Three Russian schooners, *Konstantin, Mikhail* and *Nikolay*, were used to survey the Aral Sea, and maps from these expeditions were published in both St Petersburg and London.

Tsar Alexander II sent a mission to Khiva in 1858 and the delegation carried with them gifts for the khan, including, somewhat ridiculously, an organ. The Russians recorded scenes of devastation resulting from the Karakalpak Uprising and famine which had happened not long before their arrival. Leading the delegation was N P Ignatyev, who spent six weeks in Khiva. His visit was a tense one: Sayyid Muhammad Khan was not unreasonably suspicious that the Russians were spying on him and at the same time was terrified he was going to be assassinated by one of his own officials. Ignatyev and his colleagues were kept under armed guard and although they were given audiences with the khan, they were fruitless.

The power dynamic in Khorezm shifted in the 1860s as Russia increased its presence in Central Asia. Russian garrisons controlled the Syr Darya Valley and General Konstantin von Kaufmann was appointed Governor General of the territories the Russians called Turkestan. The khanates of Kokand and Bukhara fell to the Russians, and when Kaufmann attempted to negotiate a friendship treaty with the latest khan of Khiva, Muhammad Rahim Bakhadur Khan II (r. 1864–1910), his entreaty was rebuffed. Kaufmann reported back to St Petersburg that a military solution would be the only way to bring Khiva to heel, and transported by the Aral Flotilla, Kaufmann attacked Khiva with 13,000 men in 1873.

We have a detailed account of Kaufmann's campaign as, by a quirk of fate, an American journalist from the *New York Herald* was embedded with the Russian forces. The Russians crossed the Amu Darya at Hazarasp and entered the citadel there without firing a shot as the local governor simply surrendered. In fact, there was no significant resistance until they reached Mangit (page 166), where the khan's forces attacked the Russian column but suffered heavy losses. The Russians bombarded Khiva with artillery and the khan quickly surrendered. The Russians, however, were happy to keep him on the throne as a puppet ruler, and a treaty was signed between the two parties in August 1873.

Legally the khan was still king, but he was subservient to the tsar. The Russians could conduct tax-free trade and annexed the khan's lands on the eastern bank of the Amu Darya, adjoining them to Russian Turkestan. They built Fort Petro-Aleksandrovsk close to what is now Tortkul and a second garrison at Nukus, where there was soon a dock for the Aral Flotilla. The lower Amu Darya was surveyed and mapped by Russian geographers and the photographer Grigoriy Krivtzov captured the first photos of Khiva.

Largely, the Russians pursued a policy of non-interference in Khiva's affairs, but there was some cultural exchange. Muhammad Rahim Bakhadur Khan II was invited to attend the coronation of Tsar Alexander III in Moscow in 1883, returning with Russian products including cigarettes and a telephone. The first Russian school in Khiva opened the following year. Elsewhere in the region the Russians built the first hospital, more schools, and a library. Russian merchants became a regular presence in the markets and the overland trade route to Russia flourished, with the volume of trade quadrupling from 1873 to 1898.

Rising opposition to the tsar around the turn of the century had little impact on far away Khorezm, but from 1905 onwards there were signs of unrest, including protests over pay and conditions. Already living at a subsistence level, there were reports of peasants being on the verge of starvation, especially after the failed harvest in 1910. The Russian governor's response was to crack down on perceived dissidents, and at the same time there were calls for change from the Jadids, Muslim reformers.

Muhammad Rahim Khan II was succeeded by his son, Isfandiyar Khan (r. 1910–18), who would be the last khan of Khiva. Isfandiyar Khan's advisors made many trips to Russia, introducing new technologies and ideas, and encouraged the khan to build Khiva's first post office and city hospital, as well as a larger building for the school, a pharmacy and a cotton mill. Khorezm became much better connected to the rest of the world thanks to the launch of a regular steamboat service across the Aral Sea and the introduction of the telegraph.

It was in the early months of World War I that the situation in Khorezm began to deteriorate. The recently installed General von Martson began extorting payments from Isfandiyar Khan, apparently in exchange for weapons, and the khan raised taxes to pay for them. When the Turkmen attacked Khiva in 1915, they were supported by the Russians. The khan's requests for arms were ignored. The Uzbeks marched on Khiva the following year, and rebellions broke out across Turkestan when it was announced that non-Russians were no longer exempt from military conscription. Chimbay's chief of police and his wife were killed in the ensuing violence, and due to the instability the cotton harvest was only half what it was the previous year. Order was restored in Khorezm in January 1917, just a month before Tsar Nicholas II's abdication.

The Tashkent Soviet of workers was established very soon after the tsar's abdication, as the city was already home to exiled Russian emigrés, Bolsheviks and union leaders. They set an example that others in Central Asia would quickly follow. It didn't help Isfandiyar Khan's cause that he was on vacation in Crimea at the time and had to be escorted home by Russian troops. Khiva's Jadids allied with the newly formed Soviet at Khiva's Russian garrison, and together they pressed the khan for a list of reforms, including an elected government, civil liberties, and financial support for schools, the postal service, the railway, and other public services. The parliament that was assembled initially excluded Turkmen representatives, causing tension. In quick succession there was an uprising, a coup d'état that put the khan back in power, and an overthrow of the provisional government in Turkestan.

On 6 November 1917, far away in St Petersburg, Leon Trotsky and his fellow Bolsheviks stormed the Winter Palace. Vladimir Lenin would soon establish the All-Russian Congress of Soviets, with civil war engulfing the former Russian Empire. Khorezm would not be spared. Isfandiyar Khan hunted down Jadids and other supposedly radical elements. The short-lived parliament was abolished and many Jadids put on trial and executed, but the Petro-Aleksandrovsk Soviet (the elected council based in the fort) had plans to annex Khiva, and by autumn 1919 the tide had turned in the Soviets' favour. The Red Army forced Sayyid Abdullah Khan (r. 1918–20) to abdicate, the First All-Khorezm Congress of Soviets agreed to abolish the khanate, and an independent Khorezm People's Soviet Republic was born.

THE SOVIET UNION As early as 1920 there was debate as to how many national republics should be created in Turkestan. At first, there were two, Bukhara and Khorezm, but in the 1920s they were subdivided, probably to reduce their power.

Khorezm was split into three: the western part of the region joined the Turkmen Soviet Socialist Republic (SSR); the Karakalpak Autonomous Oblast was created within the Kyrgyz Autonomous Soviet Socialist Republic (ASSR), but then in 1932 upgraded to be an ASSR in its own right, under the Uzbek SSR, with Tortkul as its first capital; and Khiva and Urgench became Khorezm Oblast, part of the Uzbek SSR. This is the origin of the administrative divisions that exist today, and it was the first time that the Karakalpaks were the titular owners of a homeland.

What would fundamentally change Karakalpakstan, however, was Joseph Stalin's first Five Year Plan, which would abolish the private sector and collectivise agriculture across the Union of SSRs (USSR). This would forcefully settle nomadic populations and eliminate their traditional lifestyles, disconnecting them from their livestock and land. Those who resisted forced collectivisation were punished; some were sent to a gulag on Resurrection Island (page 133) in the Aral Sea. Economically and humanitarianly speaking, the policy was an unmitigated disaster. Agriculture collapsed and people starved. Those who challenged Stalin were purged.

Collective enterprises were established across Karakalpakstan in the 1930s, including *sovkhoz* (state farms) and *kolkhoz* (collective farms). The former were state owned and state run; the latter, in theory at least, were cooperatives. This model wasn't just for agriculture, however, as the fishing community in Muynak also formed a *kolkhoz*. The first Five Year Plan included a target that the USSR would become self-sufficient in cotton production, so Karakalpakstan's grain producers were pressured to switch to growing cotton. Cotton is an exceptionally water intensive crop, so this necessitated the large-scale construction of canals (page 144).

Stalin's Communist Party consolidated its authoritarian control in the late 1930s. Any potential challenger – including elites, entrepreneurs, religious figures and academics – was eliminated or branded a traitor. Previous tolerance of local traditions evaporated. There were, however, some investments in Karakalpakstan, including a power station at Tortkul, factories in Nukus and a cannery in Muynak. The expansion of the irrigation network and use of fertilisers did ultimately have the desired effect of boosting agricultural production, including of cotton.

World War II, known in the USSR as the Great Patriotic War, did not impact Karakalpakstan directly, though many local men fought and died in the Soviet army. Despite being on the winning side, Stalin and later his successor, Nikita Khrushchev, were paranoid about the USSR's industrial and military weakness and invested heavily in military expansion, including the nuclear weapons testing programme in Kazakhstan. There are plenty of rumours that nuclear weapons were tested on the Ustyurt Plateau, or under water in the Aral Sea, but these claims are unsubstantiated. The only known nuclear tests in Ustyurt took place in the 1970s and they were civil (though still environmentally damaging) tests. Bioweapons were developed and tested at Aralsk 7 (page 133), however, and also in Nukus (page 79).

Khrushchev committed to yet more canal building in Central Asia. At the same time, poor management of irrigation infrastructure left much farmland waterlogged or too salty to use. His Virgin Lands campaign was also unsuccessful, and when combined with the Cuban Missile Crisis, it was to be his downfall. He was pushed to resign in 1964, by which time there were already concerns about falling water levels in the Amu Darya and Aral Sea (page 4). At Muynak, which a decade earlier had been the home of 3,000 fishermen catching and processing 26,000 tonnes of fish a year, the water had already dried up. By 1970 the former port was 10km from the coast.

Agricultural production was also starting to stagnate. There was a succession of crop failures in the late 1970s and early 1980s, and in Karakalpakstan cotton yields were falling as the soil became more and more saline. Excessive use of chemical fertilisers and pesticides was also taking its toll.

By the time Mikhail Gorbachev became General Secretary of the Communist Party in 1985, the USSR was economically and politically in decline. He called for *glasnost* (openness) and *perestroika* (restructuring), but this would not halt the fall of the USSR. One by one the SSRs proclaimed independence, including the Uzbek SSR (which contained Karakalpak ASSR) on 31 August 1991.

KARAKALPAKSTAN SINCE INDEPENDENCE The nature of Karakalpakstan's independence and relationship with Uzbekistan was negotiated in the early 1990s when both republics drafted their first constitutions (page 24). This decade was a period of extreme economic challenges for Karakalpakstan, but there were some important achievements, not least the adoption of the multilateral Aral Sea Basin Programme in 1994; and a bilateral agreement with the US to clean up the Chemical Research Institute in Nukus and Aralsk 7 and other contaminated areas on Resurrection Island.

GOVERNMENT AND POLITICS

Legally speaking, the Republic of Karakalpakstan is an autonomous republic of Uzbekistan. Although not exactly the same, this means that the relationship between Karakalpakstan and Uzbekistan is similar to that between Scotland and the United Kingdom: Scotland has its own parliament in Edinburgh and can

2022 PROTESTS

In June 2022, the Uzbek President Mirziyoyev proposed 170 amendments to Uzbekistan's constitution. Many of the proposed changes were minor, but one draft amendment removed the clause that gave Karakalpakstan the right to secede from Uzbekistan. The amendment had purportedly been approved by the Jokargy Kenes, but on 1 July people took to the streets of Nukus in protest. Lack of consultation on this issue was the primary grievance, but there was also a background of discontent relating to the belief that Karakalpakstan was being left behind other parts of Uzbekistan in terms of economic development.

Tragically, the protests became violent. At least 18 people were killed and 243 injured. The authorities imposed a State of Emergency and blocked access to the internet, which may have inadvertently contributed to the sense of panic and spreading of rumours. There were allegations that protestors attacked law enforcement officers and attempted to storm public buildings, but this is contested. The majority of casualties were civilians, some of whom seem to have been innocent bystanders caught up in the violence.

President Mirziyoyev visited Karakalpakstan twice in quick succession. He immediately withdrew the controversial constitutional amendment, which quelled the violence, and castigated local deputies for not having briefed him on the likely opposition to it earlier. On 31 January 2023, 22 Karakalpaks were found guilty of crimes against the state, and as of March 2023 the trials of 39 more were ongoing.

1

legislate on certain policy areas, but on other matters it is subordinate to the British Government in Westminster.

Karakalpakstan's constitution was adopted on 9 April 1993. The constitution declares that Karakalpakstan is a sovereign democratic republic which forms a part of the Republic of Uzbekistan, and that the relationship between the two republics shall be regulated by treaties and agreements. The territory of Karakalpakstan shall be inviolable and indivisible, and the republic has the right to secede from Uzbekistan on the basis of a nationwide referendum. An attempt to change this last point was the trigger for violent protests in Karakalpakstan in July 2022 (page 23).

Karakalpakstan's legislature is the Jokargy Kenes (Supreme Council). It has 65 deputies who are elected for a five-year term. Any citizen of Uzbekistan who is over the age of 25 is eligible for election to the Jokargy Kenes, and the Chairman is elected by the deputies. There is also a Council of Ministers, an executive body of the Government of Karakalpakstan, which provides guidance on economic, social and cultural development. Amanbai Orynbaev was elected Chairman of the Jokargy Kenes (and, simultaneously, Deputy Chairman of the Senate of Oliy Majlis, the parliament of Uzbekistan) in July 2022. He was previously Minister of Internal Affairs and has a background in political science and law.

For administrative purposes, Karakalpakstan is divided into 16 districts, plus one district-level city, Nukus, which is the capital. Each district has its own administrative centre, which is usually but not always the largest town or city.

ECONOMY

According to Uzbekistan's Center for Economic Research and Reforms, Karakalpakstan's total foreign trade turnover in 2021 was US$657.2 million, an increase of 21.9% on the previous year. By far and away the greatest proportion of exports comprised products from the chemical industry (67.9%), followed by food products (11.3%) and cotton fibre (2.8%). This presents a very limited picture of Karakalpakstan's present economy and its future potential, however, as the republic's total GDP reached US$2.37 billion in 2021 and per capita income in the region more than doubled between 2017 and 2022.

The reason for this is that Karakalpakstan's economy is still mostly geared to domestic consumption. The main sectors – industry, construction, agriculture and services – sell their products within Uzbekistan. New initiatives to stimulate economic growth include tax exemptions and reductions, combined with infrastructure investments paid for from the state budget. When these projects and the new gas fields (page 26) come online, it is expected that there will be not only a jump in GDP but also in exports.

As you drive across Karakalpakstan, the importance of the agricultural sector as a wealth creator and employer is clear. Gradually, farmers are transitioning away from cotton and wheat to higher-value crops; this is for environmental reasons as well as economic ones. Crop diversification is a key part of the agricultural development strategy, as is reducing state involvement in the sector. Investments including the World Bank's South Karakalpakstan Water Resources Management Improvement Project are improving irrigation and drainage, increasing productivity and sustainability.

Karakalpakstan is rich in minerals (page 7), though the mining sector is underdeveloped. *Invest in Karakalpakstan*, a guide published by UNDP, identifies the

1 Cotton picker. 2 Fishing. 3 Farmers at work in spring. ▶

Karakalpakstan has some of the greatest gas reserves in Central Asia: it is estimated that there could be as much as 1.7 trillion cubic metres of natural gas here, most of it within the Ustyurt Plateau and the Amu Darya Basin, and more reserves are still being discovered. For comparison, the total gas reserves in all of Uzbekistan is 1.88 trillion cubic metres, so you can see why Karakalpakstan is so critical to the energy sector.

Gas exploitation began in Karakalpakstan in the 1960s at Shakhpakhty on the Ustyurt Plateau, and though this site is no longer in use, it proved Karakalpakstan's worth and stimulated widespread gas exploration. Production from the Urga gas field is used domestically, but at other sites such as the Akchalak and Chandir group of gas fields the gas is exported.

Karakalpakstan is also a corridor for gas exports, crisscrossed with transcontinental pipelines. The Bukhara-Urals pipeline runs from the Gazli gas field via Kungrad and the western side of the Aral Sea to Kazakhstan; meanwhile the Central Asia-Centre pipeline connects gas fields in southern Uzbekistan and Turkmenistan with Beyneu and, ultimately Moscow, routing via Jaslyk. Gas compression stations are dotted along the route, including at Karakalpakiya. The gas corridors are operated by Uztransgaz, a subsidiary of Uzbekistan's state-owned gas company Uzbekneftegaz.

Significant funds are still being invested in gas exploration in Karakalpakstan, spurred on by the recent discovery of new industrial reserves at sites such as the Jel gas field on the Ustyurt Plateau. It is anticipated that in the first ten years of exploitation, this field could produce 1.5 billion cubic metres of gas and 76,000 tonnes of condensate, making a huge and much needed contribution to the local economy. It is not without cost, however. There are serious concerns about the impact of gas exploration on the already fragile landscape and on the long-suffering people and wildlife and it's not easy to strike the right balance between these competing interests.

potential for mining iron ore from the Tebinbulak deposit, and producing cement and vermiculite in Karauzyak District, both projects which are likely to be realised in the next few years.

Manufacturing is varied and contributes more than 30% of GDP. The production of chemicals and petrochemicals is critical to the economy, production of construction materials is growing, and there's growth in textiles manufacturing, too. There is a major soda plant in Kungrad, a glass factory in Khujayli, and the Ustyurt Gas and Chemical Complex produces ethylene, polyethylene and polypropylene among other products. Special clusters and small industrial zones are being created for the higher value-added processing of cotton and wool.

PEOPLE

Karakalpakstan is a multi-ethnic, multicultural republic of almost 2 million people. The largest communities are the Karakalpaks, after whom Karakalpakstan is named; the Uzbeks, and the Kazakhs. There are also smaller but significant populations of Turkmen and Russians, and of course many people are of mixed heritage.

KARAKALPAKS The name Karakalpak combines two words, *kara* (black) and *kalpak* (hat), and it is an endonym that is used by the Karakalpaks to describe themselves. Karakalpaks are a heterogenous people and a recent DNA study showed that they are a confederation of different tribes with no common origin. They are a Turkic group, subdivided into two divisions, the On Tort Uriw and the Qonirat, with a worldwide population of around 600,000 people, around 80% of whom live in Karakalpakstan. Even here, though, they are outnumbered by Uzbeks.

Traditionally, the Karakalpaks were a semi-settled people who raised livestock (in particular cattle) and fished. Because of this, they tended to live close to the rivers and marshes. The modern population is divided between urbanites, most of whom live in Soviet-era apartment blocks, and the rural population, who live in single-storey mud-brick houses called *tams*. Although the yurt (page 150) is culturally significant, very few if any Karakalpaks live in these felt tents today.

UZBEKS Uzbeks are the largest Turkic ethnic group in Karakalpakstan – around a million live in the republic – and in Central Asia, and have a total worldwide population of around 35 million. The origin of the name Uzbek is disputed, but it is found in written sources as early as the 12th century. Genetically, Uzbeks have a higher proportion of Middle Eastern and West Asian DNA than the Karakalpaks and Kazakhs, whose gene pool leans more towards East Asia.

KAZAKHS With an estimated 400,000 Kazakhs in Karakalpakstan today, Kazakhs are the third-largest ethnic group in the republic, closely related to the Karakalpaks in their language and culture. They are of Turco-Mongol origin and have been known by the name Kazakh since the 15th century; in Karakalpakstan, the Kazakhs were traditionally nomadic and bred sheep. They are spread across the republic but there are certain communities, such as Kubla Ustyurt, where almost all the residents are Kazakh.

LANGUAGE

Karakalpakstan has two official languages, Karakalpak and Uzbek. They are both Turkic tongues but belong to different branches, so are not mutually intelligible.

KARAKALPAK Karakalpak is a Kipchak language, a group that includes Kazakh, Kyrgyz and Tatar. In fact, Karakalpak and Kazakh are so close that speakers have no difficulty understanding one another.

Until the 1920s, Karakalpak was written in the Arabic script. The Russians then enforced the use of Latin script, followed two decades later by Cyrillic, albeit with the addition of a few extra letters to represent all the necessary Karakalpak sounds, as there are 21 native consonant phonemes. The Latin script was reintroduced after independence, in 1995, but the older generation educated in the Soviet period still tends to write in Cyrillic.

In general, the word order in Karakalpak is subject, object, verb (SOV). The language is agglutinative, meaning that you keep adding affixes to the verb and each one has a grammatical category. Words are usually stressed on the final syllable, and the vowels of the word stem must harmonise with any suffixes.

UZBEK The Uzbek language is also Turkic, but belongs to the Karluk branch and hence is closer to the extinct language of Chagatai and to modern Uighur. Like Karakalpak, the script was changed multiple times in the 20th century, but officially

THE KOREANS OF KARAKALPAKSTAN

Although Nukus is far away both geographically and culturally speaking from either North or South Korea, the city has a number of Korean restaurants. That's because there is a small but permanent Korean population in Karakalpakstan, some of whose ancestors have lived here since the 1930s.

Koreans first arrived in the Russian Far East in the 1860s, with a second wave of migrants escaping Japanese occupation in 1917. They settled there and might well have stayed, but during the 1930s Stalin, viewing them as a potential insider threat, issued a decree that forcefully relocated 170,000 Koreans and 7,000 Chinese to Central Asia. As many as 50,000 of these poor people died en route or within the first year of arrival, from starvation or other harsh conditions, and about 2,500 were shot by the Soviet authorities for opposing their deportation.

It was planned that 2,300 Korean families would be resettled in Karakalpakstan, though in the end a little over half of these families (approximately 6,800 people) came. They were housed initially in Kungrad, Muynak and Khujayli, and Karakalpakstan's authorities also provided food and basic household items, as the families had been forced to leave pretty much everything they owned behind. Korean-language schools opened in the towns where the Korean families lived, and the settlers were also given access to medical care. In some places the Koreans established their own collective farms, and from 1945 onwards they were able to travel around Central Asia (though not further afield within the USSR) as regular Soviet citizens. The Koreans, together with Germans who had suffered a similar fate, were given full rights only in 1982.

Immediately after the fall of the USSR there were about 9,200 Koreans living in Karakalpakstan. This figure has fallen significantly since then, as many Koreans have left to work or study abroad, including in South Korea. There is, however, still an Association of Korean Culture Centres in Karakalpakstan, which has helped establish strong ties between Nukus and the Institute of Asian Culture and Development (IACD), Korea International Cooperation Agency (KOICA), and other organisations from South Korea.

at least it is now written in Latin script, making it easy for English speakers to read. Words follow SOV order and there are two main categories of words: nominals and verbals.

RELIGION

For the majority of people in Karakalpakstan, religion is a personal matter. You will rarely see overtly religious dress and only a minority of people regularly attend a place of worship. In part that is because the USSR attempted to wipe out religious practice, and the political ambivalence towards organised religion continued into the early years of independence. That is not to say that faith isn't important, however. Only around 2% of the population admit to being atheists when surveyed, and deeply held beliefs and traditions come to the fore at times of birth, marriage and death.

ISLAM It is unknown exactly what proportion of Karakalpakstan's population is Muslim, but assuming the republic matches the trend of the rest of Uzbekistan, it will be at least 90%. This is mostly a form of cultural identification, however; not all of them are practising.

The dominant form of Islam is Sunnism, which was first introduced to Central Asia during the Arab Conquest in the 8th century. It would take several centuries for the new religion to become widespread, however, and it was Sufi missionaries who introduced Islam to the masses. This is why there are so many small shrines dedicated to Sufi saints in Karakalpakstan, plus larger religious complexes such as Sultan Uvays Dag (page 179).

The form of Islam practised in Central Asia was never acceptable to the Orthodoxy because it incorporated local, pre-Islamic beliefs and practices. Even today you can see the skulls of sheep or cattle mounted on sticks to provide protection from the evil eye, or ribbons tied to trees and wooden staffs at sacred places. Each ribbon represents a wish or prayer.

The political attitude towards Islam remains cautious – a legacy of the Soviet Union – but it has relaxed significantly in recent years. Mosques closed by the Soviets have reopened and been renovated, and some new mosques have been built.

ZOROASTRIANISM There are only a handful of Zoroastrians in Karakalpakstan today (and an estimated 7,000 in all of Uzbekistan), but what is believed to be the world's first monotheistic religion is worth mentioning here because it was the dominant religion in Karakalpakstan prior to the arrival of Islam. There are also numerous archaeological sites across the republic – most notably Chilpik Dakhma (page 167) – linked to Zoroastrian beliefs.

Zoroastrianism is an Iranic religion that probably has its roots in the 2nd millennium BC. There are some who believe it developed in Khorezm, but more likely it evolved in what are now Azerbaijan or Iran. It was the state religion of the Achaemenids (550–330BC) and subsequent Iranian empires, which accounts for its extensive spread.

The religion has a dualistic cosmology: every concept has an opposite. There is a god, Ahura Mazda, and his antithesis, Angra Mainyu: good and evil; heaven and hell; angels and demons, and so on. Zoroastrians also believe that mankind has free will and that we will be judged after death, all concepts that were later incorporated into the Abrahamic faiths.

Fire has a sacred status in Zoroastrianism, and its worshippers build fire temples. There is archaeological evidence of these across Karakalpakstan, including at Toprak Kala (page 182). Zoroastrian burial practices (page 167) are designed to ensure the polluted body does not contaminate the sacred elements, which is why large numbers of ossuaries have been excavated at sites like Mizdakhan (page 162).

EDUCATION

Education is managed by the Ministry of Public Education of the Republic of Karakalpakstan. In the academic year 2021/22 there were 734 general educational institutions in the republic, plus more than 300 preschool facilities. Education is mandatory from the age of seven and lasts for 11 years.

Preschool education is a top priority for the government in Karakalpakstan, as just over 30% of children are currently enrolled. The intention is to scale up the network of private and state-run preschools and kindergartens so that all children in the republic can benefit from early years education. It's not just about increasing numbers of institutions, though: quality is also important. Karakalpakstan is learning from South Korea's experience, building brightly coloured, well-equipped classrooms and social spaces, and encouraging the graduates of teacher training colleges to work in preschool institutions.

All children in Karakalpakstan are expected to complete primary and secondary school, and education is free of charge. There is a national curriculum and the National Program for the Development of Public Education for 2022–26 is intended to improve the quality of education, including teaching new subjects and skills necessary for the modern world. The top-performing students are selected to attend the Presidential Schools, one of which was founded in Nukus in 2019 and has 142 students in grades six to 11.

The majority of schools in Karakalpakstan teach in Karakalpak, though there are Uzbek and Kazakh language schools, too. Foreign languages are considered to be an important part of the curriculum, with Russian and English being the most widely offered options. The British Council is supporting the government to update the English curriculum and improve the quality of training for English teachers.

Karakalpakstan has around half a dozen well-respected higher educational institutions. The oldest and most prestigious of these is Karakalpak State University, which opened in 1935. At first it was a teacher-training college; now students study a wide range of subjects at undergraduate and postgraduate level. Several universities from Tashkent, including Tashkent University of Information Technologies and Tashkent State Agrarian University, have branches in Nukus, as does the Uzbekistan State Institute of Arts and Culture.

ARTS AND CRAFTS

The Savitsky Museum (page 89) is the reason many tourists want to come to Karakalpakstan in the first place, so it would be completely remiss not to talk about arts and crafts.

Until the 20th century, 'Karakalpak art' meant folk art. The Karakalpak branch of the Uzbek Academy of Sciences began collecting examples in the 1950s, which were then transferred to the Savitsky Museum, which has the world's most complete collection. The majority of items were made to decorate either yurts (page 150) or people.

Karakalpak domestic textiles were usually produced by young girls as part of their dowry. A yurt should be decorated with felt and knotted carpets, woven panels, and ribbons and runners made from cotton, silk or wool. No fabric was ever wasted, as *kurak* (patchwork) was used to make everything from tablecloths to pillows, and wedding canopies to baby clothes. The colour palette – which is dominated by red, ochre and brown – reflects the natural colours of Karakalpakstan and the local plants from which dyes could be made. The exception is the blue dye indigo, which had to be imported. You will see many recurring patterns in domestic items, many of which are amulets believed to have protective properties. The motifs include multiple horns, which are symbols of fertility and prosperity, and are used not only in *kurak* but also in *suzanis* (embroideries).

Wood carving was also related to yurt building, as yurts needed doors, hearths, tables, and trunks for storing clothing, tools and other household items. The decoration was done entirely by hand and traditional patterns included zoomorphic elements such as fish, birds and animal horns. There were also floral motifs and geometric forms.

Historically Karakalpaks were semi-settled and often herded cattle, so it is unsurprising that leatherwork featured prominently in folk art. Much of the

1 A traditional Karakalpak yurt. 2 Knotted carpets. 3 Karakalpak dresses. ▶

leatherwork was for saddlery, and the leather was embossed and then embroidered to make it beautiful. Footwear, including rigid heeled shoes and boots with turned-up toes, is another obvious example of leatherwork, but craftsmen also produced things like leather teapots and cup cases, making the most of the material's waterproof qualities.

Fine art emerged in Karakalpakstan only in the 20th century. Collector Igor Savitsky (page 92) encouraged the artistic development of young artists, as well as providing a space for them to exhibit their work. Kdyrbay Saipov (1939–72) was one of the first professional Karakalpak artists. He worked as a theatrical art director and produced beautiful still lifes and landscapes. His *In the Evening on the Amu-Darya River* hangs in the Savitsky Museum. Other Karakalpak artists of note include Amangeldy Utegenov (1951–), who is known particularly for his autumnal landscapes; sculptor Daribay Toreniyazov (1928–2003), who worked predominantly in wood; and Zholdasbek Kuttimuratov (1934–), a protégé of Savitsky, who depicts mostly female forms.

A number of important artists work in Karakalpakstan today, continually developing the contemporary art scene. Sculptor and painter Daribay Tadjimuratov's workshop in Chimbay (page 149) is open to the public, as is painter Bakhtiyar Serekeev's studio in Nukus (page 94).

CLOTHING AND JEWELLERY Weaving has always been regarded as a women's craft in Karakalpakstan. Prior to mechanisation in the Soviet period, yarns were made on a spindle or spinning wheel, and the textile was then woven on a narrow loom. Most weavers produced simple cotton fabrics for everyday use, which were boiled in groats or starch to make them more durable, but in southern Karakalpakstan there was also a small production of *zhipek*. This dark red-and-white striped silk was a luxury product used to make elegant capes and coats.

Traditional women's costumes, which were worn well into the 20th century, were made to tell you something about the women wearing it: her age, clan affiliation, social and marital status, etc. One item of women's clothing, the *kok koylek*, was an ankle-length tunic with long sleeves and a round collar worn by young women and occasionally brides from northern Karakalpakstan. It was made from cotton, usually dyed blue, and decorated with a panel of embroidery on the front. There are excellent examples in the Savitsky Museum and the State Museum of History and Culture of Karakalpakstan (page 93).

Popular from the 16th until the early 20th centuries, a *kiymeshek* (veil or cloak) would be worn by married women on special occasions, covering their head and shoulders but leaving their faces exposed. The *kiymeshek*, worn with a matching headdress, has an embroidered triangular panel at the front and a diamond-shaped shawl at the back. By looking at the style of the *kiymeshek* you would know the age of the woman.

For everyday use, there was a *jegde*, a cloak worn over the head rather than the shoulders. Usually these cloaks were made from cotton, though finer silk examples are known. The most popular colour was maroon, and the collar panel was embroidered. Ethnographers believe that these weren't originally part of the traditional Karakalpak costume but were introduced when the Karakalpaks migrated south in the 18th and 19th centuries and encountered women wearing *paranajas* (horsehair veils) in Khorezm.

◀ 1 A *takiya* or skull cap worn by a Karakalpak man. 2 & 3 Examples of *sawkele* – a ceremonial headdress worn by women.

Perhaps the most distinctive and dramatic item of traditional women's costume, however, was the *sawkele*, a ceremonial headdress with three components: a felt *tumaq* (domed hat) lined with cotton; a netting encrusted with coral beads and jewels, which hangs across the forehead and down the sides of the face; and the *halaqa*, a decorative panel which hangs down the back, covering the woman's hair. The very best example, one of only seven known to be preserved in museum collections, belongs to the Savitsky Museum. It dates from the 19th century and has been beautifully restored.

Both the *sawkele* and the *tobelik*, a kind of crown, were rare, but there were plenty of more common types of jewellery Karakalpak women could use to accessorise their outfits. Jewellery was worn by all levels of society, and some items were believed to have protective properties. Photographs from the early 20th century typically show women weighed down with heavy silver jewellery, though this was probably only worn for special occasions, and lighter pieces became more popular as the century wore on. Young girls wore pairs of *shashbaw*, silver plait decorations, in their hair until they were married. Large nose rings were common, particularly in northern Karakalpakstan, and earrings were similarly large, described by one 19th-century visitor as looking almost like bracelets. In some cases the earrings were connected with a decorative necklace strung with pendants, known as a *halqaplı sırg'a*. There are plenty of examples of traditional jewellery exhibited in Karakalpakstan's museums but if you are interested in how it is made, the best bet is to visit Adilbay Tadjimuratov's Karakalpak Jewellery Workshop (page 147) in Chimbay.

In the same period, men's costume was less decorative than women's and the colours of the fabrics tended to be more muted. Men wore a loose cotton shirt, tied at the waist, over baggy trousers, with a waistcoat or *chapan* (coat) over the top. In winter, heavier attire was required to keep out the cold, so the trousers were often quilted and coats made from sheepskin or lined with fur. The main decoration was a triangular amulet, usually embroidered on to the back of a coat, which symbolised the Mother Goddess and was thought to protect against evil forces.

Traditionally, Karakalpak men always covered their heads. This could be with an *oramal* (a twisted handkerchief worn as a simple turban), a *takiya* (skull cap) or a *qurash* (a sheepskin cap). Simple belts were obligatory accessories, and on special occasions these would be upgraded to a silk scarf or leather belt made from cowhide. Wealthier men had silver pendants hanging from their belts.

ARCHITECTURE

Karakalpakstan is quite diverse in its architectural styles, materials and construction methods. Most of the buildings you see in Nukus date from the Soviet period, which has its own architectural legacy. The planned streets are typically wide and the buildings low-rise, but there is an abundance of concrete, including the three- to five-storey apartment blocks known as Khrushchyovka. A few of these are decorated with mosaic panels, which you can see on a self-guided walking tour (page 96). Some of the public buildings, built by the Soviets and in the post-independence period, are more aesthetically interesting, however. These include the Berdaq Theatre (page 88), the Berdaq State Museum of the History of Karakalpak Literature (page 94), and the three buildings that make up the Savitsky Museum (page 89). The modern Mosque of Imam Ishan Muhammad is also quite impressive with its turquoise tiled dome.

---

1 Ayaz Kala (page 185). 2 The Savitsky Museum (page 89). 3 Mizdakhan (page 162). ▶

KIRILL SKOROBOGATKO/S

MEHMETO/S

Elsewhere in Karakalpakstan, residential architecture varies from single-storey adobe or breezeblock houses to modern apartment blocks. In towns, houses are typically built around a courtyard, occupied by several generations of the same family, and arranged within *mohallas* (neighbourhoods), which are the social building block of the community.

For architecture lovers, generally Karakalpakstan's historic architecture is more intriguing, and there is more than 2,500 years of architectural development on show, starting with desert fortresses such as Ayaz Kala (page 185) and Djanbas Kala (page 191). As these structures were often damaged in battle and had to be repaired, or were updated to meet contemporary needs, it is possible to chart their evolution over time. Another important ancient site is Chilpik Dakhma (page 167), a rare surviving example of Zoroastrian religious architecture.

Many of these early structures were decorated with motifs associated with magic and protection from supernatural forces. The use of red colour symbolised energy and life forces; green was nature, and later the colour of Islam; and yellow represented the sun and wealth. Zoomorphic motifs reveal a sacred attitude towards animals, and monumental paintings have been made since ancient times to decorate buildings and tell stories. Archaeologists excavated wall paintings at Toprak Kala (page 182) and the tradition continues to the present day, as you will see, for example, inside the Berdaq State Museum of the History of Karakalpak Literature (page 94).

The best place to learn about medieval architecture and urban planning in Karakalpakstan is at Mizdakhan (page 162). Here, municipal houses, ranging from single-room dwellings to large houses with courtyards and *ayvan* (verandas), had adjacent workshops and shops. Some of the mud-brick compounds accommodated yurts. Archaeologists have found plenty of examples of vaulted ceilings, especially in the ceremonial buildings, and of windows covered with *pandjara* (lattice screens).

THEATRE AND CINEMA

The Karakalpak State Theatre was formed in 1930. Performances took place not only in Nukus but across Karakalpakstan as the company toured widely, even visiting collective farms. This reflected the Soviet ideology that culture was for everyone and that if you couldn't get to the theatre, the theatre should come to you. Some of the performances were new dramas written in Karakalpak, others were plays by famous playwrights such as Nikolai Gogol and Alexander Ostrovsky, translated into Karakalpak from Russian.

Theatre and cultural performances flourished at every level. By the 1970s it is estimated that there were eight folk theatres and ensembles in Karakalpakstan, plus more than 900 amateur groups whose members included everyone from students to farm workers. More new plays were written: S Khodzhaniyazov's *Taluas*, a musical comedy; and N Eshmatov and R Eshimbetov's *Zhaylaudatoi* (*Wedding in the pasture*) were particularly popular with audiences. Two figures were at the forefront of the development of theatre (including bringing Karakalak folk traditions to the stage) in Karakalpakstan in the mid 20th century, Amet and Ayimkhan Shamuratov. Their house museum (page 93) is in Nukus.

Cinema became popular in Karakalpakstan from the 1930s onwards, and by 1960 there were 120 venues where you could watch a film. This figure would more than double by 1989. Most of the films shown were made elsewhere in the USSR, but the first local film, *Fishermen of the Aral Sea*, was produced by N Zhapakov and M Melkumov in the 1960s; Tashkent Film Studio opened a branch in Nukus

Ask anyone in the know about dance in Uzbekistan and sooner or later they will tell you about Tamara Khanum (1906–91), one of the first women in the country to dance on stage without a veil, who was awarded the Order of Lenin. Less well known is her younger sister, Elizaveta Petrosova (1913–97), who played a critical role in the development of theatre in Karakalpakstan.

Petrosova began her career in her native Andijan in the Fergana Valley and refined her art in the companies of Samarkand Drama Theatre and the Uzbek State Philharmonic Theatre in the 1930s. During World War II she performed on the battlefields with the Women's War Song and Dance Ensemble, who attempted to boost Soviet troops' morale. It is in the post-war era that her career became most fascinating, however, as in 1956 Petrosova was appointed as the artistic director of the Berdaq Theatre in Nukus (page 88). She immersed herself in Karakalpak folk culture, spending much of the next three years travelling from village to village learning about local traditions and observing dances, songs and games.

With this first-hand exposure, Petrosova was able to replicate traditional dances on stage, carefully choreographing more than 70 Karakalpak dances. Many of these dances reflected the everyday work of the communities who had originally created them, and so they have names like *Fishermen* and *Beating Felt*. With Petrosova's patronage, such dances were performed for an international audience for the first time, including at the Moscow International Festival of Democratic Youth and Students in 1957. Petrosova's choreography won numerous awards at international dance competitions, and in tribute to her important work she was named People's Artist of the Uzbek SSR and the Karakalpak ASSR in 1957.

in 1970, mostly making documentary films; and a full film studio, Karakalpakfilm, opened in 1989. Four important Karakalpak films were made in the final years before independence: *Gum-gum*, *Nepokornaya*, *Aral-kum* and *Year of the Snake*.

Since 1991, many of the films made in or about Karakalpakstan have focused on promoting national heritage. *Alakoz* (2006) is a biopic about the Karakalpak hero (page 139) and the two-part *Golden Heritage* (2006) explores Karakalpakstan's ancient sites. Intangible cultural heritage is a popular topic, too. *Ulg'ayiw* (1994), *Yar-Yar* (2004) and *Betashar* (2004) are all about marriage traditions; and *Kelinchak* (2005) is about women's costume, make-up and customs. You are highly unlikely to find such films at your local cinema at home, but some are available on YouTube or other online platforms.

MUSIC

Traditional Karakalpak music and oral folk traditions are closely entwined, as stories were sung or recited out loud with a musical accompaniment. The main type of musical work is called a *kosik*, which is a poem set to music. Songwriters – who are usually also singers themselves – typically take inspiration from legendary folk heroes, and popular themes include the fight for independence and the pain of separation from one's homeland.

There are two main musical styles in Karakalpakstan: *Bakhshi* and *Zhirau*. *Bakhshi* is recognised by UNESCO on its list of Intangible Cultural Heritage. The *dostons*

(poems) are based on myths, folk tales and ancient chants, and are performed by a *Bakhshi* who must be able not only to recite the epic poems from memory, but to do so in a captivating way. This entails a creative use of language: word games and proverbs are popular. The Karakalpak poet Ajiniyaz (page 98) was also a famous *Bakhshi*.

The poetic recitation is accompanied by music, played by the *Bakhshi* himself (traditionally it was a role for men) or by other members of the group. The typical instruments are the stringed *dombra*, which is plucked; and the *kobuz*, which is played with a bow. You can see such instruments in museums in Nukus, but the best place to learn about them is from master instrument maker Azat Pirniyazov at his Traditional Instrument Workshop in Chimbay (page 149).

The second style, *Zhirau*, became widespread in Karakalpakstan in the late 18th century. It is a form of throat singing, also known as overtone chanting, which is accompanied by a *kobuz* strung with horsehair. Performers believe it is an innate gift which cannot be taught. Many of the stories have a tragic twist, a reflection of Karakalpakstan's often difficult history (page 14).

The foundation of the Aykulash (meaning 'moonlight') folk ensemble in the 20th century helped not only preserve but also promote Karakalpakstan's traditions of music and dance. *Bakhshi* and composer Japaq Shamurodov wrote down around 200 chants and songs, many of them for the first time; and composers such as A Khalimov created numerous new works, including musical dramas and comedies, inspired by Karakalpak folk poems. Najimatdin Mukhammeddinov's ballet, *Ayjamal*, and opera, *Ajiniyaz*, demonstrated the versatility of Karakalpak styles and the musicians who performed them, introducing them to new audiences in large concert halls. Notable modern performers include singer and *kobuz* (two-stringed instrument played with a bow) player Janibek Piyazov; singers and *dutar* (long-necked, two-stringed lute) players Tengelbay Qalliev and Gayratdin Otemuratov; and duo Ziyada Sheripova and Injegul Saburova, one of very few Karakalpak women to play the *ghirjek* (spike fiddle), an instrument that is normally taught by a father to his sons.

Contemporary music in Karakalpakstan owes something to Karakalpakstan's folk traditions, but also draws influence from other Central Asian and international styles. There are often live pop concerts at the Amphitheatre in Nukus (page 88), and for electronic music, the Stihia Festival founded in Muynak (page 128) is an extraordinary showcase for acts from Karakalpakstan and beyond.

LITERATURE

Although the Karakalpaks were only semi-nomadic, until the 19th century all of their literature was oral. Epics were performed by bards, who were trained by bards of the previous generation. This oral literature, though, didn't have set texts that were memorised and could be transcribed. Each epic had a framework of stories, characters and formulaic phrases and was recomposed each time it was recited. It mixed verse and prose, the proportion (and the length of the epic) depending on the skill of the bard and the time available for the performance. This purely oral tradition continued until recently. Jumabay-jiraw, the last exponent of it, died in 2006.

One of the most important of these epics is *Edige*, the story of a historical figure, an emir of the Golden Horde and a contemporary of Amir Timur (page 18). The

◀ 1 Concert Hall in Nukus. 2 Musicians playing folk instruments.

epic adds myth and legend to its historical source. Edige's father becomes Baba Tukli Aziz, who was important in bringing Islam to the Golden Horde. His mother becomes a *peri* (a beautiful winged spirit in Persian mythology). Edige is raised by the khan of the Golden Horde, then flees to the court of Timur, enabling him to claim legitimacy by his association with these two great powers. He rescues Timur's daughter from an ogre and marries her. There are more adventures, involving the son Edige left behind in the court of the Golden Horde, a 360-year-old bard, a dragon, an argument between father and son, and a final reconciliation. A number of recitals have been recorded and some details of the story, especially the ending, vary between them. Unusually for Karakalpak literature, an English translation was published by Academia Scientiarum Fennica in 2007, and the book is accompanied by a CD of Edige being performed by Jumabay.

Another epic poem handed down through the generations, and arguably more influential than *Edige*, is *Kyrk Kyz* (40 Girls). There are variations of this story across Central Asia, as well as sites associated with it in the Surkhandarya and Navoi regions of Uzbekistan, but the original tale is Karakalpak. *Kyrk Kyz* is the story of a 16-year-old girl, Gulaim, who sees in a dream a Khorezmian warrior, Arislan, and knows he is intended to be her husband. Many eligible young men want her hand in marriage, but she refuses them all. Meanwhile, the Iranian ruler Nadir Shah sees and falls in love with Arislan's sister, Altinay, but she declines his advances, provoking his fury. Nadir Shah attacks Khorezm and makes Altinay his slave. Gulaim, leading her own army of 40 female warriors, marches to fight the Kalmyks, but on the way meets Arislan and immediately recognises him from her dream. Together they fight the Kalmyks and then turn their attention to Nadir Shah, defeating him and rescuing Altinay. And for once, the story has a happy ending: Gulaim and Arislan get married and live happily ever after. You can watch a 2020 recording of a live performance of *Kyrk Kyz* by artist and documentary maker Saodat Ismailova, created with the support of the Aga Khan Music Programme, on YouTube.

Poetry has always been a key component of Karakalpak literature, historically and in the present day. The 19th-century poet Berdaq is regarded as Karakalpakstan's answer to Shakespeare and the father of Karakalpak literature; closely followed in importance by Ajiniyaz. You can find out more about both these writers in the box on page 98 and read their poetry in English in *Three Karakalpak Poets*, translated by Andrew Staniland and Karakalpak co-translators Aynura Nazirbaeva, Gulbahor Izentaeva, Gulnaz Jadigerova, Nargiza Urazimbetova, Nilufar Abdullaeva and Shaxnoza Tursınbaeva.

The third poet in that collection is Ibrayim Yusupov, a contemporary writer who was known for using idioms linked to the human body, something common in the Karakalpak language. Examples might include 'to put a straw in one's eye' (to cheat), 'to take dust into the mouth' (to be silent), or 'to put a rope through the nose' (to be subordinate). Yusupov also found inspiration in the earlier poetry of Berdaq, attempting to reveal aspects of Berdaq's character in his own work and thus to form a link with the past. He was awarded the title People's Poet of Uzbekistan and Karakalpakstan and died in 2008.

Novels became an established genre for Karakalpak literature only in the 20th century. One of the writers we have to thank for this was journalist and novelist Gulyasha Esemuratova (1930–), who was born in a village just outside Chimbay. Her father, a wealthy man and a religious figure in the community, was executed during Stalin's purges, so she was raised by her uncle, a linguist with an extensive library. Esemuratova graduated in language and literature from the Nukus State

Pedagogical Institute and started her journalism career in 1951 at the newspaper now called *Qaraqalpaqstan Jasları*.

Esemuratova was a keen observer of the lives of Karakalpak women and wrote about them extensively in her journalistic work and in her fiction. She joined the Karakalpakstan Union of Writers, established her own literary journal *Aral qızlar* (Girls of Aral), and is the author of more than a dozen books, as well as a biography of Yusupov. Now well into her 90s, Esemuratova remains an inspiration to the latest generation of women writers in Karakalpakstan and still makes appearances on TV and radio.

2

Practical Information

WHEN TO VISIT

Karakalpakstan has an extreme continental climate, meaning that it gets very hot in the summer with temperatures well into the 40°Cs, and is very cold in the winter, with average temperatures in January between -5 and -8°C. With climate change, extreme temperatures are more common, as are dust storms. Although this doesn't actually prevent you travelling at those times, it does mean that outdoor sightseeing will be uncomfortable, and in winter the off-road tracks to the Aral Sea can become blocked by snow and ice. The yurt camps there will in any case be closed in wintertime.

We recommend, therefore, that you plan your trip to Karakalpakstan between March and June or September and November. Not only will the weather be more comfortable in these months but there will also be plenty of things happening that you might want to see or participate in. This includes Navruz, the pre-Islamic Persian New Year celebration on 21 March (spring equinox); the archaeological excavation season; biannual bird migrations; Stihia, an annual electronic music, arts and science festival founded in Muynak that now moves between different locations each year; and plenty of live performances and exhibitions in Nukus.

HIGHLIGHTS

The appeal of Karakalpakstan is the huge variety of destinations and experiences it offers. In a matter of days you can explore vast salt flats and geological formations that are millions of years old; go paddling in the Aral Sea; contemplate the enormous historical importance of ancient fortresses and burial grounds; visit national parks and nature reserves protecting critically endangered species of animals and birds; and, remarkably, view the world's second largest collection of Russian avant garde art. We have attempted to distil the main attractions into this short list of highlights, the must-see sights of Karakalpakstan.

ARAL SEA (page 121) Far more famous, sadly, than Karakalpakstan itself is the Aral Sea, an endorheic lake (ie: a body of water with no outflow) that until the late 20th century covered a large proportion of this region but is now but a shadow of its former self. The shrunken sea rightly demands the attention of scientists and has caught the curiosity of disaster tourists, but those are far from the only reasons to visit. Even now, the Aral Sea is a place of extreme beauty. There are

---

1 Craft workshops at Chimbay (page 147). 2 One of the paintings hanging in the Savitsky Museum; the museum is an undisputed highlight of a trip to Karakalpakstan. 3 Barsakelmes salt flats, Ustyurt. 4 Look for Bukhara deer at Lower Amudarya State Biosphere Reserve. ▶

MAXIMUM EXPOSURE PR

SHCHIPKOVA ELENA/S

PAUL A CARPENTER/S

important wildlife populations in the newly created Aralkum National Nature Park and in the Saigachy Reserve, which flank the sea on either side. Driving along the Ustyurt Chinks looking out towards the Aral Sea is an unforgettable lesson in geology. And most of all, travelling here is a chance to reflect on how mankind is destroying our planet and the need for us all to be more responsible in our use of natural resources.

BARSAKELMES (page 105) Reminiscent of the Salar de Uyuni in Bolivia, the world's largest salt flats, from a distance Barsakelmes looks like a layer of snow has fallen on the desert of the Ustyurt Plateau. Get closer, however, and you will see that the white colour is a thick crust of salt, crunchy under foot, stretching as far as the eye can see. Thirty million years ago this area was at the bottom of the a salt water lake but the water has long since evaporated, leaving only the salt behind.

CRAFT WORKSHOPS (page 147) Karakalpakstan's folk art traditions are thankfully not confined only to its museums but are being preserved and further developed by a new generation of artisans. The best way to see and learn about their work is with a visit to Chimbay where a number of workshops are open to the public. Here you can watch anything from yurt building and reed weaving to jewellery making, felt making and embroidery. Contemporary artist Daribay Tadjimuratov has his studio here, too.

DESERT FORTRESSES The Desert Castles of Ancient Khorezm are on UNESCO's Tentative List and are likely to be given World Heritage Site status in the foreseeable future. There are more than 50 of these extraordinary mud-brick structures spread across Karakalpakstan and neighbouring Khorezm, the oldest of which date back to the 7th century BC. The most impressive examples include Ayaz Kala (page 185), Toprak Kala (page 182) and Jampik Kala (page 157), but even the smaller fortresses give a good feel of just how fiercely this territory was fought over and the lengths communities had to go to to protect their safety and ways of life.

LOWER AMUDARYA STATE BIOSPHERE RESERVE (page 169) LABR is the most developed protected area in Karakalpakstan, with basic tourism infrastructure and a well-run breeding and conservation programme for the highly endangered Bukhara deer. Visitors are guaranteed to be able to see the deer within their enclosure, but as it is now estimated that there are in excess of 1,600 deer in the reserve, you stand a very good chance of seeing them in the wild, too. During our visits in August and September we saw dozens of them wandering through the tugai forest and drinking from and swimming in the Amu Darya, which runs through the reserve.

MIZDAKHAN (page 162) Founded in the 4th century BC, Mizdakhan is one of Karakalpakstan's most ancient and sacred sites. A local legend says that it is the burial place of Adam and that when the last brick falls from his mausoleum, the world will end. It's what is called an armageddon clock. Whatever your religious beliefs, archaeologists are confident that this was the second largest city in Khorezm after Konye Urgench and, even after the Arab Conquest, Zoroastrian practices continued to be entwined here with the newly introduced faith of Islam.

SAVITSKY MUSEUM (page 89) Often described as the Louvre of the Steppe, the Savitsky Museum is Karakalpakstan's greatest treasure. Founded in the 1960s to exhibit archaeological finds and Karakalpak folk art, the museum has become world famous thanks to its remarkable collection of Central Asian and Russian avant garde art. The story of how these artworks – many of which were by artists purged by Stalin – came to be in Nukus is almost as extraordinary as the paintings, sculptures, graphics and prints themselves.

SUDOCHYE LAKES (page 130) There are multiple birding sites across Karakalpakstan but few can compete with Sudochye Lakes for the variety of species or the natural beauty of the landscape. It is a quiet place, relatively easily accessible from both Nukus and Muynak, and the biodiversity is particularly high in the spring and autumn when the migrant species stop by. The pink flamingos are a colourful addition to the scene, but of greater interest to serious birders are the 24 rare and vulnerable species recorded here, 13 of which are included in the International Red List of IUCN.

SUGGESTED ITINERARIES

The amount you will be able to see and do in Karakalpakstan will depend on whether or not you have private transport. The first two itineraries below are doable on foot and with shared taxis and buses; the longer itineraries assume you have access to a car and driver or are prepared to combine public transport and private taxis to reach your final destination.

TWO DAYS If you are planning a flying visit to Karakalpakstan and have just two days available to explore, base yourself in Nukus. Book accommodation within walking distance of the Savitsky Museum (page 89) and allow a full day for the museum, starting with a guided tour with one of the passionate English-speaking guides. There is a small café within the museum for lunch, or you can pop across to one of the coffee shops nearby (page 84). If you do finish early at the museum and you haven't yet overdosed on culture, head to the House Museum of Amet and Ayimkhan Shamuratov (page 93) nearby. In the early evening, you can sit outside and enjoy a beer at Chillout (page 86): an idyllic spot in the park beside the river.

On the second day, have breakfast at the Main Bazaar (page 88) and then visit the State Museum of History and Culture of Karakalpakstan (page 93). A couple of hours will be sufficient but it is well worth a visit, especially if the second building at the Savitsky is still closed for renovation. If the weather is fine, spend the afternoon on a self-guided walking tour of Nukus's Soviet era mosaics (page 96), which are gradually being restored. End your time in Nukus with a meal at Artizen (page 84): *juyeri gurtik* is a local delicacy and absolutely delicious.

THREE DAYS With three days in Karakalpakstan, spend your first day at the Savitsky Museum in Nukus as above, then plan two day trips out of the city. The first of these excursions should be west of Nukus to Khujayli District in order to visit Mizdakhan (page 162) and, while you are close by, Gyaur Kala (page 156). On day three, drive or take the bus to Chimbay to tour the town's many craft workshops. The Kara Uy yurt workshop (page 147) is a must-see, and you can arrange to have lunch with yurt maker Azamat Turekeev and his family. This is also an excellent opportunity for souvenir shopping; items from the Felt Workshop (page 141) and Karakalpak Jewellery Workshop (page 147) make thoughtful, easily transportable gifts.

As an alternative three-day itinerary, you can combine Nukus and one of these day trips and then head south on the third day, stopping at the Lower Amudarya State Biosphere Reserve (page 169) and a couple of the fortresses. This makes particular sense if your next destination is Khiva or Urgench. Gyaur Kala (page 156) and Jampik Kala (page 157) are both easily accessible from the A380, as is the LABR, so you don't need to make significant detours.

FIVE DAYS If you want to visit the Aral Sea, allow five days. After a day in Nukus, drive to Muynak and overnight there, making sure you visit the Ship Graveyard (page 126) and the Museum of the Aral Sea (page 126). Continue on to the BesQala Yurt Camp (page 110), which looks out on to the sea and is within easy reach of the Saigachy Reserve (page 108) and the canyons (page 115). On day four, drive to Sudochye Lakes (page 130) for birding, staying at the yurt camp at Old Urga (page 132), and then on the final day return to Nukus via Barsakelmes (page 105).

TEN DAYS Spending ten days in Karakalpakstan gives you enough time to see almost all the main sites without having to rush. Start in Nukus and spend two days visiting the museums (page 89) and getting a good grounding in the history and culture of Karakalpakstan. Drive to Muynak via Hakim Ata (page 128) and the Jantemir Ishan Mausoleum (page 130). You will arrive in the afternoon, so check into a hotel for two nights so you can have all of the next day in Muynak. On day five, go to Sudochye Lakes, and from there go north to the Aral Sea, booking into the BesQala Yurt Camp for two nights. This will give you a full day to explore the Saigachy Reserve, including its ancient cemeteries, two evenings of watching the sunset over the Aral Sea, and two nights of unforgettable stargazing (page 116). On day seven you will see herds of camels near Kubla Ustyurt (page 108) as you drive across the Ustyurt Plateau to Jaslyk to pick up the main road back to Kungrad. Stop at Barsakelmes (page 105) on the way and walk down from the cliff top to the salt pan.

After Kungrad, return to Nukus via Mizdakhan. The most physically challenging part of this itinerary is now over, and you can use Nukus as your base for a day trip to Chimbay (page 145). Allocate the final two days of your trip to visiting Chilpik Dakhma (page 167), a selection of the desert fortresses, and LABR, ending your journey either back in Nukus or in Urgench.

TOUR OPERATORS

It is possible to visit some parts of Karakalpakstan independently, but given the large distances involved, limited public transport, and the language barriers faced outside of Nukus, many international tourists decide to book a tour to reduce the hassle and ensure they get the most out of the time they have available. In fact, the cost of a tour package booked with a local company can often be comparable or even cheaper than booking your own accommodation and ground transport. We have listed here some of the most experienced and reliable local tour operators in Karakalpakstan and other parts of Uzbekistan, as well as a selection of international tour operators selling tours in Central Asia.

KARAKALPAKSTAN

Ayim Tour S Kamalova 50, Nukus; `61 224 2525; e ayimtourtravel@gmail.com; w ayimtour. com. Run by the owners of the two Jipek Joli hotels in Nukus, Ayim Tour has run tours in Karakalpakstan since 2005. It has itineraries to Barsakelmes & the Aral Sea but we particularly

recommend 'A Night in the Desert', a two-day trip which includes Chilpik Dakhma, four fortresses, & the Lower Amudarya State Biosphere Reserve. The night is spent at the Ayaz Kala Yurt Camp (page 181).
BesQala A Navoi 121, Nukus; `91 377 7729; w besqala.com. Also known as Aral Sea Discovery,

BesQala owns the BesQala Guesthouse in Nukus & the BesQala Yurt Camp at the Aral Sea, & also supplies most of the 4x4 vehicles required to get there. It offers shared & private tour options to help keep costs low. The three-day 'Aral Sea Discovery Eco Tour' includes Mizdakhan, Sudochye Lakes, the Aral Sea & Muynak.

UZBEKISTAN

Advantour Tashkent 100015; +998 78 150 3020; e tashkent@advantour.com; w advantour.com. Advantour offers tours across Central Asia but specialises in Uzbekistan, with regular scheduled departures throughout the year that include Nukus & the desert fortresses. It also books train tickets.

Akbar Travel Urgench 220100; +998 91 429 9777; e info@akbartraveluz.com; w akbartraveluz.com. Islom Ibragimov runs Akbar Travel from Urgench & specialises in tours to Karakalpakstan & Khorezm, though he can also provide nationwide itineraries.

Compass Tour Tashkent 100070; +998 90 356 3551; w compass-tour.org. Compass' Humoyun Magdiev is particularly strong on Islamic cultural heritage & pilgrimage sites, & on catering to the needs of religious tourists.

DOCA Tours Samarkand 140117; +998 93 350 2020; e info@doca-tours.com; w doca-tours.com. DOCA offers a wide range of Uzbekistan itineraries including the 15-day Adventure Trip to the Aral Sea, four days of which is spent in Karakalpakstan.

✳ **International Caravan Travel Service** Tashkent 100000; +998 71 237 1241; e sales@caravantraveluz.com; w caravantraveluz.com. ICTA prides itself on organising high-quality cross-border tours so will be the first choice for Uzbekistan – plus Turkmenistan once the border between the two countries reopens. In Karakalpakstan it also has access to knowledgeable nature guides from the Academy of Science.

✳ **Peopletravel** Tashkent 100077; +998 71 232 2333; e info@peopletravel.uz; w people-travels.com. Co-organisers of Stihia Festival & enthusiastic supporters & travelling companions during the creation of this guide, Sanjar Halmuradov & Farrukh Rakhmanov are leaders in adventure travel, including self-driving tours.

✳ **Veres Vert** Samarkand 140100; +998 66 233 6126; e info@veres-vert.com; w veres-vert.com. Founded in 2009, Veres Vert is one of the most highly regarded tour operators in Uzbekistan. It focuses on carefully curated, mostly cultural experiences & is used to handling VIPs & unusual requests.

UK

Jules Verne London SE1 0BE; 020 3811 5126; e sales@vjv.co.uk; w vjv.com. Experience the best of Central Asia on VJV's 26-day 'Legends & Empires' tour, which covers all the region's republics & includes Ayaz Kala, Toprak Kala & the Savitsky Museum in Karakalpakstan.

Silk Road Adventures Brecon LD3 0DD; 0117 427 0129; e travel@silkroadadventures.com; w silkroadadventures.com. Marley Burns & Ants Bolingbroke-Kent are the people who brought Joanna Lumley to Uzbekistan for the TV show *Joanna Lumley's Silk Road Adventure*. The Ayaz Kala is included in their 'Classic Uzbekistan' tour, but to see more of Karakalpakstan approach them for a tailor-made itinerary.

TransIndus London W5 5RH; 020 8566 3739; e enquiries@transindus.com; w transindus.co.uk. Discover both Turkmenistan & Uzbekistan on TransIndus' 15-day 'Silk Road Explorer' itinerary, which focuses on Ancient Khorezm (on both sides of the modern border) & then adds Bukhara, Samarkand & Tashkent.

Travel Local w travellocal.com. A UK-based website where you can book direct with selected local travel companies, allowing you to communicate with an expert ground operator without having to go through a 3rd party. Your booking with the local company has full financial protection, but note that travel to the destination is not included. Member of ABTA, ASTA.

Travel the Unknown Purley CR8 2EL; 020 7183 6371; e enquiries@traveltheunknown.com; w traveltheunknown.com. Long-term champion of off-the-beaten-track destinations, Travel the Unknown includes Nukus & the desert fortresses in its popular 11-day 'Uzbekistan Odyssey'.

✳ **Trotting Soles** Staines TW18 4AX; 07553 709314; e info@trottingsoles.co.uk; w trottingsoles.co.uk. Sunita Ramanand has a passion for history, archaeology & culture, & loves Central Asia almost as much as we do. She aims to deliver transformational travel experiences & all her tours are bespoke.

Wild Frontiers London EC1V 4JB; 020 3925 9104; e info@wildfrontiers.co.uk;

2

w wildfrontierstravel.com. Wild Frontiers'
14-day Uzbekistan & Turkmenistan: Cities of
the Silk Road' does include a night in Nukus &
a morning at the Savitsky Museum, but if you
want longer in Karakalpakstan then ask for a
tailor-made itinerary.

☀ **Indy Guide** Schönenberg 8824, Switzerland;
☏ +41 79 100 55 00; e info@indyguide.com;
w indyguide.com. Indy Guide is not a tour
operator but rather the leading online marketplace
for independent guides, drivers & tour operators
to sell their services. Its initial focus was on
Central Asia but it has since expanded to offer
other destinations.

Kalpak Travel Nussbaumen 5415, Switzerland;
☏ +41 44 585 2961; e info@kalpak-travel.com;
w kalpak-travel.com. Run by Swiss-Kyrgyz couple
Luca & Aijan Lasser, Kalpak Travel sells small-group
& private tours to Central Asia. Most of its guests
opt for multi-country itineraries but 'Uzbekistan
Tour in Two Weeks' is an excellent option if you
want to focus your attention on just one country &
it does include Karakalpakstan.

Soviet Tours Berlin 10999, Germany; ☏ +49
152 0463 9635; e info@soviettours.com;
w soviettours.com. Photojournalist Gianluca
Pardelli is the proud & passionate founder of
Soviet Tours, which runs private & escorted
tours to the least-visited parts of the former
USSR, including Karakalpakstan. It also offers
volunteering programmes.

Bestway Tours & Safaris Burnaby BC V5C 3T8,
Canada; ☏ +1 800 663 0844; w bestway.com.
The 10-day 'Splendours of Uzbekistan' and 12-
day 'From Ashgabat to Tashkent' itineraries both
include a visit to Karakalpakstan.

MIR Corporation Seattle WA 98102, USA;
☏ +1 800 424 7289; w mircorp.com. The USA's
Russia & Central Asia experts (with an office in
Tashkent), MIR Corporation offers exceptional tours
of Uzbekistan, including not only multi-country
Silk Road tours, but also one-off art, dance &
cultural tours.

Odyssey Traveller Haymarket NSW 2000,
Australia; ☏ +61 300 888 225; w odysseytraveller.
com. With a slower pace of travel ideal for older
travellers, the 31-day fully escorted 'Central
Asia Silk Road Small Group Tour' has guaranteed
departures & identifies the Savitsky Museum as a
highlight of the trip.

Sundowners Overland Melbourne
VIC 3000, Australia; ☏ +61 396 725 386;
e travel@sundownersoverland.com;
w sundownersoverland.com. Sundowners
Overland doesn't include Karakalpakstan in its
standard Uzbekistan itineraries but it is available
as part of a tailor-made trip & it specialises in
journeys by rail.

RED TAPE

VISAS Uzbekistan's Ministry of Foreign Affairs (w mfa.uz/en) sets the visa policy
for the entirety of the Republic of Uzbekistan, including Karakalpakstan. More than
90 nationalities are now eligible for visa-free entry to the country for up to 30 days.
This includes those with passports issued by the UK, EU, Australia, Canada, Israel
and New Zealand. You can check the latest list of eligible countries here: w mfa.uz/
en/pages/visa-republic-uzb. If you wish to stay longer than 30 days you can leave
Uzbekistan and re-enter, which restarts the clock; otherwise you can apply for a
paper visa at an Uzbek Embassy.

Travellers from nearly 60 countries which are not yet eligible for visa-free entry
are permitted to apply for an e-visa. The list of countries is available at the same
MFA link above. At the time of writing, US and Indian passport holders both
require an e-visa but it is hoped that they will be added to the visa-free list during
the lifetime of this edition. You should apply at w e-visa.gov.uz. It costs US$20 and
is valid for 90 days from the date of issue. You can stay in Uzbekistan for up to 30
days within that 90-day period. Payment is by credit or debit card but the payment

processing is temperamental so you may need to try several times with different cards to get the transactions to go through.

All remaining nationalities require a print visa. You should complete the online form at w visa.mfa.uz, download and print it out, and sign it in black ink. You will need to submit the form along with your letter of invitation, passport, a photocopy of the photo page of your passport, and two passport photos to an Uzbek Embassy (page 50). The cost of this visa is dictated by your nationality, where you are applying, the length of your stay and whether it is for single, double or multiple entry. Note that your passport must have at least two empty pages and be valid for at least six months after the end of your visit to Uzbekistan.

If Uzbekistan does not have diplomatic representation in your country of residence, it is sometimes possible to arrange in advance for a visa to be issued on arrival at Tashkent International Airport but not at other entry points. You should contact a tour operator (page 46) to arrange this, and you will need both your letter of invitation and approval letter (a form you will be issued to present on arrival) to check in for your flight.

Extending your visa once you are in Uzbekistan is difficult: most visitors prefer to leave and re-enter. However, it is in theory at least possible to obtain a seven-day extension from the Office of Visa and Registration (OVIR) at Tashkent Airport or at 22 Chekhov (⌕71 256 95 86/71 256 96 14) for US$40.

LETTER OF INVITATION If you require a print visa, you will need to get a letter of invitation before you submit your visa application. The letter of invitation has to be prepared by a tour operator in Uzbekistan (if you book through an international tour operator then this will be their ground agent in Uzbekistan) and approved by the Ministry of Foreign Affairs.

It is worth checking with the tour operator before booking but in general you will be expected to provide them with a colour scan of the photo page of your passport, and a colour scan of a letter from your employer confirming your job title and that you are employed. The latter is not required for retired people and a declaration on headed paper is adequate if you are self-employed. The tour operator will submit these documents to the Ministry of Foreign Affairs, who will review the application within seven working days (three working days for the expedited service). If your letter of invitation application is approved, the Ministry of Foreign Affairs will send a Telex confirmation to the Uzbek Embassy where you intend to apply for your visa, and the tour operator will send you a scan of the letter of invitation which includes that Telex number.

REGISTRATION The requirement for foreigners to register within three days of arriving in any given place in Uzbekistan is an irritating overhang from the Soviet period that is long overdue for abolition. Hotels now use an online registration system, but may sometimes still give you paper slips to confirm your stay. If you take an overnight train journey, keep the ticket stub or booking confirmation as proof of your whereabouts. If you are camping, staying with friends or at a homestay for more than three nights, you should register at the local OVIR (foreigner's registration office) to ensure you and your hosts are in the clear. The OVIR in Nukus (⌕ 09.00–13.00 & 14.00–18.00 Mon–Fri) is at Islam Karimov 104A. There is no cost to register at the OVIR but if you do not register you may be fined.

ADDITIONAL PERMITS Access to some areas of Uzbekistan, including national parks and reserves, sometimes requires a permit and the process for acquiring it is often poorly defined. Where permits are required in Karakalpakstan (for example to visit the Saigachy Reserve, page 108) we have given details in the relevant sections.

EMBASSIES For a full list of Uzbekistan's embassies overseas and foreign embassies in Tashkent, visit w embassypages.com/uzbekistan. For quick reference, the embassies listed below can all be found in Tashkent.

Kazakhstan A Chekhov 23; +998 71 152 1654; w mfa.gov.kz/en/tashkent
Kyrgyzstan Niyozbek 30; +998 71 237 4794; w mfa.gov.kg/en/dm/uzbekistan-en
Tajikistan A Qahhor 61; +998 71 254 9966; w mfa.tj/tashkent

Turkmenistan Afrasiab 19; +998 71 256 9402; w uzbekistan.tmembassy.gov.tm
UK Gulyamov 67; +998 78 120 1500; w gov.uk/world/uzbekistan
USA Moyqorghon 3; +998 71 120 5450; w uz.usembassy.gov

GETTING THERE AND AWAY

Karakalpakstan is a remote destination and there is no quick and easy way to get there. However, regional connectivity is improving rapidly and it is expected that more flight connections will become available during the lifespan of this guide. A high-speed train connection to Nukus has also been announced (page 52), which would connect the city to Tashkent, Samarkand, and Bukhara, and should be operational by the end of 2026.

BY AIR If you are visiting Karakalpakstan from abroad, the likelihood is that you will have to fly first to Tashkent, Bukhara, Samarkand or Urgench. Nukus does have an international airport (page 81), but its only international flights are to Aktau in Kazakhstan and Moscow. From Tashkent there are two domestic flights a day with Uzbekistan Airways (1hr 40mins; from US$80) to Nukus and three flights a week to Muynak, via Nukus; otherwise you can travel by rail or road.

A wide range of airlines now fly to Uzbekistan and the number of flight routes is increasing every month. The airlines listed below are most likely to be useful; where available, the phone numbers given are for their local offices in Uzbekistan.

Aeroflot +998 71 120 0555; w aeroflot. ru. Russia's largest airline has daily flights from Moscow to Tashkent & Samarkand.
Air Astana +998 90 936 2533; w airastana. com. Kazakh national carrier. Daily flights from Almaty to Tashkent.
China Southern Airlines +998 71 231 8880; w csair.com. Daily flights from Beijing to Tashkent. Good connections from the Far East, Australia & domestic destinations within China.
Fly Dubai w flydubai.com. Daily flights from Dubai to Tashkent.
Turkish Airlines +998 71 147 0849; w thy. com. Daily flights from Istanbul to Tashkent (also 4/week to Samarkand, 2/week to Bukhara, & 2/

week to Urgench) with connections from Europe & the US.
Uzbekistan Airways +998 78 140 4623; w uzairways.com. Uzbekistan's national carrier serves a wide range of destinations from Tashkent & some regional airports including Almaty (Kazakhstan; daily), Bishkek (Kyrgyzstan; 3/week), Dubai (UAE; daily), Dushanbe (Tajikistan; 2/week), Frankfurt (Germany; 3/week), Istanbul (Turkey; daily), London (UK; 2–3/week), Moscow (Russia; daily), New Delhi (India; 4/week), New York (US; 3/week), Paris (1/week) & Tbilisi (Georgia; 1/week). The airline also operates an extensive domestic flight network which includes 2 flights/day (1hr 40mins) from Tashkent to Nukus.

1 Getting around by train is a possibility in Karakalpakstan. 2 Taxis in Kungrad. ▶

Wizz Air w wizzair.com. The budget airline flies twice a week from Abu Dhabi to Samarkand. It is expected Wizz will launch additional routes to Uzbekistan, including from its Budapest hub, during the lifespan of this guide.

BY RAIL Karakalpakstan's railway infrastructure mostly dates from the Soviet period, but as a consequence it is linked to Kazakhstan and Russia as well as to other parts of Uzbekistan. In 2022 President Mirziyoyev announced that the line to Nukus would be electrified, connecting the city into Uzbekistan's high-speed rail network and reducing the travel time between Tashkent and Nukus from 16 hours to 7 hours. The completion date of this project is yet to be set but it should be before the end of 2026. This will be a much faster, more comfortable option than the slow and very basic existing trains.

There are daily departures from Tashkent (16hrs) and Bukhara (9hrs) to Nukus, and from Tashkent (21hrs) to Kungrad. Twice a week there is a train from Andijan to Kungrad (27hrs). Trains also cross the international border from Kazakhstan: there are four trains a week from Volgograd (39hrs) to Nukus, which stop en route in Karakalpakiya, Kungrad, and Khujayli; and three trains a week from Beyneu (8hrs 30mins) to Nukus, which also stop in Karakalpakiya and Kungrad.

The easiest way to check timetables and buy tickets for trains within Uzbekistan is online (w chipta.railway.uz/en/home). If tickets appear to be sold out on the website, the route you want isn't listed, or you need to buy a ticket for an international train, contact Advantour (page 47).

Ticket classes On the regular trains, these are categorised in the Russian style. First-class accommodation (*Spalny Vagon*; SV or es-veh; also known as deluxe) buys you an upholstered seat in a two-berth cabin. The seat turns into a bed at night. Second class (*Kupé*) is slightly less plush, and there are four passengers in a compartment. Third class (*Platskartny*) has open bunks (ie: not in a compartment) and leads to lots of interaction with fellow passengers.

If you are travelling on the Afrosiyob trains (Uzbekistan's high-speed trains) then there are three classes of tickets: economy, business and VIP. These all get you seats but with increasing levels of comfort, and even economy class has AC, plenty of legroom, and free cups of tea and snacks.

BY ROAD The combination of border closures between Uzbekistan and Afghanistan and Turkmenistan, and the ongoing attack on Ukraine by Russia, means that it is now much more difficult to reach Uzbekistan by road, especially from Europe, than it was a few years ago. We do live in hope that the situation will improve during the lifespan of this guide, however, at which point regional movement across land borders will also become easier, and overlanders, cyclists, hitchhikers and long-distance bus enthusiasts can rejoice. For now, the land border with Kazakhstan is open and you can cross directly into Karakalpakstan. The conveniently located border with Turkmenistan was closed owing to Covid-19, but reopened March 2023. However, at the time of going to press, there were no reports of tourists having crossed. You can check the latest status and requirements of all Central Asia's border crossings at w caravanistan.com/border-crossings.

If you are bringing your own vehicle into Uzbekistan (regardless of the entry point) you will have to declare it on the usual customs form, plus fill in additional paperwork to be entered on to the customs computer system. Theoretically at least, you will not be allowed to leave the country unless you take the vehicle with you. Occasionally, you may be told by border officials looking for a bribe that right-hand-drive vehicles cannot enter Uzbekistan; this is not true, so stand your ground and ask to speak to a more senior member of staff. Expect to have the vehicle thoroughly inspected and to have its contents passed through the X-ray machine.

From Kazakhstan There are several crossing points between Kazakhstan and Uzbekistan but to enter directly into Karakalpakstan you need the **Tejen** crossing near Karakalpakiya (page 117). The border opens at 09.00 and on the Kazakh side trucks, processed in batches of 30, are given priority over private cars, so you may have to wait for up to 2–3 hours at busy times. If you are crossing on foot, you will need to take a taxi from the border post to the closest town, Karakalpakiya, which is 20km away and has a train station; or arrange for a car and driver to meet you at Tejen. There are no buses, minibuses or shared taxis.

From Turkmenistan When Turkmenistan reopens its borders, there are two conveniently located border posts for Karakalpakstan. The **Khujayli–Konye Urgench** border crossing (09.00–12.30 & 13.30–18.00) is a 30-minute drive southwest of Nukus. Shared taxis wait on both sides: it should cost you no more than US$2 from Konye Urgench to the border, and a maximum of US$10 from the border to Nukus.

Further south in Uzbekistan's Khorezm Region, but convenient for the southern part of Karakalpakstan, is the **Shavat–Dashoguz** crossing (09.00–12.30 & 13.30–18.00), which is around 50km west of Urgench. It can only be reached by taxi (around US$15 from Urgench or Khiva) and requires a shuttle (US$1) between the border posts; on the Turkmen side, there are shared taxis to Dashoguz (US$1).

Within Uzbekistan As Karakalpakstan is within Uzbekistan, no border formalities are required when entering from the neighbouring regions of Bukhara, Navoi and Khorezm: it is like driving between England and Wales. Upgrading road infrastructure is a priority for the government and construction work is ongoing, but with such vast distances to cover, the road conditions are still patchy and driving can be slow.

The drive from Urgench to Nukus is 180km and takes approximately 3hrs. There is a daily bus and numerous taxis and shared taxis ply the same route. There are also daily buses to Nukus from Bukhara (8hrs), Navoi (10–12hrs), Samarkand (12–14hrs) and Tashkent (16–18hrs) but given the distances involved you should plan to break your journey en route, or perhaps consider flying or taking the sleeper train.

HEALTH   *With Dr Daniel Campion*

BEFORE YOU GO Comprehensive **travel insurance** should be high on your list when you contemplate travelling to Karakalpakstan. Choose a policy that includes medical evacuation (medevac) and make sure you fully understand any restrictions: it is not uncommon for insurance companies to exclude certain activities from cover. Leave a copy of the policy documents at home with someone you trust and keep a copy of them, along with the emergency contact number, on you at all times.

Your GP or a specialised travel clinic (page 54) will be able to check your immunisation status and advise you on any additional **vaccinations** you might need. It is wise to be up to date on tetanus, polio and diphtheria (now given as an all-in-one vaccine that lasts for ten years), and hepatitis A.

The hepatitis A vaccine comprises two injections given about a year apart, though you will have cover from the time of the first injection. Once completed, the course gives you protection for 25 years. The vaccine is sometimes available on the NHS. Hepatitis B vaccination should be considered for longer trips (one month or more)

2

and by those working in a medical setting or with children. The standard vaccine schedule comprises three doses taken over a six-month period, but for those aged 16 or over it can be given over a period of 21 days if time is short. The rapid course needs to be boosted after a year. A combined hepatitis A and B vaccine, 'Twinrix', is available, though at least three doses are needed for it to be fully effective. For those under 16, the minimum time is over eight weeks.

Typhoid vaccine (injected or oral) is recommended for those travelling in rural areas and when there may be difficulty in ensuring safe water supplies and food.

Rabies is prevalent throughout Uzbekistan and vaccination is highly recommended for those travelling more than 24 hours from medical help or for those who will be coming into contact with animals as there is unlikely to be treatment available within the country.

Uzbekistan is recognised by the World Health Organisation as a malaria-free country, so there is no need to take antimalarials.

TRAVEL CLINICS AND HEALTH INFORMATION A full list of current travel clinic websites worldwide is available on w istm.org. For other journey preparation information, consult w travelhealthpro.org.uk (UK) or w nc.cdc.gov/travel (US). All advice found online should be used in conjunction with expert advice received prior to or during travel.

PRESCRIPTION MEDICATION If you require prescription medication it is best to bring adequate supplies with you for the duration of your trip as you cannot guarantee to be able to get the same products locally. Bring a copy of the prescription with you and try to keep the medication in its original packaging.

Psychotropic and narcotic medications (including opioids such as codeine and anxiolytics like diazepam or Xanax) are tightly controlled in Uzbekistan and you should declare these on a customs form before arrival. The interpretation of the regulations by the Uzbek Embassy in London is that you can bring up to seven days' dosage of these medications provided that you have a signed letter from your doctor and declare them to customs on arrival.

IN KARAKALPAKSTAN The medical system in Karakalpakstan, as across Uzbekistan, is seriously overstretched. The quality of medical training fell after the

---

TICKS

Precautions against tick bites should be taken by inspecting the skin daily for ticks. Ticks should ideally be removed complete, and as soon as possible, to reduce the chance of infection. You can use special tick tweezers, which can be bought in good travel shops, or failing this with your finger nails, grasping the tick as close to your body as possible, and pulling it away steadily and firmly at right angles to your skin without jerking or twisting. Irritants (eg: Olbas oil) or lit cigarettes are to be discouraged since they can cause the ticks to regurgitate and therefore increase the risk of disease. Once the tick is removed, if possible douse the wound with alcohol (any spirit will do), soap and water, or iodine. If you are travelling with small children, remember to check their heads, and particularly behind the ears, for ticks. Spreading redness around the bite and/or fever and/or aching joints after a tick bite imply that you have an infection that requires antibiotic treatment. In this case seek medical advice.

While pharmacies in Karakalpakstan are numerous, especially in the towns, and some are well equipped, you should still pack a first-aid kit and any prescription medicines you require. A minimal kit should contain:

- An antiseptic such as iodine or chlorhexidine
- A few small dressings (plasters)
- Suncream
- Insect repellent, ideally containing around 50% DEET
- Aspirin or paracetamol
- Imodium (loperamide) and rehydration salts
- Ciprofloxacin or norfloxacin (for severe diarrhoea)
- A pair of fine-pointed tweezers (to remove thorns, splinters, etc)
- Tick tweezers
- Alcohol-based hand sanitiser or bar of soap in plastic box
- Clingfilm or condoms for covering burns (for anyone with a camping stove)
- A small needle and syringe kit

end of the Soviet era: many doctors left to find work abroad, and today hospitals are rundown and equipment is out of date. Outside the major cities there is also a shortage of drugs and other medical supplies. If you are ill or have an accident, you will be able to receive emergency treatment at a basic district hospital, but will then require medevac to a country with more developed medical infrastructure for ongoing care. British citizens should be aware that the reciprocal healthcare agreement between the UK and Uzbekistan formally ended in 2016, though the reality is that hospitals do still provide emergency treatment for free.

Every town in Uzbekistan has countless pharmacies (marked 'Apteka' or 'Darikhana'), selling a range of generic drugs. You do not need a prescription to purchase medication but should read the instructions carefully (or get someone to explain them to you).

POTENTIAL MEDICAL PROBLEMS
Travellers' diarrhoea Diarrhoeal diseases and other gastrointestinal infections are very common, and perhaps half of all visitors will suffer in this way at some point during their trip to Karakalpakstan. Travellers' diarrhoea, as well as more serious conditions such as typhoid, comes from getting bacteria in your mouth. To avoid getting ill you should ensure that you observe good hygiene practices, such as regular hand washing, using bottled or purified water (including for cleaning teeth), and avoiding foods of doubtful provenance. Many travellers use the following maxim to remind them what is safe:

PEEL IT, BOIL IT, COOK IT OR FORGET IT

This means that fruit you have washed and peeled yourself and hot foods should be safe, but raw foods, cold cooked foods, salads, ice cream and ice are all risky, and foods kept lukewarm in hotel buffets often harbour numerous bugs. That said, plenty of travellers and expatriates enjoy fruit and vegetables, so do keep a sense of perspective: food served in a fairly decent hotel in a large town or a place regularly frequented by expatriates is likely to be safe.

Practical Information   HEALTH

2

Although Uzbekistan is not an area with a high risk of malaria, mosquitoes can carry other diseases and their bites are, in any case, uncomfortable. As the sun is going down, don long clothes and apply repellent on any exposed flesh. Pack a DEET-based insect repellent (roll-ons or sticks are the least messy preparations for travelling). Repellents should contain between 30 and 50% DEET and can be used by children and pregnant women. Insect coils and fans reduce rather than eliminate bites. Travel clinics usually sell a good range of nets, treatment kits and repellents. Acceptable alternatives to DEET include Icaridin (or picaridin), Eucalyptus citriodora oil, hydrated, cyclized (also known as p-menthane diol or PMD) or 3-ethlyaminopropionate (IR3535).

Mosquitoes and many other insects are attracted to light. If you are camping, never put a lamp near the opening of your tent, or you will have a swarm of biters waiting to join you when you retire. In hotel rooms, be aware that the longer your light is on, the greater the number of insects will be sharing your accommodation.

For advice on tick bites, see page 54.

If you are struck down with diarrhoea in spite of your precautions, remember that dehydration is your greatest concern. Drink lots of clear fluids. Sachets of oral rehydration salts give the perfect biochemical mix to replace all fluids you are losing. If you don't have rehydration salts, or dislike the taste, any dilute mixture of sugar and salt in water will do you good: try Coke or orange squash with a three-finger pinch of salt added to each glass (if you are salt-depleted you won't taste it). Or add eight level teaspoons of sugar (18g) and one level teaspoon of salt (3g) to one litre of safe water. A squeeze of lemon or orange juice improves the taste and adds potassium, which is also lost in diarrhoea. Drink two large glasses after every bowel motion, and more if you are thirsty. These solutions are still absorbed well if you are vomiting, but you will need to take sips at a time. If you are not eating, you need to drink three litres a day plus whatever is pouring into the toilet. If you feel like eating, take a bland, high-carbohydrate diet. Plain rice, dry bread or digestive biscuits are ideal. Moderate diarrhoea in adults (without fever or blood in the stool) can be made more bearable with loperamide (Imodium).

If the diarrhoea is severely affecting your daily activities, you are passing blood or slime or you have a fever, you may need antibiotics in addition to fluid replacement. Consult a doctor as soon as possible. An antibiotic self-treatment kit may be prescribed to higher-risk travellers, particularly those who may develop severe illness because of underlying health conditions.

Prickly heat Karakalpakstan can become exceptionally hot in summer: temperatures above 40°C are common. A fine pimply rash on the chest or forearms is likely to be heat rash; it is caused by sweat becoming trapped beneath the skin and causing a histamine reaction. Taking cool showers, dabbing dry, and applying talc will help, as will wearing only loose, 100%-cotton clothes and sleeping naked under a fan. An antihistamine tablet may help reduce the itching, as will 1% hydrocortisone cream.

Sunstroke and dehydration The sun in Karakalpakstan can be very harsh, especially in the desert. Sunstroke and dehydration are serious risks. Wearing a hat, long loose sleeves and sunscreen helps to avoid sunburn. Prolonged unprotected exposure can result in heatstroke, which is potentially fatal. Stay out of the sun between noon and 15.00.

In the heat you sweat more, so dehydration is likely. Don't rely on feeling thirsty to tell you to drink. A good guide is to make sure your urine looks clear and colourless at least once a day. Carry bottled water with you at all times and make sure you stop to drink it.

Rabies Uzbekistan is classified as a high-risk rabies country. Rabies can be carried by all warm-blooded mammals and the disease is transmitted to humans through contact with an infected animal's saliva. If you are bitten, scratched or even licked on your face or over broken skin, you must assume that the animal has rabies. Scrub the area with soap under a running tap for around 10 to 15 minutes or while pouring water from a bottle, then pour on antiseptic (or alcohol if none is available). This helps stop the rabies virus entering the body and will guard against other wound infections.

Vaccination before travel is strongly recommended as there is almost certainly going to be a shortage of the specific post-exposure treatment in Uzbekistan. If you are unvaccinated before exposure, then you are likely to require a blood product Rabies Immunoglobulin (RIG) and definitely four doses of vaccine, given over 21 days. The RIG and first dose of vaccine should be given as soon as possible and ideally within the first 24 hours. RIG is not usually available at the time of writing in Uzbekistan and there have been some problems with sourcing rabies vaccine, too. If neither of those products is available, evacuation would be the only recourse. Having three doses of the vaccine before travel over a minimum of 21 days (it can be compressed over seven days if time is short, but requires an extra booster after a year) simplifies the post-exposure treatment by removing the need for RIG and reducing the post-exposure treatment to two doses of vaccine given three days apart. While evacuation may still be necessary, it is less of an emergency. Three doses of vaccine cost around £190 in the UK. Routine booster doses are not recommended for most travellers, but those at risk of occupational exposure (such as veterinary surgeons working overseas) will need regular boosters and antibody testing. Without the correct treatment for rabies following exposure, the mortality is almost 100%.

Tetanus Tetanus is caused by the *Clostridium tetani* bacterium and though it can accumulate on a variety of surfaces, it is most commonly associated with rusty objects such as nails. Cutting yourself or otherwise puncturing the skin brings the bacteria inside the body, where it will thrive. Clean any cuts thoroughly with a strong antiseptic.

Immunisation against tetanus gives good protection for ten years, and it is common practice to give a booster injection to any patient with a puncture wound. Symptoms of tetanus may include lockjaw, spasms in any part of the body, excessive sweating, drooling and incontinence, and the disease results in death if left untreated.

SAFETY

The UK's Foreign, Commonwealth and Development Office (FCDO) generally considers Uzbekistan to be a safe country for foreigners to travel in. It regularly updates its travel guidance, and the latest advice is available online at w fco.gov.uk.

Petty crime is rare but not unheard of, so do exercise usual caution regarding your belongings, especially when travelling on public transport. Some tourists do experience low-level corruption from traffic police and other officials, including at border crossings. If someone tries it on, ask for a receipt and don't hand over documents or cash on the street. Ask to be taken to the police station instead.

Driving standards in Uzbekistan are generally poor, and Karakalpakstan is no exception. The wide variety of vehicles on the roads, from decrepit Soviet-era makes to large modern 4x4s, makes for traffic travelling at different speeds. Overtaking on the inside and illegal U-turns are among many common infringements in the cities. The poor state of repair of many roads, with potholes and often inadequate or nonexistent street lighting, adds to the difficulties. In rural areas, animals and pedestrians wandering into the road present a considerable risk.

If you are driving yourself you will need to be careful and cautious, always wear a seatbelt, and never drink and drive. Try to avoid driving outside cities after dark as roads are poorly lit and other vehicles may not have working lights. Bad driving also creates a risk to pedestrians.

When on foot, you should avoid the local practice of crossing busy roads by walking out to the centre and waiting for a gap in the oncoming traffic, even if this means taking a detour to cross at the next set of traffic lights. Do not expect cars to stop for you, even if you are on a zebra crossing.

WOMEN TRAVELLERS

Uzbekistan is generally a safe country for women to travel in, and there are no specific legal or cultural restrictions imposed on women (either locals or foreigners). The social conditions of women improved significantly during the Soviet period, and the enrolment of women in education and in the workplace remains high. Gender roles remain traditional but relaxed.

Women should, however, exercise the usual personal safety precautions. Unaccompanied women may receive unwanted attention in bars and clubs, but this is usually deflected with a few terse words. If the harassment continues, alert the management or leave the premises and find a more pleasant alternative. Try to avoid physical confrontation, as alcohol-fuelled violence and being tailed home are not uncommon. Domestic violence is high in Uzbekistan, as it is across Central Asia. There have been suspected cases where 'date rape' drugs have been used; keep a close eye on your drink, and do not accept drinks from strangers.

You should dress practically and do not need to be overly worried about modesty: in summertime wearing loose sleeves to avoid sunburn is more of a priority. However, if you do intend to visit mosques and shrines it is polite to cover your head, shoulders and legs, and local people will appreciate your consideration.

LGBTQIA+ TRAVELLERS

Homosexuality (specifically sodomy) is illegal in Uzbekistan and Article 120 of the country's penal code punishes voluntary sexual intercourse between two men with up to three years in prison. Sexual intercourse between two women is not mentioned in the code.

Many people in Uzbekistan are deeply conservative, especially when it comes to the issue of sexuality, and homosexuality is still often seen as a mental illness (a hangover from the Soviet period). Muhammad Salih, leader of the People's Movement of Uzbekistan, said publicly in 2012: 'I support a civilised way of isolating

The UK's **gov.uk** website has a downloadable guide (w gov.uk/government/publications/disabled-travellers/disability-and-travel-abroad) giving general advice and practical information for travellers with a disability (and their companions) preparing for overseas travel. The **Society for Accessible Travel and Hospitality** (w sath.org) also provides some general information.

gays and other sick members of society so that they could not infect healthy people with their disease.' Sadly, his views are widely shared. Homosexuals in Uzbekistan regularly experience harassment, including from the police, who heavily monitor LGBTQIA-friendly establishments, often forcing them to close. Police detention and the threat of prosecution are regularly reported.

If you are travelling with a same-sex partner you should refrain from public displays of affection and be exceptionally cautious when discussing your relationship with others: it is often simplest to allow others to assume you are simply travelling with a friend. Double rooms frequently have twin beds, so asking for one room is unlikely to raise eyebrows in any case.

TRAVELLING WITH A DISABILITY

Travellers with disabilities will experience difficulty travelling in Uzbekistan. Public transport is rarely able to carry wheelchairs, few buildings have disabled access, and streets are littered with trip hazards. Hotel rooms are often spread over multiple floors without lifts and assistance from staff is not guaranteed. If you have a disability and are travelling to Uzbekistan, you would be advised to consult a local tour operator (page 46) in advance and travel with a companion who can help you when the country's infrastructure and customer service fall short.

TRAVELLING WITH KIDS

All communities in Karakalpakstan attach great importance to family life. Children are welcomed in restaurants and shops, but you may have difficulty manoeuvring pushchairs in and out of buildings and along broken pavements. Nappies, baby food and other similar items are available in supermarkets and larger stores, but you are unlikely to find European brands.

Journeys by car and public transport are often long and uncomfortable, however, and food supplies are erratic, which may deter families with younger children travelling beyond Nukus and those tourist sites accessible on a day trip from the capital. Ensure you stock up with plenty of snacks before leaving a town, and take plenty of entertainment options along for the ride.

WHAT TO TAKE

You may wish to consider the following, in addition to the usual holiday packing.

- **Plug adaptors** Sockets in Uzbekistan are the twin round-pin, continental European type. The voltage is 220V.
- **A torch** Many parts of Uzbekistan, including city streets, are unlit at night, and pavements may conceal dangers such as uncovered manholes. Power cuts are

Practical Information WHAT TO TAKE

2

not uncommon. If you are planning to stay in a yurt camp, or use homestays in rural areas, you'll need a torch to navigate to the toilet at night.

* **Filter bottle** The environmental cost of single-use plastic bottles is huge, so do your bit for the planet and bring a reusable water bottle with a three-in-one filter. We recommend Water-to-Go (w watertogo.eu). Alternatively you can use a regular bottle and add chlorine or iodine tablets, but you have to wait for these to work and they make the water taste strange.
* **Mosquito repellent** Uzbekistan is not a malarial country, but the swarms of mosquitoes you may encounter in the marshes and forests of Karakalpakstan can still damage your enjoyment of your holiday. Make sure you also pack long-sleeved shirts. For more information on avoiding insect bites, see page 56.
* **Warm clothing** If you are planning a trip to Karakalpakstan in the winter months (November to April), or plan to head up into the mountains or spend a night in the desert, you need to treat its cold temperatures with respect, with good warm clothing minimising areas of exposed skin. The locals often wrap themselves in sheepskin or furs, but outdoor adventure shops are probably the best source of suitably warm garments. Dress in several layers, with particularly warm (and preferably wind- and waterproof) outer garments.
* **Good footwear** In winter, wear strong, rubber-soled boots, preferably lined with fleece. If you are planning to go hiking in the desert, sturdy walking shoes or boots are essential.
* **Flip-flops** You'll need these inside homestay accommodation (shoes are left at the front door in Karakalpak and Uzbek homes). They also come in useful in less-than-savoury bathrooms.
* **Sheet sleeping bag** If you will be staying in bottom-range accommodation, a sleeping bag, of the kind used by youth hostellers, can help save you from unsavoury bedding.
* A **universal sink plug** is also worth packing.
* **Sun protection** Including good suncream, a lip salve and sunglasses (spare sets of any prescription glasses are also useful).
* **Toilet paper**, **wet wipes** and **hand sanitiser gel** are highly advisable and will make staying clean infinitely easier.
* **Dental floss** and a **needle**, a roll of **gaffer tape** and a packet of **cable ties** will enable you to fix almost anything while you're on the go.
* **Small gift items** related to your home country make ideal presents for hosts. Chocolates often melt, but photographs and souvenir items (think snow globes with castles or tea towels featuring cathedrals) go down a treat. Pictures of your home, family and friends are also popular.

MONEY AND BUDGETING

The unit of currency in Uzbekistan is the Uzbekistani som (UZS). It was first issued in 1993, and the current series of notes was released in 2021. Notes are printed in denominations from UZS2,000 to UZS200,000. The latter might sound like a large amount, but at the time of writing it was equivalent to less than US$18.

Uzbekistan is still a predominantly cash-based economy, though the government has been reforming the banking sector and is encouraging businesses to embrace online banking and digital payments. For now, you will only be able to pay by card (Visa, MasterCard and Union Pay, plus Uzbekistan's domestic variants) in large hotels and a few restaurants in Nukus; elsewhere you will need to pay cash.

ATMs are widespread in Karakalpakstan and you will find them in all the major towns. You need to check the logos on the front of the machines, however, as some banks can process Visa or MasterCard but not both. It is also not uncommon for ATMs to be out of cash or out of order, so make sure you plan ahead and keep some cash in reserve.

There are banks in most towns and providing they have sufficient cash behind the counter, all of them will change dollars, euros and roubles. If you need to change less common currencies (including sterling and the Swiss franc), you will need to take them to a branch of the National Bank of Uzbekistan. Uzbekistan's banks are less fussy than others in the region, but you should keep your foreign notes clean, unfolded and uncreased. If there are any marks on the notes, including ink stamps from being counted in a bank, they may be rejected. High-denomination bills are preferred, as are US dollars printed since 2006.

BUDGETING Karakalpakstan is a very cheap destination to visit, and by that we mean that even in Nukus you will find hostel accommodation for well under US$20 and can book a double room at the best hotel in the city for under US$70. Outside the capital, a double room in a guesthouse or small hotel is rarely more than US$25. The only downside to this is that all the current options are currently geared towards budget travellers: if you want to splash out on a four- or five-star hotel, you can't. At least not yet.

Cafés and restaurants tend to be similarly basic but affordable. A meat dish, bread and a couple of salads will usually cost no more than US$5, and you can have a feast at a good restaurant in Nukus for US$10 per head. Local beers are less than US$2 and often not dissimilar in price to a litre bottle of soft drink.

Museum, theatre and concert tickets in Karakalpakstan are an absolute bargain. Museum tickets are typically around US$3 with the exception of the Savitsky Museum, which still offers incredible value for money at US$5. Good seats at a theatre or for a concert are available for a similar price.

You will find the biggest variations in cost in public transport. Local buses and shared taxis are often only a couple of dollars, but if you hire a private car and driver then you will need to budget at least US$50 per day. Reaching the Aral Sea and BesQala Yurt Camp (page 110) is particularly expensive – approximately US$150 from Nukus – because you need a 4x4, and suitable vehicles and experienced drivers are both in short supply. It is possible to split the cost with other passengers, however, and tour operators (page 46) will facilitate this for you if there are others wanting to travel on the same dates.

Example costs for some basic items are:

litre bottle water	UZS2,000-3,000
½ litre beer	UZS7,000-15,000
loaf of bread	UZS2,000-6,000
street snack	UZS3,000-8,000
T-shirt	UZS40,000-200,000
litre of petrol	10,000-12,000

GETTING AROUND

Karakalpakstan is a large destination with inadequate transport infrastructure, which makes travel between many of its tourist attractions time consuming and uncomfortable. In many places you will need a taxi or other private vehicle as there is no public transport.

BY AIR Uzbekistan Airways (w uzairways.com) flies three times a week from Nukus to Muynak. The flight takes one hour, so although it is more expensive than going by road it can be a convenient option for those pushed for time.

BY RAIL A surprising number of towns in Karakalpakstan have a railway station, though not all of these have regular passenger services. Most useful for tourists is the line running north from Nukus towards Kazakhstan, as four trains a week stop at Khujayli, Kungrad and Karakalpakiya. Most tickets can be purchased in advance online (w chipta.railway.uz/en/home) but they are also available from the ticket desk at any station. If you are having difficulty finding information about trains or booking tickets, contact Advantour (page 47).

BY ROAD The majority of journeys in Karakalpakstan are by road. Upgrading the road surfaces on highways is a priority for the government and most of the work on the A380 running northwest from Nukus to the border has been completed, but there are still some sections in poor condition and trucks and cyclists alike must dodge the potholes or cross temporarily on to the parallel desert tracks for a smoother ride. Beyond the major routes, there is little signage and the road quality deteriorates significantly. In many areas roads are unsurfaced tracks through the desert. Street lighting is nonexistent outside towns (which cuts down on light pollution), but it is in any case inadvisable to drive after dark.

Karakalpakstan's cities and larger towns are linked by buses, but these are infrequent and often quite old and uncomfortable. Much more common are the shared taxis: regular cars taking multiple paying passengers heading to the same destination, which depart whenever they are full and are only a little more expensive than the bus. If you speak a few words in common, it can liven up the journey, but there is always the risk that you'll be squashed in next to someone who hasn't washed, is travelling with a live chicken, or insists on smoking in the car. If you don't want to wait – or you want more space – you can pay for the empty seats, at which point it is no different than a private taxi. Note that taxis of all kinds are not registered taxis but rather local people happy to chauffeur a paying passenger to their destination – they may or may not drive for a living. You will generally find a taxi stand near the main bazaar and/or near the bus station, but if there are two or more stands they may be going to different places. Be sure to check the *Getting there and away* section of the relevant chapter in this guide.

You will sometimes see the small white minibuses known as *mashrutkas* in Karakalpakstan. Generally these run along set routes within a city, but occasionally they shuttle back and forth between two nearby towns. Fares are very cheap but the minibuses can be overcrowded and are not always well maintained.

For longer journeys you may wish to hire a car and driver for several days. Our list of recommended drivers is on page 81. Prices start from US$50 per day but increase significantly if you want to go to the Aral Sea (page 121). There are no international car rental companies in Karakalpakstan and we seriously advise against self driving beyond the main roads due to the remoteness of these areas and the potential difficulties and dangers of driving in the desert.

STREET NAMES AND ADDRESSES Many streets are named after notable local or national figures, for example Sabir Kamalova, in which case they are listed in this guide with the first initial and the surname (ie: S Kamalova), as generally only the surname is used on the street signs and when giving directions. Amir Timur and Islam Karimov are notable exceptions to this rule. There are also multiple variations in spellings due to the difficulty of transliterating Karakalpak, Uzbek or Russian names written in Cyrillc script into Latin script. To further confuse you, some streets have two names. Usually these are a Soviet-era name and a new name, but local people may remember one and not the other, or use the two interchangeably. When listing addresses in this guide we have aimed to use the most common Latin spelling and the most common name.

For locations that do not have an easy-to-find street address we have given the what3words (page xiii) name. This is much more precise than a street address and particularly useful for identifying a location where there is no building number, or perhaps no street or building at all! A name is easier to remember and check than the long string of numbers required for a GPS coordinate of equivalent accuracy, and when reading or searching for it you are less likely to make a mistake.

MAPS The printed maps in this guide offer a reasonable level of detail and identify the location of all the points of interest mentioned in the text, but if you have a smartphone it is also well worth downloading the MAPS.ME app, which shows every street and building and works offline. In Karakalpakstan there are many more user-added points of interest on this app than on Google Maps, and you can also easily save and search your favourites and get directions between locations.

Our most-used country map is the 1:1,500,000 *Uzbekistan* published by the Russian company Roskartografia. It includes the country's road and rail networks (without the latest additions). The map comes with a separate index of place names and notes on history and geography. Its only downside is that place names are written in Cyrillic. Another reasonable option, this time in English, is the slightly newer (2008) 1:1,700,000 *Uzbekistan Tourist Map* produced by the state-run Cartographiya. It's in full colour, illustrated around the edges with a few good photographs. You may also like ITMB's (International Travel Maps and Books) *Uzbekistan* (1:1,580,000), which is the most up to date of the three options listed here (2010); ITMB also publishes *Uzbekistan, Kyrgyzstan and Tajikistan* (1:1,600,000).

ACCOMMODATION

Nukus has a fair selection of places to stay, all in the budget to mid-range bracket: there are not yet any hotels in Karakalpakstan that could be classed as upmarket or luxury. Once you leave the capital behind, however, accommodation choices are very limited, and in many locations there is no official accommodation at all.

ACCOMMODATION PRICE CODES

The price codes used in this guide indicate the approximate price of a standard double room, per night, including breakfast. In other destinations, the quality of rooms would equate to shoestring, budget, and mid-range options, as there are not yet any upmarket or luxury accommodation options in Karakalpakstan. The shoestring category also includes beds in shared rooms; property specific information is given in the accommodation listings in each chapter.

$$$ Over US$40
$$ US$20–40
$ Under US$20

Several donor-funded projects are planning to set up homestays in Karakalpakstan, and there are some ad-hoc options in Muynak that are operational during the Stihia festival, but for now if you want to book a homestay you will need to ask a local tour operator for the latest available options.

The best accommodation, equivalent to a three-star hotel, is in Nukus and is priced in the mid-range bracket, costing US$40 to US$60 per night for a double room. In these hotels you can expect modern, well-equipped rooms with AC and en-suite bathrooms, a restaurant or breakfast room, and 24/7 reception staff who usually speak a little English. They can generally be booked online or by email, and can accept foreign card payments. Such hotels tend to be a good source of tourist information, too, and staff can usually introduce you to reliable local drivers or call other hotels and guesthouses to make reservations on your behalf.

The majority of places to stay in Karakalpakstan are in the **budget** category, with double rooms priced between US$20 and US$40. They include local hotels and guesthouses; the latter tend to have a bit more character and offer a warmer welcome. Breakfast is usually included in the price, but there won't be a restaurant on site. Guesthouses may, however, offer to prepare you an evening meal. In general these accommodation options are clean but plumbing can be temperamental and staff will probably not speak English. You are unlikely to be able to book online but you can pre-book by calling ahead or, if there's a language barrier, using Google Translate and texting.

There are also quite a few **shoestring** options with prices under US$20 per night, and those we have chosen to list in the guide are not bad at all. They include a mixture of family-run guesthouses and hostels, usually offering dormitory-style rooms with a shared bathroom. In some instances, the bathroom may be outside, and squat toilets are not uncommon. Breakfast may or may not be included.

Yurt camps are increasingly popular in Karakalpakstan and an important part of the area's ecotourism development. Some of these, including the BesQala Yurt Camp (page 110) and the Ayaz Kala Yurt Camp (page 181) are large and well established; others just have a couple of yurts and are still working out how to service the tourists who want to stay. In each yurt there are usually two to five single beds with clean sheets and multiple layers of duvets and blankets, and lighting powered by a generator or solar panel. You can book a yurt for a single person or couple, or share with others to bring down the cost. Toilet and shower facilities (where available) are basic and separate to the yurts. As the yurt camps are in remote locations, breakfast and dinner are usually available and included in the price. Yurts fall into the mid-range through to budget category.

Campsites are uncommon in Uzbekistan and there are no official campsites in Karakalpakstan. While it is permitted to camp in the national parks and in the deserts, setting up a tent in other public places is generally frowned upon. If you wish to put up a tent on private land, you will need to ask the owner and will usually be expected to pay the som equivalent of a few dollars.

EATING AND DRINKING

Food in Karakalpakstan exhibits a wide range of culinary influences, reflecting the region's Silk Road and Soviet history as well as the ingredients grown and made by the Karakalpak, Uzbek, Kazakh, Turkmen and other communities living here today. As the population was traditionally nomadic or semi-nomadic, and the

◀ BesQala Yurt Camp at the Aral Sea.

dominant agricultural crop is cotton not foodstuffs, meat and carbohydrates are the dietary staples, but there is fantastic fresh produce in season, with market stalls groaning under its weight.

Whether you are eating breakfast, lunch or dinner, there will always be bread on the table. The traditional round, flat loaves are called *non* (a word with the same root as Indian *naan*), made from wheat flour. They are most delicious when eaten still warm from the *tandor* (clay oven) and are used for everything from dipping in sour cream to soaking up meat juices. In Turkish restaurants you can also find *lavash*, a thin, unleavened flat bread also cooked in a *tandor*. Every neighbourhood has local bakeries that supply families and cafés alike.

Very similar wheat doughs are used for many other Karakalpak dishes. These include *bauirsak* (thinly rolled rectangular pieces of dough fried in oil), *sozban* (large fried flat cakes), *samsa* (a stuffed, triangular pastry akin to an Indian samosa), and two local kinds of noodles, *kespas* and *kaysas*, which are cooked in milk and sour milk and, in the case of the latter, also seasoned with oil. Many restaurants also serve *laghman*, another variety of noodles that are common on Uzbek and Uighur cuisine and come soaked in a stew of meat and vegetables. *Mayek borek* is a form of layered pastry made with eggs, butter and fried onions. You will find variations of dumplings almost everywhere, including *beshbarmak,* a highly popular Kazakh dish, which is a combination of dough and boiled meat cooked in a meat broth; *manti* (steamed dumplings usually filled with meat or pumpkin); and *pelmeni*, the Russian equivalent of ravioli, which are stuffed and served in broth.

The most common meats in Karakalpakstan are beef and lamb, followed by chicken. Other meats such as horse, camel and rabbit are less commonly served, and your host would tell you proudly if they were going to give you these, so you are unlikely to eat them by accident. As Uzbekistan is a Muslim-majority country, it is very rare to see pork on a menu. It's not illegal, there's simply no local demand for it. Meats are usually roasted, boiled or grilled in kebabs called *shashlik*, which may include cubes of fat or vegetables as well as meat. Slices of meat also top *plov*, the rice-based national dish of Uzbekistan, which is included on UNESCO's Intangible Cultural Heritage list. Historically fish was an important part of the diet due to the large fish stocks in the Aral Sea, but as those are now gone, it's less common. Fish on a menu in places like Nukus and Muynak is likely to come from the Amu Darya or one of Karakalpakstan's lakes. Usually it is deep fried.

If you are in Karakalpakstan in summer and early autumn, the markets are bursting with fresh fruits, some which are grown here and others which come from more fertile parts of Uzbekistan such as the Fergana Valley. The season starts with strawberries in April, then various kinds of cherries in May, peaches and apricots in June, watermelons (the size of beach balls) in July, plums in August and grapes, pomegranates, pears and persimmons in September and October. Apples – which coincidentally evolved in what is now Kazakhstan – are available all year.

The same markets are good places to pick up snacks for long journeys. Dried fruits and nuts are always on sale, as are wrapped chocolates and sweets, biscuits sold by weight, and crisps. If you want something more substantial to eat there and then, you can watch the *shashlik* sizzling on the grill and devour it with a freshly baked *non*, or have *samsa* hot from the *tandor*.

Vegetarians are in for a tough time in Karakalpakstan, and vegans even more so. These concepts are little understood, and even less frequently catered for. It is usually possible to identify some suitable salads on a menu, plus of course bread,

---

1 Nukus's Main Bazaar. 2 Traditional round, flat loaves or *non*. ▶

but beyond that the best approach is to select a dish that could be made vegetarian with the removal or substitution of one of the ingredients. Be very specific about what you ask for; staff will do their best to help but need clear instructions. If you are going to be eating meals at a guesthouse or yurt camp, you will need to inform them of your dietary needs in advance so that they have time to plan and prepare something suitable.

DRINKS Tea is as much a cultural institution as it is a drink and the *chaikhana* (tea house) is central to any community: people go to do business as well as gossip and relax. Green tea (*zilloniy chai*) is most common, but black tea (*chorniy chai*) is also widely available. Both are drunk without milk but you will usually be offered sugar or lemon. In summer you may also be offered *ayran* or kefir (chilled yoghurt drinks).

Coffee is available in hotels and restaurants, but it is generally instant coffee and aficionados will be disappointed. The exception is in Nukus where there are several proper coffee shops grinding beans and able to serve anything from a double espresso to a frappuccino. Just don't expect to be offered non-dairy milks.

In terms of other soft drinks, bottled water is available everywhere, but if you can bring your own reusable filter bottle, please do as there are no recycling facilities for single-use plastics and every used bottle ends up in landfill. Restaurants and grocery shops always have carbonated drinks in bottles and concentrate juice in cartons, from both international and local brands, and you can get freshly squeezed fruit juices on street side stalls and in the markets.

Alcohol is consumed in Uzbekistan, though less so than in the other Central Asian republics. Both beer and spirits (particularly vodka and whisky) are widely available in shops and restaurants, as well as in many hotels, and it is sometimes possible to buy Uzbek wines. Local brands are much less expensive than foreign ones owing to the high import taxes. There is no clear distinction between bars and restaurants, because bars always serve food as well as drinks, and restaurants often have music and a dance floor.

EATING OUT Nukus's restaurant and café scene has become much more vibrant in recent years, and it is the local middle class more than foreign tourists who are driving the growth and diversification of the hospitality sector. Here you have a wide variety of places to eat, including good Turkish and Korean restaurants (page 84) in addition to those serving local cuisine. There are a number of restaurants where service is professional, there's a good ambience, and you can have a leisurely evening with several courses and a few beers or a bottle of wine. Several Western-style cafés have their own bakeries and produce coffee and excellent cakes, which is great for a pick-me-up between museums.

Outside Nukus your options for eating out are very much more limited. Towns generally have a few simple, clean if not exactly atmospheric cafés all serving

RESTAURANT PRICE CODES

The price codes used in this guide indicate the average price of a meat-based main course. The cost of side dishes, dessert, and/or drinks would be on top.

$$$ Over US$5
$$ US$2.50–5
$ Under US$2.50

a similar menu of local dishes: *shashlik*, dumplings, salads, etc. Eating out is inexpensive, and although individual dishes are often tasty, the lack of variety on menus can be quite monotonous, so it is worth also visiting local markets for fresh fruit and other snacks. Having a *non* and a few chocolate bars or packets of crisps to hand can also be a saviour on long journeys; these are widely available in grocery stores. In remote areas, you may be invited to eat in local homes. Even if your hosts initially refuse payment, try to find some way to compensate them for their hospitality as feeding you will have cost them both money and time.

PUBLIC HOLIDAYS AND FESTIVALS

14 January	Day of Defenders of the Fatherland
8 March	International Women's Day
21 March	Navruz (Persian New Year)
9 May	Remembrance Day
1 September	Independence Day
1 October	Teachers' Day
8 December	Constitution Day
31 December–4 January	New Year

These dates are public holidays when schools and government offices will be shut. Restaurants, visitor attractions, and shops generally remain open, however, and the cultural celebrations associated with the holiday may last for several days either side. This is particularly the case for Navruz, which officially marks the start of spring.

The Islamic festivals of **Eid ul-Fitr** and **Eid al-Adha** are also celebrated with public prayers and family events. As they are based on the lunar calendar their dates change from one year to the next. The anticipated dates for the next few years are as follows:

10 April/16 June 2024
30 March/6 June 2025
20 March/26 May 2026
9 March/16 May 2027

SHOPPING

The opportunities for shopping in Karakalpakstan are much less developed than elsewhere in Uzbekistan, which is disappointing as the region has a rich applied arts tradition and many tourists would happily buy souvenirs and gifts if they were more widely available. You can find a small selection of handicrafts on sale in Nukus and Muynak (the *Shopping* sections in their respective chapters give details) but the best option is to visit the crafts workshops in Chimbay (page 147) and to buy items directly from the artisans. Of particular interest are silver jewellery, felt rugs and other items such as slippers, weaving and embroidery.

You should, however, plan to visit at least one bazaar while you are in Karakalpakstan because the multisensory experience of browsing, chatting, tasting and haggling offers great insight into local life. What you buy is immaterial, but *non* straight from the *tandor*, a glass of freshly squeezed pomegranate juice, or a bag of lightly salted almonds or pistachios would invariably be good choices. The dried fruits and nuts travel well, too.

ARTS AND ENTERTAINMENT

Karakalpakstan has a proud tradition of performing arts (page 36). Theatres, concert halls and cinemas were all established here during the Soviet period and the main venues in Nukus still have regular performances of local and touring productions. As in many countries, there is insufficient investment in the arts, but supporters do their best to keep their favourite cultural institutions afloat.

Most of Nukus's theatres do not have an online presence and hence do not advertise or sell tickets for performances online. In fact, the programme is often not announced more than a week or two in advance. If you do want to go to the theatre or a concert during your visit, either call or ask one of the local tour operators (page 46) or hotels (page 83) to check what's on for you. Tickets need to be purchased from the box offices and paid for in cash. Prices vary depending on the performance, venue, and category of seat but are unlikely to cost more than US$5. It is rare for performances to sell out, unless it is a celebrity performing at the Amphitheatre.

PHOTOGRAPHY

Many of the photography and video restrictions that used to be in force in Uzbekistan have been lifted, but use of drones is still tightly controlled. You are only allowed to import or operate a drone if you have a permit, which you should apply for via an Uzbek Embassy (page 50) before you travel. Processing the application takes at least one month and there is no guarantee that approval will be granted.

As in most countries of the world, pointing any sort of camera in the direction of military installations and personnel, border crossings or government buildings is to be avoided. It is not worth having your camera kit (or camera phone) seized just for the sake of an otherwise useless picture of a typical border post or concrete bridge across the Amu Darya.

It is always polite to ask before taking someone's photo, and even if you don't speak the same language, gesturing to the camera or phone and then to them, and watching their reaction, will give you a good idea. If you are using a long lens this may not be feasible, but if you can, it's still considerate to ask permission first.

MEDIA AND COMMUNICATIONS

MEDIA A government decree officially ended state censorship of the media in 2002. In reality, however, all forms of media in Uzbekistan remain strictly controlled, and although there has been some improvement under President Mirziyoyev, Uzbekistan still falls far short of having freedom of the press. Visiting media (including bloggers) require accreditation to be allowed to report from Uzbekistan, the government broadcaster operates the main TV and radio networks, and the government also keeps a tight grip on the internet.

NEWS The readership of newspapers in Uzbekistan is low, with figures estimated to be not more than 50,000 people countrywide, and there are no regional newspapers focused on events in Karakalpakstan. The state controls newspaper distribution and materials supply, hence the market is dominated by the three state-owned papers

1 Berdakh Theatre. 2 & 4 Handicrafts for sale. 3 Visit a bazaar for a glass of freshly squeezed pomegranate juice ▶

Halq Sozi, *Narodnoye Slovo* and *Pravda Vostoka*. *Halq Sozi* is published in Uzbek and the other two papers are in Russian.

Most people in Uzbekistan get their news from the television or from online sources, including popular Telegram accounts. The four state-owned TV channels dominate the television market, though there are a large number of small, private channels. The State Press Committee and the Inter-Agency Coordination Committee issue broadcast licences to such channels, and withdraw licences swiftly from those organisations that pursue too independent a line.

Uzbekistan's national news agency, the imaginatively named Uzbekistan News Agency, is state-controlled. Reuters and the Associated Press (AP) both have offices in the country, though they are only able to work within strictly enforced confines. The most balanced English-language news sources are to be found online from agencies based outside Uzbekistan, such as Eurasianet (w eurasianet. org), Novastan (w novastan.org/en), and Central Asia & South Caucasus Bulletin (w thebulletin.news).

TELEPHONE The country code for Uzbekistan is +998. To call abroad from inside Uzbekistan, dial 810 and then the country code. Mobile numbers begin with 09 (drop the 0 when calling from abroad) and do not need to be prefixed with an area code. Emergency numbers are 101 for fire, 102 for police and 103 for ambulance.

Like so many other developing countries, Uzbekistan has jumped from having almost no communications infrastructure to having mobile phone penetration of nearly 100%. For clarity, that means that there is the equivalent of one mobile phone per person, not that every person actually has a phone. Every town and most villages have signal on one or more of the local networks but there are still some signal black spots in remote areas, including large parts of the Ustyurt Plateau.

Uzbekistan has five mobile network providers, the most popular of which are Beeline, Mobiuz and Ucell. To get a SIM card you will need to take your passport to one of the providers' offices or branded stores. They can also be obtained in the arrivals hall at Tashkent Airport. Filling out the various forms and processing them takes about 15 minutes. Depending on the network, you'll either pay around US$3, or the SIM will be free when you top up by a certain amount.

Topping up your phone is easy. You can do it in any store that shows your network's logo and at any Paynet machine, found in or outside convenience stores or other places with high foot traffic. These allow you to type in your phone number, feed in bank notes and voilá! You've topped up.

If you are using a foreign handset and plan to stay in Uzbekistan for longer than 30 days (or to return for another visit), you need to register it with **UZIMEI** (w uzimei.uz/en). Follow the step-by-step instructions on its website.

INTERNET Thanks to the availability of cheap mobile data, a high proportion of people in Karakalpakstan are now online. Most people use the internet for social media, in particular the Telegram app, and more and more businesses are accepting local payment apps. In general the connection speed is good, though data is less likely to be available in rural areas.

Hotels and many cafés tend to have Wi-Fi, at least in theory; however, connections are, generally speaking, very weak and you may not be able to connect. Websites, including critical news sites, are sometimes blocked in Uzbekistan and the government has been known to turn off the internet at times of crisis, for example during the 2022 protests (page 23).

POST Uzbekistan does have a domestic postal service with a central post office (marked Uz Post or O'zbekiston Pochtasi) in most large towns, but you are likely to arrive home before your postcards (US$3), if indeed they arrive at all. Letters and parcels are generally transported internally by hand (you may be asked to carry a gift to your next destination for so and so's relative) and couriers and diplomatic bags are the preferred method to send and receive anything overseas.

BUSINESS

Uzbekistan is not an easy place to do business, either for locals or foreign investors, but it is getting better: in the last World Bank *Doing Business* index (2020), Uzbekistan ranked #69, comparable to Oman and Vietnam, a dramatic improvement since 2013 when the country ranked #154. This is the result of reforms relating to protection of minority investors, simplifying the tax system and cross-border trade, and making it easier to enforce contracts. Any legal entity, be it an individual or an organisation, may invest in Uzbekistan. Foreigners can both establish companies and buy shares in existing companies. A company will be considered a foreign investment if its fund capital exceeds US$150,000 and 30% of the share value is held by foreign entities. Investments can be made into all economic sectors, and tax exemptions of up to seven years are available for companies investing in the manufacturing of electronic components, light industry, silk production, construction materials, food production (in particular poultry, meat and dairy products), chemicals and pharmaceuticals.

The first port of call for anyone interested in investing in or doing business with Uzbekistan is the website of the Investment Promotion Agency (w invest.gov.uz; +998 71 202 0210). The English-language version of the site is well written and clearly explains all relevant legislation, as well as giving details of ongoing investment opportunities. Priority projects are categorised by region and sector, and there is a long list for Karakalpakstan. You can contact the IPA's call centre with queries, or arrange a face-to-face meeting with the trade attaché at an Uzbek Embassy (page 50). Organisations such as the Uzbek-British Trade & Industry Council (UBTIC) and AmCham Uzbekistan (w amcham.uz) are also useful sources of information, recommendations and contacts.

Doing business in Uzbekistan is strongly dependent on personal relationships. You will be expected to spend significant time getting to know potential business partners or clients and how they work, and this may include socialising and spending time with their families as well as more formal business meetings. If you are pitching for a contract, your bid will be considered not solely in terms of cost or quality; how the client feels about you and your colleagues will often be a contributing factor too.

Problems also occur from mismatched expectations; though Uzbekistan is now nominally capitalist, central planning and state ownership still dominate many people's thinking, and intricacies of concepts that Western companies take for granted, such as investment and shares, may have to be carefully explained. Understanding of what does and does not constitute corruption are often wildly different, as is the extent to which fast-tracking, the payment of fees, goodwill gestures and even all-out extortion are acceptable. You will need to maintain good lines of communication, explain everything clearly (even if you think it is obvious) and ask plenty of questions.

CULTURAL ETIQUETTE

Hospitality towards guests is an important part of culture in Karakalpakstan and it is offered frequently and genuinely, even to strangers. If you are invited to

2

someone's home, you should take a small gift for your hosts. A souvenir item, such as a picture book, from your home country is ideal, but if you have brought nothing suitable with you a gift such as a bouquet of flowers (get an odd number) or box of chocolates or sweets is fine. Note that an invitation to go to someone's house for 'a cup of tea' invariably means something more substantial: often a full meal. If you bring biscuits, dried fruit and nuts or chocolates, they might well be added to the spread. At the end of the meal, thanks are given by the act of bringing the hands together in front of the face, then moving them down in an action symbolising a washing gesture. This is the signal for everyone to get up from the table. You shouldn't continue to pick at food after this point.

On entering a home or guesthouse (regardless of whether it is a flat, a house or a yurt) you should remove your shoes at the door. There is usually a mixture of assorted slippers and flip-flops available to wear around the house.

Mosques, shrines and other holy places often have their own sets of rules and you should endeavour to observe these. If in doubt, ask the guardian or someone else who appears to work or worship there, as it is better to appear naïve than disrespectful. Requirements are likely to include removing your shoes, covering your head (women only) and wearing long trousers or a skirt that covers the knees.

In general, men do not wear shorts except when playing sport, but foreigners are generally excused. Some women also cover their legs and hair; again, foreigners are free to dress as they wish.

And finally, toilets – you'll usually find Western-style WCs in hotels and restaurants, but squat toilets are still commonplace, especially in more rural areas. In either case, the plumbing and sewage system is not designed to cope with toilet paper so you should always put used paper in the bin provided.

TRAVELLING POSITIVELY

Economic development is critically important for Karakalpakstan, and tourism has an important role to play in delivering growth and jobs. As a responsible tourist, think about where and how you spend your money, remembering that staying in family-run guesthouses, eating in local restaurants, hiring local guides and drivers, and buying local crafts and foodstuffs are all great ways to put your money directly into the local community.

There are lots of other ways you can contribute to the improvement of Karakalpakstan, the development of its communities, and the protection of its natural spaces and wildlife. Stihia (page 128), the festival founded in Muynak and now changing location each year, relies on a huge tribe of enthusiastic volunteers before and during the festival, which is a fun if exhausting way to give back. Donating to UN-supported **#GreenAralSea** (w greenaralsea.org) funds the planting of drought-resistant saxaul on the dried seabed of the Aral Sea. You might also consider donating to or volunteering with the **Saiga Conservation Alliance** (w saiga-conservation.org), which not only protects saiga antelope but also provides educational and economic opportunities for communities living near saiga herds.

Part Two

THE GUIDE

3

Nukus

Many travel writers, including the British journalist A A Gill, have been far from complimentary about Nukus. Those who paid but a fleeting visit to the city have frequently described it as grim or depressing, but by and large their reporting is lazy and out of date. Yes, there was a time when tourists would arrive on the morning flight from Tashkent, visit the Savitsky Museum and leave that same evening for Khiva, but in recent years Nukus has come into its own. You only have to walk or drive down any of the main streets to see how much money has been invested in modern public buildings and commercial real estate. The Nukus Free Economic Zone (FEZ) established in 2019 is attracting investment, and the profits from Karakalpakstan's booming gas sector are clearly evident, too. It seems a new restaurant or café is opening almost every week, and the growing middle class has plenty of money in their pockets to spend.

This isn't to say that Nukus is a pretty place polished for tourists: it is a working city of around 330,000 people, with an economy based on industry, manufacturing and agriculture. As the Karakalpak capital, it also has a political function: the Supreme Council of the Republic of Karakalpakstan is here, housed in a large and impressive building, and so too are government ministries. There are national museums, theatres and concert halls, parks, major banks, hospitals and all of the other infrastructure, including an international airport, which citizens and visitors alike need. There's plenty to see and do to plan a two- to three-day itinerary entirely within the city limits, but as the hotel accommodation in Nukus is the best in Karakalpakstan, we also recommend using the city as a base for exploring nearby destinations such as Mizdakhan (page 162), the Lower Amudarya State Biosphere Reserve (page 169) and the desert fortresses (page 182).

HISTORY

As recently as the early 1930s, Nukus was little more than a village. One of the few Western travellers to visit in the early 20th century was the Swiss adventurer, photographer and writer Ella Maillart, who came in 1932. She described a shortage of accommodation caused by an influx of construction workers building the new hospital, and also the regular arrival of steamer ships which had crossed the Aral Sea and brought timber (even then in short supply) from the Urals. At that time, the administrative capital of the recently created Karakalpak ASSR (Autonomous Soviet Socialist Republic) was Tortkul (page 189), more than 180km to the south. But the Amu Darya on which both settlements lie is a fickle neighbour, often changing course, and substantial flooding in Tortkul in 1932 caused significant damage. The capital needed to be moved, and in 1939 political power and economic investment shifted north to Nukus.

The settlement then began to grow. By 1940 there were already factories for brick making, woodworking and processing alfalfa. The output of agricultural produce (much of which was processed or sold in Nukus) increased, and there was demand for much larger and more sophisticated irrigation schemes. The construction of the Turkmen Canal began in 1950 and was intended to run from the southern side of Nukus all the way to Turkmenbashi on the Caspian Sea, though the project was abandoned after Stalin's death in 1953.

From the late 1950s onwards, Igor Savitsky (page 92) began collecting archaeological and ethnographic artefacts and, later, artworks, including those from Soviet artists who had been purged. He campaigned for the local authorities to build a museum in Nukus, and what has become known as the Savitsky Museum opened in 1966, with Savitsky as its first curator. Thanks in part to the remoteness and relative isolation of Nukus, Savitsky's avant-garde art collection went largely unnoticed or ignored by the Soviet authorities, and thus survives to the present day.

Nukus was regionally important, but this didn't mean it was easy to visit. The Soviet authorities wanted to keep people – and foreigners in particular – out. This is because in the dying decades of the USSR, Nukus was also the location of the infamous Chemical Research Institute – a closed military complex where scientists worked on the Soviet Union's chemical weapons programme. Their projects included the development of the nerve agent Novichok, which became infamous in 2018 when the Russian government used it to poison double agent Sergei Skripal in the UK and killed two unconnected British nationals; and also in an unsuccessful assassination attempt against political opposition figure Alexei Navalny in 2020. After independence in 1991, the first president of Uzbekistan, Islam Karimov, renounced weapons of mass destruction and invited American

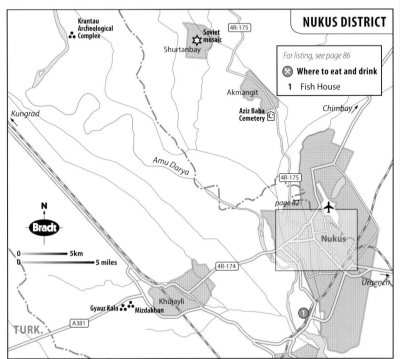

experts to dismantle and decontaminate the complex under the Pentagon's Cooperative Threat Reduction programme. This paved the way for Nukus to open up, inviting investment, businesses and tourists in.

GETTING THERE AND AWAY

Nukus has the best transport infrastructure in Karakalpakstan, and consequently you are likely to start and/or end your visit here.

BY AIR **Nukus International Airport** (A Dosnazarov; 61 226 0023) is on the northeastern side of the city centre, though still within the city limits. At the time of writing there are two flights a day (1hr 40mins) from Tashkent with Uzbekistan Airways, two flights a week from Moscow (3hr 30) and Aktau (1hr), and three weekly flights from Muynak (1hr). See page 123 for more details.

The drive from the airport to most hotels and tourist sites is under 10 minutes and there are usually taxi drivers waiting outside arrivals. If there aren't any there, or you prefer to book a taxi in advance, call one of the local drivers (see below).

BY CAR Driving to Nukus with your own vehicle is relatively straightforward, as the main roads through Karakalpakstan and connecting to Kazakhstan, Turkmenistan and other parts of Uzbekistan all intersect in the city. There are no international car-hire companies in Nukus, but it is possible to book a car with a local driver; either contact a local tour operator (page 46) or get in touch with one of the following drivers by phone or on Telegram (w telegram.org), all of whom are highly recommended.

Bakhtijar 97 789 5866. Bakhtijar speaks Russian only but is professional & reliable.
Kasim 99 095 8841. Kasim speaks just a few words of English but is a superb off-road driver & knows the Aral Sea region like the back of his hand.

Oktyabr 99 535 3228. Oktyabr is an archaeologist & guide in addition to being a driver & speaks fluent English.

BY BUS AND TAXI Buses and taxis leave from different places, depending on their destination. Buses for Muynak (3½hrs; UZS20,000) depart from the **bus station**, 3km southwest of Nukus on the main road to Khujayli, at the T-junction with Takhiatashskoye. They depart three times a day (09.00, noon & 15.00). Shared taxis depart from the same location throughout the day as soon as they are full (3½hrs; UZS60,000 pp).

The informal **taxi stand** for Urgench (3hrs) is at the junction of G Sheraziev and Pushkin. The journey costs UZS100,000 per person in a shared taxi, or UZS400,000 for the whole car. The shared taxis leave when they are full.

Qubla bus station is the station for long-distance services, found to the southeast of the city at the junction of the A380 and the A381. There are daily buses to Tashkent, departing at 14.00 (UZS150,000) and two buses a day to Bukhara, Navoi and Samarkand, departing at noon and 14.00 (UZS71,500, UZS85,500 & UZS106,000 respectively). There are also buses to more local destinations including Mangit (frequent but non-scheduled departures; UZS9,000), Beruni (10.00; UZS18,000), Buston (13.00; UZS18,000), Tortkul (11.30; UZS22,000) and Urgench (14.00; UZS22,000), which is the closest transport hub for Khiva.

◀ 1 The Savitsky Museum opened in 1966. 2 State Museum of History and Culture of Karakalpakstan. 3 Mosque of Imam Ishan Muhammad.

3

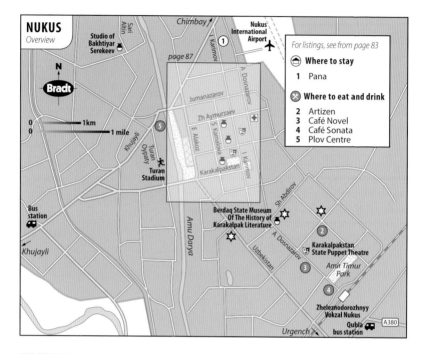

Within the map:

NUKUS
Overview

Studio of
Bakhtiyar
Serekeev

Chimbay

Nukus
International
Airport

For listings, see from page 83

Where to stay
1 Pana

Where to eat and drink
2 Artizen
3 Café Novel
4 Café Sonata
5 Plov Centre

N

page 87

Sari Altin

A Dosnazarov

Jumanazarov

Zh Aymurzaev

E Alakoz

S Kamalova

I Karimov

K Karimov

Khujayli

Turan Oypday

Turan
Stadium

Karakalpakstan

0 1km
0 1 mile

Bus
station

Khujayli

Amu Darya

Uzbekistan

Berdaq State Museum
Of The History of
Karakalpak Literature

Sh Abdirov

A Dosnazarov

Karakalpakstan
State Puppet Theatre

Amir Timur
Park

Zheleznodorozhnyy
Vokzal Nukus

Urgench

Qubla
bus station

A380

BY TRAIN Nukus's train station, **Zheleznodorozhnyy Vokzal Nukus** (📞 61 223 2952), is on the southern side of the city in Microdistrict 22. There are daily departures to/from Tashkent (16hrs; from UZS166,650) and Bukhara (9hrs; from UZS115,940), and on Wednesday, Thursday, Friday and Sunday there are trains to Volgograd in Russia (39hrs; from UZS1,050,000). The Volgograd train stops at Khujayli, Kungrad and Karakalpakiya, which may be convenient if you are planning to explore northern Karakalpakstan. There are also three trains a week from Nukus to Beyneu (Tue, Fri & Sun; 8½hrs; from UZS64,435), where you can connect to Aktau and other destinations in Kazakhstan.

The easiest way to check timetables and buy tickets is online (w chipta.railway. uz/en/home). If tickets appear to be sold out on the website, it is worth going to the ticket desk at the station as they usually have more available for sale over the counter.

Note that the overnight train to Tashkent doesn't always have a restaurant car, but there is no indication of this on the website. You can check by calling the station a couple of days before the train's departure date, but to be safe pack a picnic as well.

It was announced in 2022 that the high-speed train line linking Tashkent to Samarkand and Bukhara would be extended to Urgench, Khiva and Nukus by 2026. This may be an ambitious timetable, especially for the Nukus link, but those travelling to Karakalpakstan in 2026 onwards should check the Uzbekistan Railways website (w railway.uz.en) for the latest news and schedules.

ORIENTATION

Nukus is a modern, planned city mostly laid out as a grid. Its centre is bound on the west by the Amu Darya, the river that runs almost due north, the airport lies to the northeast and the railway station is to the southeast. The two main bus stations (page 81) are beyond these boundaries, however, which necessitates taking a taxi from the centre.

The main roads in Nukus are wide, straight and typically lined with public buildings and shops. Most streets are named, with periodic street signs on the buildings at first-floor level so you know where you are. Somewhat confusingly, many streets in Nukus have two names: their Soviet-era name and the new name they have been given since independence. Local people sometimes use the two names interchangeably – for example S Kamalova and Tatibaev are one and the same. For consistency, we have used the street name most likely to be found on online maps, though there are discrepancies even between different apps.

The majority of sites of interest to tourists are concentrated between the river and A Dosnazarov to the east, J Amurzaeva in the north, and Amir Timur in the south. Within this zone, no two sights are more than 1.5km apart and it is quick, convenient and safe to walk between them. If you ever get lost, the two easiest landmarks to ask for and make towards are the Savitsky Museum in the city centre, or the multi-storey Hotel Tashkent to the west of the centre near the river. Both are known to everyone in Nukus and have English-speaking staff who can help you continue on your way.

GETTING AROUND

Central Nukus is easily walkable, with wide, well-maintained pavements and clearly marked pedestrian crossings with traffic lights. If needed, you can hail a taxi on the street safely or call 1191, 1053 or 1222 (noting that dispatchers are unlikely to speak English) and a car will be sent to your address. Not all taxis are marked, so if you call you will be given the registration number and colour of the vehicle to help you identify it when it arrives. Taxi drivers have meters on their smartphones that automatically calculate the distance and the cost, and they do actually use them, so you are unlikely to need to haggle over the price. The standard fare is UZS10,000–15,000 within the city centre.

TOURIST INFORMATION

There is not yet an official tourist information office in Nukus, but the English-speaking staff at Hotel Jipek Joli (see below) and Tashkent Hotel (page 84) are able and willing to provide basic information and recommendations for visitors.

WHERE TO STAY   *Map, page 87, unless otherwise stated*

Nukus has the widest selection of accommodation options in Karakalpakstan, which is why it works so well as a base for exploring the surrounding areas, as well as for sightseeing in the city itself. There aren't any high-end or luxury properties yet, or hotels belonging to international chains, though we live in hope that one of these might open within the lifespan of this edition.

Hotel Jipek Joli (21 rooms) S Kamalova 50; 61 222 1100; e jipekhotel@gmail.com; w jipekjoli.com. The newer of Jipek Joli's 2 properties is a 5-min walk from the Savitsky Museum on a quiet residential street. The English-speaking reception staff are professional & helpful & used to hosting tour groups as well as independent travellers. Rooms are large & simply decorated but comfortably equipped, with immaculate en-suite bathrooms. Free Wi-Fi, but the signal is weak in some rooms. $$$

Pana Hotel [map, page 82] (36 rooms) Miymandos 2; 97 220 1996; e aytmuratov96@ gmail.com; w bit.ly/3SPtAat. Very close to Nukus International Airport, this clean, modern hotel is well looked after, & staff are welcoming & helpful. All rooms have kettles with tea & coffee, TV & AC. The hotel also organises tours to the Aral Sea, Muynak & to the other family business, a dairy farm with goats & cows (@panaevfarms). $$$

Tashkent Hotel (72 rooms) Uzbekistan 59A; 61 224 0200; e tashkenthotel2018@gmail. com. Close to the main bridge across the river, the Tashkent is a large, modern hotel predominantly catering to business visitors. All rooms are en suite & have AC, a kettle & a fridge. There is good Wi-Fi throughout & an ATM in the lobby. Staff at reception speak English. $$$

BesQala Guesthouse (7 rooms) A Navoi 121; 91 377 7729; w besqala.com. BesQala is the most popular budget option in Nukus, with clean twin rooms & 3- & 5-bed dorms. There is a courtyard with traditional tables out front, & a decorative yurt. Reception staff are friendly & can organise trips to the Aral Sea with BesQala Tours (page 46). $$

FriendsJ (11 rooms) Sayahatchilar 26A; 97 500 4029; e janhyr76@gmail.com; w bit.ly/3LWBlci. With a décor typical of Soviet houses, this family-owned guesthouse is a new addition to Nukus's accommodation scene. The family is friendly & will help with any queries, though they speak more Russian than English. Rooms have AC & are well maintained & clean; budget travellers can opt for a bed in a room with other guests (UZS110,000), or you can have a private room with an en suite. There is Wi-Fi throughout, though the signal is not the best & sometimes doesn't work. B/fast & dinner can be ordered the day before for UZS33,000 each. $$

Jipek Joli Inn (26 rooms) Jipek Joli; 61 224 2525; e jipekhotel@gmail.com; w ayimtour.com. The original Jipek Joli property is just 1 block along from the Savitsky Museum, older & smaller than its sister hotel (page 83) but still offering a friendly welcome & good service. There are a variety of sgl, dbl & trpl rooms, plus a yurt with 4 sgl beds. $$

Sofram (8 rooms) Sayahatchilar; 91 388 0005. This clean & well-run hostel is behind the restaurant of the same name, which is the best place to eat in Nukus (page 86). Dorm-style rooms can be shared with other travellers, but there are private rooms, too, all with AC. All showers & toilets are communal & unisex, but sometimes lack soap & toilet paper so be prepared & bring your own. $

✕ WHERE TO EAT AND DRINK *Map, page 87, unless otherwise stated*

There was a time in the not-too-distant past when Nukus had limited places you would want to eat, but thankfully that's all changed; it seems that a new café or restaurant opens almost every week, and some of them are very good indeed. The availability of international cuisines like Italian, Korean and Turkish makes a welcome change if you have had your fill of local fare, and the large number of European-style coffee shops means you will never be far away from a good espresso and a slice of cake.

Artizen [map, page 82] Microdistrict 23; 90 095 2424; noon–23.00 daily. Stylish modern restaurant serving Karakalpak & Uzbek dishes, including excellent soups, salads & a local delicacy of *juyeri gurtik*, handmade pasta made with sorghum flour served with chicken, carrots & boiled potatoes. The mixed meats platter is rather impressive, though you'll need several friends to do the portion size justice. There's a large event hall on the ground floor, which has music & space for dancing in the evening & is popular with Nukus's youth, plus a quieter dining room upstairs. $$$

Cake Bumer T Kayypbergenova 54; 09.00–23.00 daily. On the corner across from the Savitsky Museum, the pink telephone box bedecked in flowers outside the door is the giveaway that this is Nukus's premier influencer hangout, as well as a popular photo spot for newlyweds. The large variety of cakes are the stars of the menu, but it also serves pizza,

Vendors at Nukus's Main Bazaar. ▶

burgers, pasta & salads. The interior is suitably stylish for the 'gram & has plenty of seats, though it can be difficult to find a place to sit at busy times. On summer days, Bumer sometimes looks as though it is closed because they pull the window blinds down, but open the door to the left of the building & the chances are it'll be buzzing inside. On cooler days & in the evening, sit outside where the patio-style seating area is decorated with fairy lights. $$$

Neo Restaurant S Kamalova 21; ✎ 91 255 6161; ⏱ 10.00–midnight daily. This Nukus hotspot has been refurbished & now looks very funky indeed, with a long modern bar, stylish yellow chairs & blue feature walls. There's also a terrace at the front, covered to protect you from the sun. The menu offers an eclectic mix of international cuisines, including sushi (be wary this far from the sea…), burgers, Korean dishes & *laghman*, a noodle dish that is a Central Asian favourite. There's a selection of beers to accompany your meal, plus plenty of soft drinks. $$$

☀ **Sofram** Sayahatchilar; ✎ 91 388 0005; ⏱ 10.00–midnight daily. This colourful Turkish café & restaurant near Hotel Jipek Joli & the Savitsky Museum is the city's best place to eat. The covered courtyard serves coffee, snacks & surprisingly good ice cream in half a dozen different flavours, though it can be a little smoky so ask for a table in the brightly decorated inside room if you plan to eat. Opens midmorning for b/fast & serves tasty grills later in the day. The skewers with alternate cubes of aubergine & shish kebab are particularly good & come with proper Turkish *lavash* (bread). $$$

☀ **Fish House** [map, page 79] Shadly Aul; ✎ 93 713 7830; ⏱ 08.00–01.00 daily. Although on the outskirts of Nukus, it is well worth jumping in a taxi to dine here, especially if you're staying in the city more than one night. The journey takes 10–15 mins & costs around UZS20,000. As the name suggests, the whole menu revolves around local fish, much of which is caught in the Amu Darya. It's a popular place with locals & is often busy, even at lunchtime. The 2 large main halls have tables in booths, or you can opt for a private dining room. $$

Café Novel [map, page 82] A Dosnazarov 11A; ✎ 93 369 3333; ⏱ 10.00–midnight daily. This bright, modern café opened in 2022 & is run by

young, friendly staff, some of whom speak English. The proper espresso is a relief for caffeine addicts suffering from too much instant coffee elsewhere, & there's also a good menu of freshly squeezed juices, smoothies & mocktails. There's plenty of cake, too, for when you're feeling peckish; for something more substantial try the selection of tasty salads, pastas & pizzas, many of which can be made suitable for vegetarians. $$

Café Sonata [map, page 82] A Dosnazarov 3; ✎ 61 223 3106; ⏱ 09.00–22.00 daily. This café, restaurant & bakery specialises in Korean food. The fried chicken gives KFC a run for its money, but if you want something a bit more authentic & with a hit of spice – a rarity in Karakalpakstan – choose the *kimchi-bokkimpab*, a fried rice dish with slightly salty pickled cabbage. There are plenty of Korean salads to have as sides, plus a small selection of beers & wines to wash it down. Service is generally attentive – eat on the terrace on a warm evening, but otherwise sit inside where there are attractive murals of cherry blossom, birds & bamboo on the walls. $$

Chillout A Shamuratova; ✎ 91 305 6161; ⏱ noon–03.00 daily. Round pavilion within the riverside park, with some outdoor tables on the terrace looking towards the river. Serves beer on tap & in cans, plus cold drinks, tea, coffee & various flavours of hookah. There's a reasonable menu of homemade pizzas, but not all of them are always available. Can be smoky in the evenings if you're inside. $$

Premier Lounge J Aymurzaeva; ✎ 97 358 7007; ⏱ 10.00–22.00 daily. A favourite for those craving a good burger; the lounge has dark-wood décor with comfortable seats & suede sofas. The atmosphere is relaxed so you might well want to stay on for an extra drink after eating. $$

Tiffany's Cafe S Kamalova 30; ✎ 90 714 4274; ⏱ 11.00–23.00 daily. Modern décor & friendly staff make Tiffany's a welcoming place to grab a quick bite. The menu consists mostly of pizzas & burgers, but you can also get some delicious soups & salads. Its take on a Caesar salad is excellent. $$

Café Karakalpagym Jumanazarov; ✎ 99 956 7007; ⏱ 10.00–21.00 daily. This non-touristy café, popular with locals, has simple décor & an outside courtyard with picnic tables & *tapchans* (a square daybed with a central table shared by multiple diners). It serves local cuisine, including

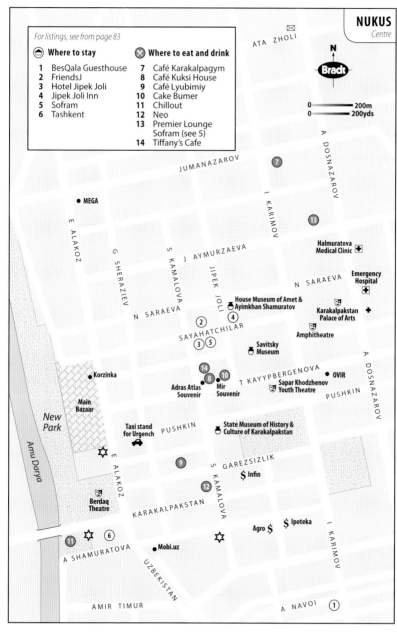

For listings, see from page 83

Where to stay

1 BesQala Guesthouse
2 FriendsJ
3 Hotel Jipek Joli
4 Jipek Joli Inn
5 Sofram
6 Tashkent

Where to eat and drink

7 Café Karalpagym
8 Café Kuksi House
9 Café Lyubimiy
10 Cake Bumer
11 Chillout
12 Neo
13 Premier Lounge
   Sofram (see 5)
14 Tiffany's Cafe

NUKUS
Centre

0 _____ 200m
0 _____ 200yds

a variety of shashliks, but its must-eat items are the *samsas* – some of the best we have ever had. $

Café Kuksi House T Kayypbergenova 56; ☎ 91 301 0105; ⏰ 10.00–21.00 daily. This simple café serves tasty but not particularly traditional Korean food. In addition to the ramen & kimchi, it also serves Eastern European dishes such as Russian potato salad & *pirozhki* (fried buns filled with meat). A good place for lunch. $

Café Lyubimiy Chekhov; ☎ 90 735 8444; ⏰ 10.00–23.00 daily. Generous portion sizes make up for the lack of authenticity at this Korean café, so make sure you're hungry – especially if you are ordering the ramen! $

Plov Centre   [map, page 82] Khujayli 1; ☏ 97 348 1006; ⏰ 11.00–22.00 daily. Situated next door to the Mosque of Imam Ishan Muhammad, this is the most popular spot in Nukus for *plov*. Come before 14.00 though, as after that it's likely to have run out & you'll be left with a less exciting choice of salads & soups. $

ENTERTAINMENT

There is a significant number of cultural venues in Nukus, with performances of everything from classical music to puppetry. The challenge is that they rarely publish or publicise their event calendars in advance or answer their phones (if indeed they have one), so you need to turn up at the venue on the day to see if anything is on. Tickets cost under UZS50,000, even for the best seats in the house, and should be booked and paid for on the spot in cash.

Amphitheatre   I Karimov 118. Preferred venue for outdoor concerts & festival events, including Karakalpak & Uzbek pop stars on tour.

Berdaq Theatre   E Alakoz 1; ☏ 61 224 0638. National drama theatre of Karakalpakstan named after the 19th-century writer (page 98). It's an attractive modern building by the river with a large auditorium.

Karakalpakstan Palace of Arts   A Dosnazarov 103A. Nukus's main Concert Hall hosts mostly classical music performances, often with a full-size orchestra.

Karakalpakstan State Puppet Theatre   A Dosnazarov 14A; ☏ 61 223 4090; w kukla-teatr. uz. The tower on the corner of this theatre is built to look like a castle with a crenellated top, making it the perfect setting for the performance of fairy tales & other children's stories. Local school groups make up the majority of the audience but it is possible to buy individual tickets.

Sapar Khodzhenov Youth Theatre T Kayypbergenova 47. Attractive theatre near the Savitsky Museum with performances by students & up-&-coming actors.

Turan Stadium   Turan Oypaty. The bigger of the city's 2 football stadiums. There are regular men's & women's matches, & you will often see members of the national teams on the pitch. There's a relaxed, friendly atmosphere in the stands & visitors are welcome.

SHOPPING

Adras Atlas Souvenir   T Kayypbergenova 56; ⏰ 10.00–20.00 daily. There are limited places to buy souvenirs in Nukus, but centrally located Adras Atlas has probably the best selection, including hand-painted ceramics, embroidery & traditional clothing. It is named after the traditional Central Asian textiles, *adras* and *atlas*, which have a distinctive zigzag pattern in their weave & have been awarded UNESCO Intangible Cultural Heritage status.

Korzinka   E Alakoz 162; ⏰ 08.00–01.00 daily. The local answer to Tesco is well stocked with local & international brands. If you are planning to visit remote areas of Karakalpakstan, including the Aral Sea, it is well worth stocking up on food & bottled water here before you go. Accepts Visa & MasterCard as well as cash.

Main Bazaar   E Alakoz; ⏰ 09.00–21.00 daily. Nukus's main bazaar is still the commercial heart of the city. It hasn't been dressed up for tourists, which is part of its appeal, & is a good place for peoplewatching as well as to buy fresh bread, *samsa* & dried fruits & nuts. If you want to try something unusual, look out for the small white balls of *qurut*, dried fermented yoghurt balls that are quite salty but make a good bar snack.

MEGA   E Alakoz 60; ⏰ 08.00–23.00 daily. This 4-floor mall selling electronics & clothing is the place to come if you need a replacement phone charger, plug adapter, camera battery, etc.

Mir Souvenir   T Kayypbergenova 56; ⏰ 08.00– 23.00 daily. Small store selling knickknacks & souvenirs, some of which are made locally. The embroidered hats & model yurts make cheap, easily transportable gifts.

OTHER PRACTICALITIES

COMMUNICATIONS Useful if you need to buy a local SIM card for your phone, **Mobi.uz** (09.00–18.00 daily) has a conveniently located office at Tortkul 138A. You need to show your passport. Prices start from UZS20,000 for 5MB data and 250 minutes of calls.

Nukus's main **post office** (w pochta.uz; 09.00–17.00 Mon–Fri) is at Ata Zholi 2. Ignore other locations on online maps: they are incorrectly marked.

MEDICAL CARE Nukus has a large number of hospitals and clinics. In case of a serious accident or severe illness, you need to go to the **Emergency Hospital** (A Dosnazarov 101; 24hrs); for non-emergency treatment, the **Halmuratova Medical Clinic** (A Dosnazarov 110) is a few buildings further along the same street. There are multiple **pharmacies** on both sides of the same road.

MONEY Forex counters and ATMs are much more readily available in Nukus than elsewhere in Karakalpakstan, so make sure you change or withdraw cash before leaving the city. There's a cluster of banks located in the centre, including **Agro Bank** (A Shamuratova 101A; 09.00–16.00 Mon–Fri), **Infin Bank** (Garesizlik 65; 09.00–18.00 Mon–Fri), and **Ipoteka Bank** (A Shamuratova 97A; 09.00–17.00 Mon–Fri). All three have 24-hour ATMs which accept Visa and UnionPay cards, & those at Infin and Ipoteka also accept MasterCard.

REGISTRATION If you need to go in person to a foreigners' registration office, head for the **OVIR** (09.00–13.00 & 14.00–18.00 Mon–Fri); it's at Islam Karimov 104A, but most easily accessed using the lane down the side of T Kayypbergenova 27. For more information about registration, see page 49.

WHAT TO SEE AND DO

The Savitsky Museum is the jewel of Karakalpakstan, known internationally as the Louvre of the Steppe and the subject of the 2010 documentary film *Desert of Forbidden Art*, voiced by Ben Kingsley, Sally Field and Ed Asner. If you are passionate about art, the museum's avant garde collection alone justifies a visit to the republic, but there are plenty of other attractions in Nukus to build an engaging city tour over two to three days. The city's Soviet-era mosaics are particularly colourful and the State Museum of History and Culture is well worth a few hours of your time.

SAVITSKY MUSEUM (T Kayypbergenova 52; 91 222 2556; 09.00–18.00 Tue–Thu, 09.00–19.00 Fri, 10.00–18.00 Sat–Sun; UZS55,000 for 1 building, UZS82,000 for 2, camera fee UZS23,000) Without a shadow of doubt, the Savitsky Museum – also known as Nukus Museum or the State Museum of Arts of the Republic of Karakalpakstan – is the most important museum in Central Asia. It was founded by Igor Savitsky (page 92) in 1966 and, since his death in 1984, the collections have been cared for equally passionately by his successors.

In total, the Savitsky Museum has more than 100,000 exhibits, though only a fraction are on show at any one time. Request a guide when you buy your ticket: guided tours (UZS92,000 pp per building) are available in English, Russian and several other European languages, and you will get much more out of the visit if you are with someone who knows the collection and the significance of individual exhibits and artists.

MAXIMUM EXPOSURE PR

MAXIMUM EXPOSURE PR

As tempting as it is to skip the archaeological and ethnographic galleries and go straight to the paintings, don't. One of the reasons Savitsky collected such a variety and breadth of items is that he believed in the importance of context. The 15,000 or so archaeological artefacts chart the development of Karakalpakstan from the Bronze Age through the emergence of the earliest states, the medieval period, and then to the 14th century when this region was incorporated into the Timurid Empire (page 18). Of special interest are the petroglyph of a Bactrian camel from Bukantau, which dates from the 2nd millennium BC; the Tuya-Muyun horse sculpture (8th–7th century BC); and wall paintings excavated from Toprak Kala (2nd–3rd century AD), which clearly show the fashionable hairstyles and clothing of the time. In the ethnographic displays, the *tobelik* and *sawkele* headdresses (page 34) are exquisite, and there are some wonderful textiles, too. The presentation of these items is much better than at the State Museum of History and Culture of Karakalpakstan (page 93), but only a fraction of the Savitsky's artefacts are currently on display so it is well worth visiting both museums if you are interested in costumes and jewellery.

The vast majority of the Savitsky Museum's collection of visual artworks are by 20th-century Russian and Central Asian artists, including some 10,000 avant garde paintings, prints, sculptures and graphics. In fact, the museum has one of the world's largest Russian avant garde collections, second only to that of the Russian Museum in St Petersburg. The Savitsky Museum owns all the surviving paintings by Vladimir Lysenko, the purged Soviet artist whose oil painting *The Bull* (also known as *Fascism Approaching*) has become the museum's calling card, the creature's eyes just as unnerving as those of the *Mona Lisa*. The museum also has 100 works by Alexander Volkov, founder of Uzbek avant garde, who was heavily influenced by Cubo-Futurism; as well as a large number of paintings by neo-impressionist artist Robert Falk, one of the founders of the Jack of Diamonds group of artists; and 400 paintings and 1,600 graphics by painter and graphic artist, Arkadiy Stavrovskiy.

Some of the most poignant artworks are by artists who were purged by Stalin and his successors because the style of their art or their lifestyles challenged Soviet ideology – and, in particular, what constituted 'good' or 'moral' art. Lysenko was confined to a mental asylum for much of his life. Aleksandr Nikolayev, better known as Usto Mumin, was imprisoned for his sexuality and banned from painting during the four years he was in prison, while Mikhail Kurzin was imprisoned and later exiled because the authorities believed his paintings were anti-Soviet propaganda. Mikhail Sokolov was sent to the gulag in Siberia where, in spite of the deprivations, he nevertheless produced miniature paintings of the camp and the surrounding landscape, many of which you can see in the museum.

Please note that Building 1 was closed for renovation at the time of writing and is not expected to reopen until 2024. When it does, it will contain galleries for archaeology, ethnography and Karakalpak painters, plus a temporary exhibition space; and the galleries of Russian and avant garde art will be in Building 2. In the meantime, an illustrative selection of artworks and artefacts from all these collections, including archaeology and ethnography, is on display in Building 2. The third building you see, confusingly located between Buildings 1 and 2, houses the museum's storage and conservation facilities. It is closed to the public but visiting researchers can request permission to enter (for a UZS92,000 fee) and study items from the collection which are not on public display.

◀ 1 *Capital*, Mikhail Kurzin, 1931. 2 *Cotton Picking*, Alexander Volkov, 1931.

Igor Vitalyevich Savitsky (1915–84) was born into a wealthy family in Kyiv shortly before the Soviet-Ukrainian War that would bring the short-lived Ukrainian People's Republic under Bolshevik control. The family had Polish and Jewish roots and moved to Moscow while Savitsky was a child. Here he initially studied to be an electrician – a good proletariat job – but he took drawing lessons on the side and ultimately refined his skills at the Moscow Polygraphic Institute, Moscow Art School and the Institute for the Advanced Studies of Artists in the 1930s. Among others in Moscow, he got to know the Ukrainian impressionist Lev Kramarenko and the Russian painter and graphic artist Reuben Mazel, and as students from Moscow Art School were evacuated to Uzbekistan during World War II, he was exposed to Central Asian artists, too.

Savitsky's first visit to Karakalpakstan occurred in 1950 when he was invited to become an artist for the Khorezm Archaeological and Ethnographical Expedition, led by the pioneering archaeologist Sergei Tolstov. Savitsky fell in love with the history, landscapes and people he encountered in Karakalpakstan, and it sparked a life-long passion for the region.

In the mid to late 1950s, Savitsky began collecting ethnographic items and folk art. He was particularly interested in traditional Karakalpak jewellery, costumes and textiles, yurt decorations, and other distinctive local items that he feared would be lost as Karakalpakstan modernised and became homogenised with other parts of the Soviet Union. Savitsky's personal collection became so large and unusually comprehensive that he was able to convince the local authorities to build a museum to house it all, and in 1966 the Savitsky Museum opened with Savitsky as its first curator.

With a premises and a budget, albeit one which he had to supplement with his own funds, Savitsky's acquisitive nature went into overdrive. In addition to his ethnographic and archaeological collections, he wanted to buy art. He believed strongly that future generations of Karakalpak artists needed to be inspired by and learn from every kind of artist, including those whose work was underappreciated or controversial. He found that he could buy avant garde paintings made by purged Soviet artists relatively cheaply, and at the same time save them from ignominy or destruction. This became his obsession, and thanks to Savitsky's determination and, frankly, bravery in defying the Soviet authorities and norms, he amassed tens of thousands of paintings, sketches, graphic work and sculptures.

It helped that there was a thaw in attitudes during the Khrushchev era in the early 1960s, and while it was too late for many of the repressed artists to be rehabilitated, their work was at least less politically sensitive than it had been in previous decades. Many of the works Savitsky collected were not exhibited in Nukus during his lifetime, but were safely kept in storage; others like *The Bull* did go on show, but largely passing under the radar of the local authorities. Perhaps they weren't interested in visiting art galleries or didn't realise what they were looking at.

Savitsky died in Moscow, where he was seeking treatment for lung disease, in 1984. It is believed his disease was caused by overexposure to formalin (formaldehyde dissolved in water), a chemical he used in his conservation work.

HOUSE MUSEUM OF AMET AND AYIMKHAN SHAMURATOV (Saraeva 29; 61 222 3452; 09.00–18.00 daily; UZS22,035) The only non-state-run museum in Uzbekistan was opened in 1999 by the children of Amet and Ayimkhan Shamuratov in their family home. The pair were the doyens of Karakalpakstan's cultural scene in the mid 20th century, remarkable creatives in their own right but also a magnet for other artists, writers and statesmen visiting Nukus.

Amet Shamuratov (1912–53) was a polymath, born to a poor peasant family and orphaned at an early age. He was able to get an education, however, and graduated from the Zoo-Veterinary Institute in Moscow. Over the course of his short but eventful life, he was a writer, translator, publisher and statesman, working in a variety of roles with the Minister Council of the Karakalpak ASSR and the Nukus Executive Committee. Twice he was elected as a deputy of the Supreme Council of Karakalpakstan.

Arguably his wife, Ayimkhan (1917–93), was even more interesting. From childhood she was passionate about singing and acting, in particular the performance of Karakalpak folk songs. Elsewhere in Uzbekistan, a number of young actresses had been killed for taking off their veils and performing in public, but the timing was right for Ayimkhan: the Soviet Union opened up new opportunities for women and built theatres. Her teacher, Abdiraman Otepov, founded the first Karakalpak theatre, and Ayimkhan's first professional performance was in the title role of Seifulgabit Majitov play, *Baghdagul*. Shortly afterwards she signed for All-Union Radio in Moscow, where she met her husband, and she recorded countless songs and toured extensively. Famously, during World War II she performed on the streets, collecting money for the Soviet Army. In total she raised 70,000 rubles, and for this she received a telegram from Stalin offering his thanks. After the war, like her husband, Ayimkhan became a deputy of the Supreme Council, though she didn't stop performing: her stage career lasted for 60 years.

The Shamuratov house museum is the best place to learn about this cultural and political power couple and the influential circles they moved in. The collection is displayed in three halls, and it focuses on personal items belonging to the family. The highlights are the many costumes that Ayimkhan performed in; recordings of her songs, which you can listen to; Amet's original manuscripts, written in Farsi, Latin, Russian and Karakalpak; and letters and photographs of Soviet writers, artists and celebrities. The museum also has some interesting ethnographic items, including a decorative yurt, a 19th-century bullock cart and Karakalpak women's clothing from the 19th and early 20th centuries.

STATE MUSEUM OF HISTORY AND CULTURE OF KARAKALPAKSTAN (S Kamalova 24; 61 222 3021; 09.00–17.00 Tue–Sun; UZS30,000) Founded in 1929, the State Museum of History and Culture (also known as the Museum of Regional Studies) is one of the oldest museums in Central Asia. Originally it was located in Tortkul, but moved to Nukus in 1944. The current building is of more recent construction. It is estimated that there are more than 65,000 artefacts in the museum's collection, grouped into three departments: Archaeology and Ethnography, Nature, and Modern History. You will get the most out of your visit by asking one of the museum's enthusiastic volunteers for an English-language tour.

The centrepiece of the museum's main hall is a traditional Karakalpak yurt, attractively decorated with woven textiles and other accessories. Although the presentation of some of the exhibits is dated, the museum prides itself on its collection of folk art and it is a good opportunity to learn about Karakalpak costume, textiles and jewellery, and to see musical instruments, horse tack and even armour and weapons. The accompanying portraits of modern women wearing

Karakalpakstan's traditional clothing and jewellery aids your imagination as you can see exactly what the ensemble looked like when put together. There are also displays of Karakalpak, Uzbek and Kazakh jewellery side by side, enabling you to compare and contrast three different but related styles.

It is well worth visiting the archaeological galleries if you plan to visit Karakalpakstan's desert fortresses and other ancient sites, as many of the artefacts excavated from them are on display here. These include a 2,500-year-old pillar cap from the Sultan Uvays Dag mountains, which is carved with a strange figure with rams' horns and a human face; tombstones from the sacred Narindjan Baba Mausoleum (13th–14th centuries; page 186); and large numbers of ossuaries and coins. There's a collection of historic manuscripts, too.

Probably the most depressing part of the museum are the rooms dedicated to natural history, which is unfortunate as the guided tours (available in Karakalpak, Russian and Uzbek) start with taxidermy of birds and mammals that once inhabited the Aral Sea. Not only are they dusty and unnaturally displayed, but you know deep down that many of their populations were ultimately killed off by hunters or climate change. The 'Last Turan Tiger' – shot by locals in 1949, and then stuffed and brought to the museum – is a particularly sad affair, and though the pelt is undoubtedly beautiful, the tiger's face is somewhat bewildered. Technically he's not even the last tiger: another one was shot in Turkmenistan in 1954.

BERDAQ STATE MUSEUM OF THE HISTORY OF KARAKALPAK LITERATURE (Sh Abdirov; ⏲ 09.00–17.00 Mon–Fri, 10.00–15.00 Sat; UZS30,000) Berdaq (page 98) is regarded as the Karakalpak Shakespeare, so it's very fitting that this museum – and Nukus's most important theatre (page 88) – are both named in his honour. The building is a modern fantasy of oriental architecture, built in the round with multiple domes, one of which is attractively striped. The entrance is between carved white pillars, and you're greeted by golden sculptures of not only Berdaq himself but also other significant writers from Central Asia such as Abay and Beruniy, a demonstration of Berdaq's right to take centre stage in this literary pantheon.

Well-executed murals decorate the interior walls of the museum, from floor to ceiling, depicting scenes of Karakalpak life and culture, plus scenes from famous stories. Look in particular at the details on the women's costumes and headdresses, the carpets and the woven textiles decorating the yurts.

Rooms on the ground floor predominantly contain books and manuscripts by local writers, in Arabic, Russian and Uzbek as well as Karakalpak. Some of the labels are in English, but you will get more out of the experience if you ask for a guided tour: Aisul speaks English and can explain a little of the biography of the writers, as well as about their works. Scattered in between the display cases of books are traditional musical instruments, mostly stringed, made in Karakalpakstan.

Upstairs is Berdaq's Hall, a domed room with a painted ceiling and large chandelier. Here you will find personal items from Berdaq's life, including a particularly fetching green *chapan* (a traditional coat), as well as copies of his books and papers. There are also several cases of textiles, jewellery and household items that are seemingly unconnected to Berdaq or to literature, but are interesting to see nonetheless.

STUDIO OF BAKHTIYAR SEREKEEV (Sari Altin 1; ☎ 90 358 7046; ⏲ by appointment) Born in Nukus in 1990, Bakhtiyar Serekeev graduated from the National Institute of

---

Berdaq State Museum of the History of Karakalpak Literature. ▶

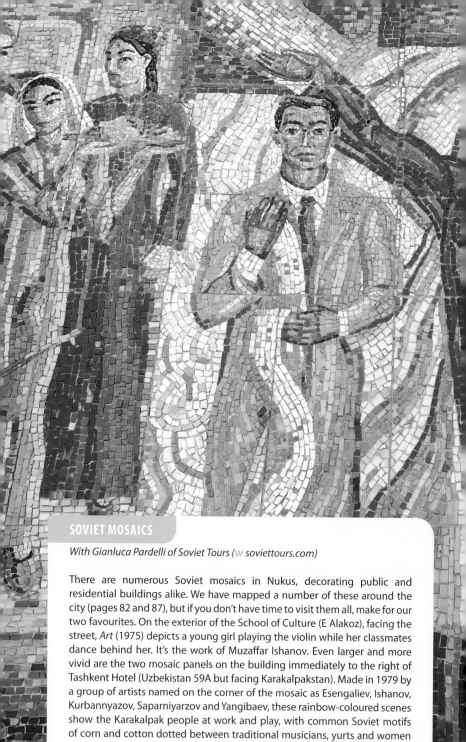

SOVIET MOSAICS

With Gianluca Pardelli of Soviet Tours (w soviettours.com)

There are numerous Soviet mosaics in Nukus, decorating public and residential buildings alike. We have mapped a number of these around the city (pages 82 and 87), but if you don't have time to visit them all, make for our two favourites. On the exterior of the School of Culture (E Alakoz), facing the street, *Art* (1975) depicts a young girl playing the violin while her classmates dance behind her. It's the work of Muzaffar Ishanov. Even larger and more vivid are the two mosaic panels on the building immediately to the right of Tashkent Hotel (Uzbekistan 59A but facing Karakalpakstan). Made in 1979 by a group of artists named on the corner of the mosaic as Esengaliev, Ishanov, Kurbannyazov, Saparniyarzov and Yangibaev, these rainbow-coloured scenes show the Karakalpak people at work and play, with common Soviet motifs of corn and cotton dotted between traditional musicians, yurts and women picking pomegranates from a tree.

A mosaic at 59A Uzbekistan, next door to the Tashkent Hotel

Written Karakalpak literature began in the 19th century, with two poets as its founding fathers: Ajiniyaz (1824–78), known by his pen name of Ziwar; and Berdaq (1827–1900). Both were born in fishing villages near Muynak, and both worked as musicians as well as poets: Berdaq earned a living by singing and playing the *dutar* at weddings and other events, while Ajiniyaz wrote the melody that transformed his most famous poem, *Bozataw*, into a folk song known to every Karakalpak.

The subject of *Bozataw* is the suppression of the Karakalpak uprising of 1858–59 (page 19). In punishment for his role as a leader in the uprising, Ajiniyaz was exiled for three years to what is now Turkmenistan. Still facing persecution when he returned home, he went to what is now Kazakhstan, where he wrote many of his best poems. It was only in 1874, shortly before his death at the relatively young age of 54 that Ajiniyaz was able to finally come back to Karakalpakstan, where he made his living teaching in village schools.

Berdaq lived long enough to experience rule by Russia as well as by the Khanate of Khiva and he wrote about the injustices of both, focusing on the suffering and struggles of ordinary people, democratic ideals and the fight for freedom of the Karakalpak people.

Both writers studied classical Turkic-Persian poetry, as well as Karakalpak folk poetry. Berdaq's own poetry is very close to folk poetry, with tales of daily life, legends and folklore. He used simple, colloquial language that was easy to understand for people without a classical education; Ajiniyaz's poems, on the other hand, are more sophisticated, combining elements of folk poetry and classical poetry.

By Andrew Staniland, adapted from the introduction to Three Karakalpak Poets, *translated by Andrew Staniland with the help of Karakalpak co-translators Aynura Nazirbaeva, Gulbahor Izentaeva, Gulnaz Jadigerova, Nargiza Urazimbetova, Nilufar Abdullaeva and Shaxnoza Tursınbaeva*

Arts and Design and has since exhibited his work around the world, most recently with solo exhibitions at the Savitsky Museum in 2019 and at the Bonum Factum Gallery in Tashkent in 2022. His dramatic experiments with expressionism and abstractionism have caught the eye of international art buyers, including Saatchi Art. Serekeev's workshop is open to the public, with four rooms to exhibit his paintings; the shop is easily spotted because of the huge graffiti artwork with three life-size human figures that covers the entirety of the gate. Do call in advance to check he will be there.

GREEN SPACES Nukus has a number of parks which, while not destinations in their own right, are nevertheless pleasant places to picnic or while away an hour or two. **Amir Timur Park** is a long thin park tucked behind the Faculty of Industrial Technology in the south of Nukus on A Dosnazarov, and **New Park** runs alongside Karakalpakstan and the riverfront. There are a couple of cafés in New Park including Chillout (page 86), and at the weekends you can watch members of the local rowing

---

1 Soviet mosaics decorate public buildings in and around Nukus; this one is in Shurtanbay.
2 Aziz Baba Cemetery. ▶

and kayaking club splashing about on the river. If you look sufficiently curious, they may even offer to lend you a kayak.

AROUND NUKUS

Outside the city limits but still within Nukus District are several interesting sites that you can easily visit on a day trip from the capital. The **Aziz Baba Cemetery** (elbows.unexpressed.purples; 24hrs; free) is about 14km north of Nukus, just off the 4R-175 before you get to Akmangit. Alaberdi, known as Aziz Baba, was a local holy man who died in the 17th century. His multi-domed mausoleum was rebuilt in 2007 and so is completely new, but it is still intriguing because of the presence of a large prayer stick decorated with ribbons and artificial flowers outside. Each ribbon represents the prayer that a pilgrim has made, asking the saint to help. Usually the prayers are from those who want to conceive a child, or to cure an illness. It's a pre-Islamic tradition that has survived in some Sufi traditions, though more Orthodox Muslims consider it heretical.

Continuing along the 4R-175 another 10km to Shurtanbay, you will come to a **Soviet mosaic** (havens.defensively.homecoming) depicting a dancer and musicians. It is on the side of the old cinema building, just before you reach the mosque.

Ten kilometres west of Shurtanbay at Baymaklyaul, on the east bank of the Amu Darya, is the extensive **Krantau Archaeological Complex**, at the heart of which lie the ruins of the Kalmak Kala (progenitors.deposited.presenting; 24hrs; free). Usually in Karakalpakstan 'Kala' refers to a fortress, but here it is a necropolis. There are around 80 separate burial enclosures, some of which are 2,000 years old, but they are particularly important because they probably include the earliest surviving monuments built by Karakalpaks. These are fortress-like burial structures dating from the 17th century. The first archaeological excavations were done in the 1950s by the Karakalpak Branch of the Academy of Sciences, whose archaeologists concluded that these are some of the oldest monuments in the region. Their architectural style is distinctly Karakalpak; you won't find anything like them in other parts of Uzbekistan. There are also two mosques within the complex: the unusually designed Bakhauddin Ishan Mosque (bargaining.chemicals.foxtrot), which is now abandoned; and on the northern side of the site, the Bektemir Ishan Mosque (grittiness.genies.congratulations). Both are made from the same kind of clay as the burial structures.

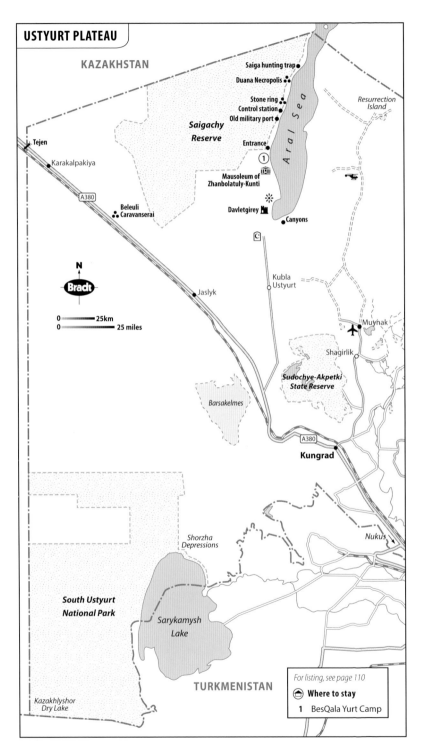

USTYURT PLATEAU

KAZAKHSTAN

Saiga hunting trap ●
Duana Necropolis ●●
Stone ring ●●
Control station ●
Old military port ●

Resurrection Island

Saigachy Reserve

Aral Sea

Tejen

Entrance

①

Karakalpakiya

A380

Mausoleum of Zhanbolatuly-Kunti

Beleuli Caravanserai ●●

Davletgirey

● Canyons

Ⓒ

N

Bradt

Kubla Ustyurt

0 ————— 25km
0 ————— 25 miles

Jaslyk ●

Muyhak

Shagirlik ○

Sudochye-Akpetki State Reserve

Barsakelmes

A380

Kungrad ●

Nukus

Shorzha Depressions

South Ustyurt National Park

Sarykamysh Lake

For listing, see page 110

⊖ Where to stay
1 BesQala Yurt Camp

Kazakhlyshor Dry Lake

TURKMENISTAN

4

Ustyurt Plateau and the Saigachy Reserve

The Ustyurt Plateau is a vast, transboundary desert shared between Karakalpakstan, Kazakhstan and Turkmenistan. It covers some 200,000km² of land with very little change in altitude and, in the Karakalpak part, Kungrad District, there is hardly any water. The population density is therefore very low: 1.7 people per km² or, to put that into perspective, just 132,800 people in an area considerably larger than the Czech Republic or the Republic of Ireland.

Tourists entering Karakalpakstan from Kazakhstan are likely to cross at the Tejen border post and then go south across the Ustyurt Plateau on their way to Nukus. It shouldn't be viewed as just a transit route, however: the Beleuli Caravanserai near Karakalpakiya and the nomadic cemeteries in the Saigachy Reserve are a reminder of the ancient human history of this land; Barsakelmes is one of the most striking, if lifeless, landscapes you will ever see; and the Saigachy Reserve and South Ustyurt National Park are both important protected areas. If you want to see what is left of the Aral Sea, including the cliffs and canyons that give way to the beach and then water, this is also where you will need to come.

KUNGRAD AND AROUND

Kungrad (also sometimes written as Qongirot) is the administrative centre of Kungrad District. The town, which has a population of around 37,000 people, is named after the Qongirot, a Turkic tribe who fought for control of Khorezm throughout the 18th century (page 19). It was situated on the trading route linking the Caspian Sea to the Urals, and caravans would have been the source of its original wealth. Kungrad remains a transport hub for long-distance travellers today, as it is the meeting point of the roads to Nukus, Muynak and the Kazakh border. There are not really any tourist attractions in the town itself, but staying here provides easy access to Barsakelmes (page 105) and Sudochye Lakes (page 130) and it is a convenient location in which to break a longer journey.

GETTING THERE AND AWAY Kungrad's **train station** is in the middle of the town on Uzbekistan, almost opposite the junction with Garezsizlik. There is an overnight train to Tashkent every day (21hrs; from UZS112,922), a twice-weekly service to Andijan (27hrs; from UZS42,185) on Tuesday and Sunday, and a train to Beyneu (9hrs; from UZS96,120) in Kazakhstan on Wednesday, Thursday and Sunday, which stops en route in Karakalpakiya. You can connect in Beyneu to Aktau and other destinations in Kazakhstan.

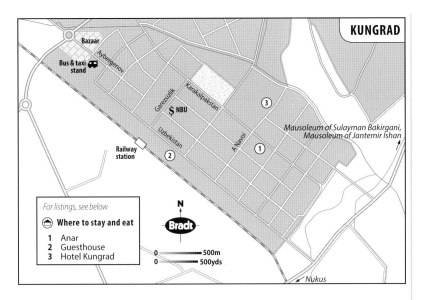

For listings, see below

Where to stay and eat
1 Anar
2 Guesthouse
3 Hotel Kungrad

KUNGRAD

Taxis and minibuses depart from the **bus station** next to the bazaar. The journey to Nukus (2hrs) costs UZS15,000 by minibus and UZS30,000 in a shared taxi. Shared taxis to Muynak (1½hrs) depart from the opposite side of the road and a seat costs UZS25,000.

WHERE TO STAY AND EAT *Map, above*

Hotel Kungrad (11 rooms) A Navoi, nr School #53; 91 098 1001. Basic, functional hotel with large en-suite rooms, comfortable beds, AC & Wi-Fi. Some bathrooms require a bit of DIY but if there's an issue with your plumbing the staff are happy to switch you to another room. $$

Guesthouse (6 rooms) Uzbekistan; 90 592 8604. Look for the sign saying 'Family Guesthouse', as houses on this street are unnumbered. Quvatbay

lives here with his family in a clean & comfortable property. The rooms share a modern bathroom with a shower & you can all eat b/fast together. $

Anar Restaurant Karakalpakstan 124; 10.00–22.00 daily. Stylishly decorated with funky artwork on the walls, Anar is a pleasant surprise in Kungrad. The menu includes salads, kebabs, soups, pizza & *manti*. There is a full bar & a good selection of soft drinks. $

SHOPPING Kungrad's **bazaar** is in the northwest end of the town, facing on to Aybergenov. The stalls here sell a range of fresh produce and basic household goods, as well as quick and tasty snacks including *shashlik* and *samsas*.

OTHER PRACTICALITIES If you need to withdraw or exchange money, the **NBU** (Garezsizlik 31; 09.00–13.00 & 14.00–17.00 Mon–Fri) is useful, with a 24hr ATM which accepts MasterCard, Visa and UnionPay.

WHAT TO SEE AND DO Seventy kilometres northwest of Kungrad, on the western side of the A380, lies the vast ✳ **Barsakelmes** salt marsh, one of the most dramatic landscapes in Karakalpakstan. To get there, turn off the main road at ▥ melodies. mister.automate and follow the track approximately 6km to the edge of the cliff: it is obvious when you can go no further!

◀ Ustyurt Plateau

4

The name Barsakelmes can be translated as 'If you go, you won't return', though we can assure you we did visit while researching this guidebook and we lived to tell the tale. Barsakelmes is a natural depression covering 2,000 sq km, which 30 million years ago was at the bottom of a sea. We know this because although most of the water has long since evaporated, it left behind a thick, crusty layer of salt, that hasn't dissolved or been washed away as it almost never rains here. From a distance it looks like a sheet of snow, and even up close the hard crystals resemble the ice on a ski run at the end of a sunny afternoon. The surface crackles and pops as you walk on it. You might well see the specks of people on the horizon: there's a local cottage industry collecting the salt for sale, though as it is a little grubby with dust and sand blown in on the wind, you probably wouldn't want to eat it.

You will need to leave your car at the top of the cliff and walk from there down the slope and out to the salt. The walk takes about 15 minutes in each direction as it is further than it looks. It is not advisable to go too far out as in places there are gaps and even small pockets of water underneath the salt, and if you tread on one you may break and fall through the solid layer. It is safest close to the shore and you'll still be able to take epic photographs.

Note that there is also a site called Barsakelmes in Kazakhstan. That Barsakelmes is an island and surrounding nature reserve in the northeastern part of the Aral Sea. They are, however, two completely different locations.

JASLYK

Jaslyk, the site of a prison which could well be described as the Alcatraz of Uzbekistan, is an infamous location in Karakalpakstan. During the Karimov era, Jaslyk Prison was notorious for torture, and for two decades human rights activists called for it to be shut down. President Mirziyoyev finally ordered the closure of the prison as a federal detention facility in 2019, though in 2021 Abdurakhmon Tashanov, head of the Uzbek human rights organisation Ezgulik, alleged that as many as 100 prisoners were still being housed there pending the completion of a new prison in Navoi Region. It is not possible to independently verify the current status of the Jaslyk Prison and its number of occupants.

Jaslyk should not be considered as a destination in its own right; rather it is a conveniently placed location to break your journey, especially if you are travelling by bike, with basic food and accommodation facilities.

GETTING THERE AND AWAY The town is 185km northwest of Kungrad, just off the A380 heading to the border with Kazakhstan. The train station is on the western side of the town but you are unlikely to want to stop in the town unless you are cycling and need to stop for the night. The most convenient accommodation is in any case on the main road, not in the centre of the town.

 WHERE TO STAY AND EAT

Hostel Alyan A380, approx 4km southeast of the junction for Jaslyk; ⬜ knockdown.irregular. rulings. This place is primarily a truck stop so you'll see lorries & cars parked on the forecourt, many of them reloading goods & passengers on their way to or from the border post. Sometimes there's even a camel tied up outside. The facilities are basic but it's a useful spot to know about if you're cycling or otherwise desperate, & it is the last spot where you can get a reasonable meal $ before reaching the border. Beds are in shared rooms & the very basic toilets & bathroom are also shared. $

◀ 1 The outskirts of Kungrad. 2 Barsakelmes salt flats.

KUBLA USTYURT

Kubla Ustyurt is a small settlement in what seems to be the middle of nowhere, but it is on the way from the A380 to the Saigachy Reserve and the Aral Sea if you are taking the cross-country route. The village is also known as K7, the reference number of the Soviet transmitter located here. Had you visited 30 years ago you would have found a much larger population, as around 200 people worked at the nearby gas compression station. Today there are just 30 families living in Kubla Ustyurt, most of whom are ethnic Kazakhs. It is a curious place, partly trapped in time and with different cultural identity to many other rural communities on account of its Kazakh population.

Driving past Kubla Ustyurt you will notice the air strip, which was built to service the gas compression station but is now in a dilapidated state. The runway is worth mentioning because it features in the opening sequence of Uzbek rock band Elektrooko's spectacular music video *Tomorrow*, which draws attention to the problems of the Aral Sea region. You can watch the full video on YouTube w youtu. be/CzaqlJltb9M.

GETTING THERE AND AWAY The unmarked turning off the A380 for Kubla Ustyurt is at blisters.crossings.broker, about 6km southeast of the junction for Jaslyk. The 50km drive through the desert from near Jaslyk along a track is almost due east, and on the way you will see herds of domesticated camels, often accompanied by a shepherd on a motorbike. It is an unsurfaced road and the condition is variable: in places drivers tend to abandon the road entirely and drive on the desert either side. There are no public transport options so you will need your own vehicle, ideally a 4x4.

WHERE TO STAY AND EAT There is no formal accommodation in Kubla Ustyurt, though local families say they will arrange a homestay if there is demand. You can stop for a home-cooked meal with Makhset and Laura in their house (pioneering.fogey.armchair; 99 951 0418; $) on the north side of the village. They are a charming Karakalpak-Kazakh couple who are used to hosting foreign guests, and they speak Russian in addition to Karakalpak, Kazakh and Uzbek. Laura will prepare a delicious lunch, typically something like beef with potatoes and carrots, tomato and cucumber salads, bread, biscuits, and plenty of fresh fruit and tea. They have an immaculately clean, modern, indoor bathroom, which is also a blessing after a long drive.

SAIGACHY RESERVE

The Saigachy Reserve (24hrs; free), which borders the western shore of the Aral Sea and stretches out on to the Ustyurt Plateau, is not a national park but rather is classed as a complex landscape reserve. It was created in 2016 and covers some 628,300ha, predominantly in Kungrad Region but also stretching into Muynak Region (page 121). The reserve has a high conservation status and is divided into two main parts: a buffer zone in the south, which is accessible to tourists with the required permit (page 110); and a restricted area in the north, close to the border with Kazakhstan.

While infrastructure in the reserve, even within the buffer zone, is minimal – rangers and staff from the State Committee for Ecology and Environment Protection

---

Stop for a home-cooked meal with Makhset and Laura in Kubla Ustyurt. ▶

work from a small control station (page 115) with the most basic of facilities – it's the wilderness of Saigachy that is its primary attraction: the landscape, including views of the remains of the Aral Sea; and the flora and fauna. Here you can see all the types of vegetation characteristic of the Ustyurt Plateau: semi-shrub vegetation of the gypsum desert, black saxaul vegetation of solina deserts, and annual saltwort vegetation of solina lands. There are two rare species of plants listed in the Uzbekistan's *Red Book* (2009) of rare and endangered species – *Salsola chlwensis* and *Euphorbia scleroscyanthum*. There are also plenty of protected species of fauna. Although the saiga (page 113) rarely stray out of the reserve's restricted areas, if you have a sharp eye and/or a pair of binoculars, you might well see other rare and endangered species. These include the Central Asian steppe tortoise, four-stripe snake, five kinds of eagle (steppe, imperial, golden, white-tailed and common short-toed), houbara bustard, Brandt's hedgehog, corsac fox, caracal, and marbled and steppe polecats.

GETTING THERE AND AWAY There is no public transport to or within the Saigachy Reserve. It is accessed via unmade dirt tracks, and due to the remoteness of this area, the lack of phone signal, signage or passing traffic, and the poor state of the roads, you should not plan to drive to Saigachy in your own vehicle unless it is a 4x4, you are an experienced off-road driver, and you are driving in convoy with another vehicle. Tour operators **BesQala** and **Ayim Tour** (page 46) both supply well-maintained vehicles with experienced drivers, but prices are high: expect to pay at least US$150 per vehicle per day, though both companies will help you find other tourists to share the car with so you can split the cost. Access is from the A380 via Kubla Ustyurt (page 108) or from Muynak via Sudochye Lake (page 130).

 WHERE TO STAY AND EAT *Map, page 102*
There is currently no accommodation within the boundaries of the Saigachy Reserve, though rangers working at the control station (page 115) are hoping to get permission and funding to build a yurt camp. For now, the best accommodation option for those visiting Saigachy is **BesQala Yurt Camp**, approximately 12km south of the reserve entrance, which is owned and run by the tour operator of the same name (page 46).

BesQala Yurt Camp 🛏 link.transpire. semiformal. Perched in an elevated position on the cliffs & looking out towards the Aral Sea are about a dozen yurts of varying sizes, all of which have single beds with clean sheets & thick duvets, & a stove for cold desert nights. There is electric lighting in the yurts but no power sockets, & the very basic toilets & showers are in wooden huts a couple of minutes' walk away. Hearty meals are served on communal tables & there are also well-placed *tapchans* where you can sit, relax & watch the sun go down over the water. What the camp lacks in facilities it makes up for in location and peacefulness, & the stargazing (page 116) is the best you will find anywhere in the world. $$

OTHER PRACTICALITIES Access to the Saigachy Reserve is restricted, so you will need permission from the State Committee for Ecology and Environment Protection (w uznature.uz/en) in order to enter. There is no fee for the permission but the official process for getting a permit is poorly defined. We were told to call **Alisher Abdurakhmanov** (📞 99 604 7979), who works at the committee, to inform him we intended to visit, and then to email our visit dates and passport copies to

1 One of almost 30 ancient cemeteries in the Saigachy Reserve. 2 A nomad grave, Saigachy Reserve.
3 & 4 Steppe polecats and corsac foxes are among species spotted in Saigachy Reserve. ▶

SAIGA ANTELOPE CONSERVATION

With Joseph Bull, Elena Bykova, Alexander Esipov and E J Milner-Gulland (w saiga-conservation.org)

Saiga antelopes (*Saiga tatarica*) used to be found in their millions across the steppe ecosystems of Eurasia, but are now constrained to Kazakhstan, Russia, Mongolia, China – and Uzbekistan. For a while the saiga had the unfortunate distinction of being the fastest declining mammal species in the world. The species declined by 95% and to the brink of extinction in the years following the fall of the Soviet Union, with the main cause of decline being poaching for horns and meat. The horns, which are only borne by males, are exported for traditional Chinese medicine, and the meat is used locally. At one point in the early 2000s, there were so few males that there were insufficient numbers to mate with all the females, limiting the number of calves being born. This population collapse led to the species being listed as Critically Endangered (the highest level of threat in the global list of threatened species). However, the saiga is an amazingly resilient species, unusual in its ability to bounce back from disaster, with a very high reproductive rate.

In the areas where saigas live, various projects aim to raise awareness about saiga ecology and conservation, reduce incentives for poaching, support protected areas for saiga conservation, enhance enforcement of national laws, and work with industry to reduce the barriers to saiga migration (eg: fencing, roads). These projects are implemented both by governments and by long-established national NGOs (including the Association for the Conservation of the Biodiversity of Kazakhstan) and international NGOs (including the Saiga Conservation Alliance, Fauna and Flora International, Birdlife, and Wildlife Conservation Society). Internationally, conservationists are working to reduce global demand for saiga horn and disrupt trafficking of saiga products.

Regarding saigas in Uzbekistan, historically this population (called the Ustyurt population) summered in Kazakhstan and migrated south into Karakalpakstan during winter. Sometimes, when winters were snowy and saiga numbers were high, they went as far south as Turkmenistan. Saiga migration is driven by weather and vegetation availability. Saigas have shifted their calving sites northwards in recent decades, in response to changes in climate and forage availability. In 2012, scientists from the Institute of Zoology of the Uzbekistan Academy of Sciences and the Saiga Conservation Alliance discovered a small permanent population in Karakalpakstan, in the Aral Sea area. Their populations are expanding back out from Kazakhstan into Karakalpakstan via the dry seabed of the Aral Sea. So although saiga numbers are small here at the moment, there is great potential for numbers to grow as long as protection is in place.

e saygachiy@eco.gov.uz. No physical permit was issued but we did then have an email chain to present to staff at the control station.

The official **entrance** to the reserve is at ▥ bubbling.lingering.handbook. There are no buildings there but there is an information board beside the track. You need to continue on, however, a further 25km to the **control station** (▥ pictured. possessions.rapidly) to show your permit to the staff. The control station has no opening times but there is always someone there as it is the base for rangers and is also used as a weather station. They will update you and your driver in Karakalpak, Uzbek or Russian with any important information such as areas with restricted access, expected changes in weather, or recent wildlife sightings.

WHAT TO SEE AND DO The primary reason for visiting the Saigachy Reserve is to appreciate the landscape, including views of the remains of the Aral Sea. For many, it is a kind of environmental pilgrimage, a chance to be alone for a couple of days in a wilderness which has borne the brunt of human actions far away. Along the length of the clifftop, which runs along the western shore of the sea, there's a dirt road in reasonable condition, from where you can stop at periodic viewpoints to see the water, the beach, and the rock formations usually referred to as the Aral canyons, though they don't meet the geological definition of a canyon. Rather, they are stacks, towers, and pyramids of rock sculpted by water and wind over millennia. You can stop anywhere along this track for memorable **views**, but you will get the best photographs from ▥ licks.jeer.timing (the first clear sighting of the sea) and from ▥ frequent.diesels.underweight (for the canyons).

It is possible to swim in the Aral Sea, though it is not necessarily a pleasant experience as it is very, very salty and rather muddy, especially around the edges. You will need to take a bottle of water and a towel with you to clean your skin afterwards, even if you only go for a paddle. The best access point is the **old military port** (▥ crutches.squared.birdhouse) where there's still the remains of a concrete slipway going down from the cliff to the water's edge. Beside the slipway there is also a depth marker for monitoring the water level. Sadly and inevitably, it is falling lower every year.

Although the herds of saiga (page 115) now tend to congregate in the restricted part of the reserve where there's a natural spring, there is evidence of their former presence across the reserve. One of the most intriguing features are the ancient **saiga hunting traps**, giant Vs which were cut into the soil to concentrate the saiga into an area where they could be easily shot with a bow and arrow or other rudimentary weapons. There are at least 16 of these traps in the reserve, the largest of which measure more than 500m long and 300m wide. To fully appreciate the size and shape of the traps you'll need to look at a satellite image, but if you head for ▥ treats.unjustly.abstracting you will be able to pick out the furrows in the land.

There are almost 30 **ancient cemeteries** scattered across the reserve and the area to its south. In the northern part of the reserve, the **Duana Necropolis** (▥ downward.bouncing.chomps) and the nearby **stone ring** (▥ rasped.disorders. reluctance) may date from as early as the 4th century BC.

Outside the reserve In addition to the natural features, there are a number of manmade sites of historical interest around the reserve. **Davletgirey** (▥ syllabus. illuminated.outflanked; 24hrs; free), also known as Kurgancha, is a 12th-century

◀ 1 A beautiful vista at Saigachy Reserve. 2 The Mausoleum of Zhanbolatuly-Kunti.

Ustyurt Plateau and the Saigachy Reserve   SAIGACHY RESERVE

Suffering from almost no light pollution, Karakalpakstan has some of the darkest night skies on earth. With the exception of Nukus, almost all of the republic is Class 1 on the Bortle dark sky scale, meaning that it is an excellent dark sky site. Assuming there is no cloud, you will be able to see zodiacal light, gegenschein (a faint nebulous light seen opposite the position of the sun), and the M33 Galaxy with the naked eye, and you may even notice the Scorpius and Sagittarius parts of the Milky Way casting shadows on the ground. It's the best view of the universe you can get without going into space.

Astrotourism is underdeveloped in Karakalpakstan, so for the time being you won't find a specialist dark sky guide or lodge, and you will need to bring your own equipment. Base yourself at the BesQala Yurt Camp (page 110): it is the remotest location of any accommodation in the region, with no nearby buildings, and they turn off the electricity, and hence all the lighting, once the guests go to bed. It will then be just you and that spectacular canopy of stars.

As a beginner stargazer you don't need a telescope. In fact, w EarthSky.org recommends starting with binoculars, which are not only cheaper but also easier to transport. A pair of 7×50 binoculars is ideal as they are small enough to hold steady without a tripod. Buying a planisphere (a rotating star locator) will help you know where to look and to correctly identify the stars and constellations you are looking at. Various apps, including Stellarium Plus and GoSkyWatch Planetarium, can help you do the same thing on your phone, but they often have a reduced dataset offline, as well as other limitations.

Many smartphones are now up to the challenge of astrophotography, though using a tripod or other stable base will improve the quality of images no end. You will need to read up on controlling the manual settings on your phone in advance, and/or use an astrophotography app such as NightCap Pro which will give you full control.

fortress about 40km south of the entrance to the Saigachy Reserve, close to the bottom end of the Aral Sea. Built from local stone and partially collapsed, it is well camouflaged against the rocky cliff. You will need stout footwear to scramble up the path, but it is well worth doing so to see the fort's walls and circular towers, which were built with stones laid in an attractive herringbone pattern. There's a good view out to the sea, which is no doubt why the original builders chose this location, but please refrain from climbing on the ruins, for your own safety but also to preserve what is left of the structure.

About 10km south of the entrance to the reserve is the **Mausoleum of Zhanbolatuly-Kunti** (anxious.spaces.instigating; 24hrs; free), an attractive yellow brick structure with a white dome. Zhanbolatuly-Kunti lived from 1723 to 1806, and the male symbol that is inscribed alongside his name and dates indicates that all those buried in the graves around his mausoleum were men. Many of the burial sites in and around the reserve are much older than this one, however. The **cemetery** (uselessness.merited.handbasket; 24hrs; free) 20km north of Kubla Ustyurt (page 108) is constructed in a similar style to the Duana Necropolis and the nearby stone ring. These were nomadic burial places, simply marked with dry stone walls encircling the graves, some of which have carved headstones.

KARAKALPAKIYA AND TEJEN

The small town of Karakalpakiya lies on the southern side of the A380, about 20km from the border post at Tejen where you can cross into Karakalpakstan from Kazakhstan. While it's not a destination in its own right, the fact that there's a train station here and other basic amenities, including a bank, makes it useful to know about, especially if you need to withdraw money from an ATM after crossing the border.

GETTING THERE AND AWAY

By road Whichever direction you are coming from, the journey to Karakalpakiya is long, slow and uncomfortable. The A380, which is the main road between Kungrad and Beyneu in Kazakhstan, is being upgraded, but work is slow due to the long distances involved and the logistics of getting workers, equipment and materials out here. Until work is finished, you are unlikely to average a speed of more than 40km/hr, and you will need your own vehicle as there are no buses or shared taxis between the towns. Most of the vehicles on the road are heavily laden trucks crossing the border, though there are a few private cars making the same journey.

Local **taxis** wait by the train station in Karakalpakiya to take passengers to the Tejen border post. This journey takes 30–40 minutes and costs UZS80,000. See page 53 for details on crossing the border.

By train The train station in Karakalpakiya is in the town centre, on the right side of the road just past the mosque. The Nukus–Volgograd train stops here, as does the Kungrad–Beyneu train. The trains are not daily, and the days they stop here depend on the direction of travel. At the time of writing, trains to Volgograd (29hrs; from UZS612,000) depart on Wednesday, Thursday, Friday and Sunday; trains to Kungrad (5hrs; from UZS79,000) are on Wednesday, Friday and Sunday; and trains to Nukus (9hrs; from UZS115,000) are on Monday, Wednesday and Saturday. The timetable is subject to change, so do check the latest departure days online at w chipta.railway.uz/en/home before planning your itinerary. You can pre-book tickets online or buy them from the ticket office (07.00–18.00 daily).

WHERE TO STAY AND EAT There is no choice of accommodation at Karakalpakiya: if you need to stay at the border your only option is the **Dinur Cafe and Hotel** (insincerity.imprisoned.antelope; $). It doesn't take advance reservations and looks unpromising from the outside but there's actually a proper building behind the shipping container, with clean rooms all with AC and Wi-Fi, a blessing given that there is no mobile signal. There are four single sofa beds in each room and you rent a bed for a 12-hour period. Staff hand out clean bedding when you check in. There is a block of fairly clean showers and toilets at the rear of the property, plus a large and lively canteen serving homemade *manti*, *samsa*, *shashlik* and salads. Cold beers, vodka and soft drinks are in plentiful supply.

OTHER PRACTICALITIES Karakalpakiya is only small – it's home to around 4,500 people – but it is the first settlement you will come to after crossing the border from Kazakhstan, and it has several important facilities you might need. The roads are not named, but as you drive into the town from the A380 you will immediately see the **Berdakh Baba Mosque** on your right, swiftly followed by **Uz Post** (09.00–17.00 Mon–Sat) and **Halq Bank** (09.00–17.00 Mon–Fri), which are just before the train station. Halq Bank has an ATM that accepts both MasterCard and Visa. There are a couple of **mini marts** here, too.

South Ustyurt National Park was created in 2020 and covers 1.45 million hectares of the extreme northwestern part of the Ustyurt Plateau. On paper, tourist activities can be carried out throughout the park, but the location is so remote and inaccessible that to date no tourism infrastructure has been built there. There is, however, potential for adventure tourism including geotourism and astrotourism – so long as you have an experienced local driver with a well-maintained 4x4 (contact BesQala; page 46) and are prepared to camp and bring all your food and water with you. Physical features of interest within the park include the Kazakhlyshor Dry Lake, a dry saline depression; the Shorzha Depressions and the wetlands of Sarykamysh Lake, which is rich in fish therefore attracting cormorants, pelicans, and other birds. Some 350 species of plants have been recorded here, including two that are endemic (*Climacoptera ptiloptera* and the recently described *Allium ravenii*). There are also 19 rare and globally endangered species of vertebrates, including four globally endangered species of mammals: ligature, goitered gazelle, Turkmen kulan and Ustyurt urial. You're unlikely to see them unless you have a lot of time, patience, and help from a local guide. In the past there were populations of saiga antelope and the Asian cheetah (a subspecies which is now extinct in Karakalpakstan), but you will no longer see them today.

On the parallel street (in the opposite direction to the railway line) is **Polyclinic #67** which is open 24/7 and provides basic healthcare services. There is a **pharmacy** (09.00–17.00 daily) in the same building.

WHAT TO SEE AND DO The **Beleuli Caravanserai** (goalpost.proclaim. ambitiously; 24hrs; free) is a remarkable historic site about 40km southeast of Karakalpakiya, 6km north of the A380 along a track. In the 14th century, when Beleuli was built, it would have been a truly impressive site. The two stone pillars of the vast monumental arch that marked the caravanserai's entrance are still standing, though the arch linking them collapsed in 2016. Originally this gate was more than 8m in height and decorated with a bas-relief of lions. Visitors in the 1960s and '70s made sketches and photographs of the relatively intact portal, and noted that its niche was decorated with white, turquoise and ultramarine majolica tiles, though these are no longer in situ.

Beleuli occupied an important location on the north–south caravan route between Khorezm and the Lower Volga. The centrepiece of the complex was the caravanserai, the medieval equivalent of a motel, with accommodation for merchants and their animals as well as storage areas for their goods. A two-storey structure with seven rooms on each floor, built around a courtyard with a well in the middle, it measured 35m by 29m, with a tower on each corner.

The limestone blocks used to build the complex were mined locally, and if you look closely at their surface you can see seashells buried within the material. Around the site you can still see the quarries, a graveyard and eight *sardobas*, reservoirs of drinking water covered with domed roofs to reduce the amount of water lost to evaporation.

◀ Beleuli Caravanserai.

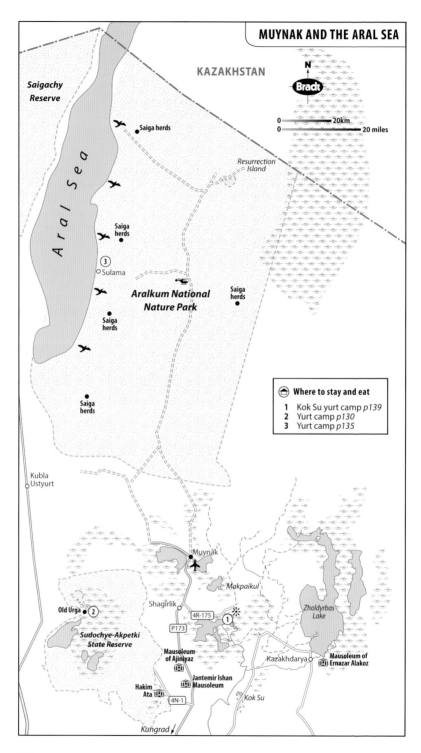

KAZAKHSTAN

N

0 ____ 20km
0 ____ 20 miles

*Saigachy
Reserve*

A r a l   S e a

Saiga herds

*Resurrection
Island*

Saiga
herds

③ ○ Sulama

*Aralkum National
Nature Park*

Saiga
herds

Saiga
herds

Saiga
herds

Where to stay and eat

1 Kok Su yurt camp *p139*
2 Yurt camp *p130*
3 Yurt camp *p135*

Kubla
○ Ustyurt

Muynak

Makpaikul

Old Urga ● ②

Shagírlik ○

4R-175
①

P173

*Zholdyrbas
Lake*

*Sudochye-Akpetki
State Reserve*

Mausoleum
of Ajiniyaz
🕌

Kazakhdarya ○

Mausoleum of
🕌 Ernazar Alakoz

Jantemir Ishan
🕌 Mausoleum

Hakim
Ata 🕌

4N-1

Kok Su

Kungrad ↙

5

Muynak and the Aral Sea

Muynak District is in the north–central part of Karakalpakstan, stretching up to the border with Kazakhstan. The district covers an area of 37,880km², larger than Belgium and only slightly smaller than Switzerland, but it is home to just 33,000 people, the largest proportion of whom live in the town of Muynak. The main reason for this low population density is that until the Aral Sea was shrunk in the late 20th century, the sea covered almost all of the district. It is within living memory that the water has been replaced by desert.

Many of those who come to Muynak District are disaster tourists: they want to see the former port of Muynak and the skeleton ships rusting in the desert; what's left of the devastated sea; and, in a few cases, the location of the infamous Aralsk 7 bioweapons base. However, the people who live here are rightly proud of their homeland, the stark beauty of the landscape, and its wildlife. They want to tell their own story – the good and the bad – and are investing in both ecotourism and adventure tourism, diversifying the economy and broadening Muynak's appeal.

Central Asia's newest national park, the Aralkum National Nature Park, was created in Muynak District in 2022, centred on Resurrection Island. This protected area complements the existing Sudochye-Akpetki State Reserve, an important location for birding. The museums in Muynak, mausolea linked to local saints and heroes, and the abandoned village of Old Urga will help you understand the district's human history.

MUYNAK

Muynak is the administrative centre of Muynak District and the only settlement of notable size in the area. Before the shrinking of the Aral Sea, the town's population numbered tens of thousands of people, most of whom were employed in the fishing industry, either on the fishing fleet or in the canneries on shore. The lighthouse still stands on the cliff above the harbour, but the ships on the seabed below are grounded on the sand: Muynak is now 150km away from the Aral Sea and for most inhabitants the former wealth of the town is but a memory. The climate change resulting from the decline of the sea is taking its toll, too: dust storms buffet the town, especially in late spring; summers are getting hotter and the winters colder. Many families have left in search of work and a better life, leaving just 13,500 people behind.

That's not to say that Muynak has been forgotten, however. The town and its inhabitants have admirable resilience and the government, development agencies, community-led groups and the private sector are working together to try and give Muynak a new identity and future as a destination in its own right – as well as being the gateway to the Aral Sea. The airport has recently been upgraded and driving along the main street you'll see plenty of new buildings, including hotels. Both the

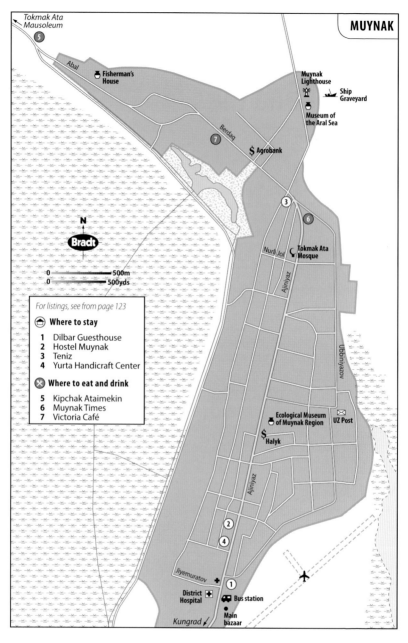

Tokmak Ata
Mausoleum

Abal

Fisherman's
House

Berdaq

Muynak
Lighthouse

Ship
Graveyard

Museum of
the Aral Sea

Agrobank

Bradt

N

0 ———— 500m
0 ———— 500yds

Nurli Jol

Tokmak Ata
Mosque

Ajiniyaz

Ubbinyazov

For listings, see from page 123

🛏 **Where to stay**

1 Dilbar Guesthouse
2 Hostel Muynak
3 Teniz
4 Yurta Handicraft Center

✕ **Where to eat and drink**

5 Kipchak Ataimekin
6 Muynak Times
7 Victoria Café

Ecological Museum
of Muynak Region

UZ Post

Halyk

Ajiniyaz

Jiyemuratov

District
Hospital

Bus station

Main
bazaar

Kungrad

museums are modern and well designed, and although some of the ships in the
Ship Graveyard have been moved to look more organised, they nevertheless give an
insight into the scale of Muynak's erstwhile fishing fleet.

GETTING THERE AND AROUND The spine of Muynak is Ajiniyaz, the main road
running roughly north–south through the town. This is where businesses and

public buildings are concentrated, with predominantly residential neighbourhoods either side. The majority of points of interest are located close to the bus station and within walking distance of one another, but you will need to take a taxi to the Ship Graveyard (page 126) and surrounding sites.

By air Muynak's recently renovated airport is on the southeastern side of the town. Uzbekistan Airways flies here three times a week from Tashkent (Tue, Fri & Sat; 3½hrs; from UZS476,262) and the plane stops in Nukus en route.

By car There is a reasonable road between Nukus and Muynak, a journey of around 200km that takes 3 hours. Driving from Muynak on to Sudochye Lakes takes 2 hours; to the BesQala Yurt Camp (page 110) overlooking the Aral Sea takes 3 hours, as much of the road is unmade and in poor condition; and to drive to Resurrection Island will take at least 2 hours.

If you want to hire an English-speaking guide and driver in Muynak to explore the town and surrounding area, we recommend **Makhmud Aitjanov** (93 489 3090). He works at the Ecology Museum (page 125) but is able to guide independently and has an excellent knowledge of regional history and geography.

By bus and taxi Muynak's bus station is on Ajiniyaz, opposite the District Hospital. From here there are buses (UZS20,000) and shared taxis (UZS60,000) to Nukus. The journey takes 3½ hours. From the same stand you can also take a taxi to the Ship Graveyard (UZS10,000), which is about a 10-minute drive away on the north side of the town.

WHERE TO STAY *Map, opposite*

After Nukus, Muynak has the greatest range of places to stay in Karakalpakstan. That is not to say that you will be spoilt for choice – there are no upmarket or luxury options – but the properties listed here are clean, well run and fairly priced, and they are used to accommodating foreign tourists as well as locals.

Teniz Hotel (32 rooms) Ajiniyaz 6/3; 93 771 1656. Functional modern hotel with clean AC rooms & good en suites. Beds are hard but have decent bedding. Cold beers, soft drinks & snacks are sold at reception. The Wi-Fi works well & the room rates are negotiable. $$

※ **Dilbar Guesthouse** (7 rooms) Ajiniyaz 8; 94 141 1031. Set back from the main street in a compound with a lovely garden & veranda is this charming family-run guesthouse. Each of the simple, clean rooms sleeps 2–4 people & has AC. There are 2 shared bathrooms with Western toilets & showers. $

Hostel Muynak (6 rooms) Ajiniyaz 39; 61 322 1554. Basic but clean accommodation with 4–6 beds per room & shared bathrooms. There is plenty of parking space within the compound, which is useful if you have your own vehicle or bikes. $

Yurta Handicraft Center (2 rooms) Ajiniyaz; 97 220 1490. Remarkably, one of the cheapest places to stay in Muynak also happens to be one of the best. Occupying the 1st floor of the building there is one huge dormitory room with 22 single beds, plus a smaller side room. Guests share 3 toilets, 4 hot showers, & a big kitchen/diner. It is light, immaculately clean, all the bedding matches, & there's AC. Individual lockers, too. No b/fast but you're close to the bazaar & can make yourself hot drinks in the kitchen. $

WHERE TO EAT AND DRINK *Map, opposite*

Muynak doesn't have a great variety of places to eat, but the following cafés are clean and dishes like soup and *shashlik* will help keep hunger at bay. Vegetarians may struggle, however, as there is rarely much choice on the menu. If you are staying at a guesthouse, ask your host to cook you dinner instead.

Kipchak Ataimekin Abai; ⊕ 10.00–21.00 daily. The fried fish is the highlight of the menu, & is best enjoyed with tomato & cucumber salad, fresh bread, & a pot of tea. The downside is it is out of the centre of Muynak, on the northern side of the town. You could walk here from the Ship Graveyard, or take a taxi from the city centre (UZS10,000). $

Muynak Times Ajiniyaz; ⊕ 10.00–20.00 daily. This place is easy to find as it is inside Muynak's Clock Tower on the main street. Simple café serving tea, coffee & snacks. $

Victoria Café Berdaq; ⊕ 09.00–22.00 daily. Serving simple snacks & conveniently close to the Ship Graveyard but not worth a specific trip out from the city centre. $

SHOPPING For basic foodstuffs, including fresh produce, go to the **main bazaar** on Ajiniyaz, which is next door to the bus station. There is not much to buy in terms of souvenirs and handicrafts, but at the **Yurta Handicraft Center** (Ajiniyaz; ⊕ 09.00–17.00) you can pop in to see local artisans producing attractive *suzanis* (embroideries) and hand-knotted carpets, both of which are made to order. They are happy to give demonstrations and also sell a small selection of paintings, ceramics and embroidered slippers.

OTHER PRACTICALITIES Muynak has several banks in the town centre. The most conveniently located of these are **Agrobank** (Berdaq 13; ⊕ 09.00–13.00 & 14.00–18.00 Mon–Fri) and **Halyk Bank** (Berdaq 13; ⊕ 08.00–18.00 Mon–Fri). Both branches have ATMs accepting MasterCard, Visa and UnionPay cards. There is a branch of **Uz Post** (⊕ 09.00–17.00 Mon–Sat) on Ubbiniyazov.

Medical care The **District Hospital** (Jiyemuratov 13; ☏61 322 1203; ⊕ 24hrs) occupies the whole block on the corner of Jiyemuratov and Ajiniyaz and can treat basic problems. There are several **pharmacies** nearby on Ajiniyaz: the easiest one to spot has a sign saying 'Hotel Moynaq', not to be confused with Hostel Muynak.

WHAT TO SEE AND DO
Ecological Museum of Muynak Region (Ajiniyaz; ⊕ 09.00–18.00 daily; UZS30,000) Confusingly, the Ecological Museum is also called the State Museum of the History and Culture of Muynak Region. It was established in 1984 but now occupies a new building opposite the Khokimat (the local council building). The artefacts on display range from a full-size Karakalpak yurt decorated with weavings and filled with traditional household items, to a slightly moth-eared selection of taxidermied animals indicative of the species that could, historically at least, be found in the local area. There is a wooden fishing boat and tackle, some interesting vintage photographs, and in the first-floor gallery, some fine paintings by Rafael Matevosyan and Faim Madgazin, two modern artists known as the chroniclers of the Aral Sea. Matevosyan's huge pen and ink panorama, *Old Muynak*, is particularly impressive and shows mid 20th century Muynak, a very different looking town to the one you see today. The museum does offer guided tours, which will help you to better understand the artefacts and their context; Makhmud Aitjanov (☏93 489 3090) speaks excellent English.

Tokmak Ata Mosque (Ajiniyaz; ⊕ 24hrs) Muynak's mosque, named after the same holy man honoured in the mausoleum (page 126), is in the centre of the town. It is a modern building but attractively designed with a striped, free-standing minaret that is faintly reminiscent of those in Khiva, but on a smaller scale. The

◀ Street scenes in Muynak.

interior includes a painted mihrab and dome, both of which are in attractive pastel colours, and multiple wooden pillars carved with a geometric pattern.

Fisherman's House
(Berdaq 106; ⊕ no fixed hrs) A white wooden fence painted with red motifs demarcates this traditional fisherman's house from its neighbours. It is loosely a house museum, but it doesn't have standard opening times or exhibitions. Nevertheless, if there is someone there to let you in, it is interesting to see the traditional architecture, simple furniture, and get a sense of how families lived in the early 20th century when Muynak was a thriving fishing community.

Tokmak Ata Mausoleum
(Nurli Jol 26; ⊕ 24hrs; free) Tokmak Ata (sometimes transcribed from Karakalpak as Topaq Ata) is thought by local people to have been a disciple of the Prophet Muhammad, which would date him to the 7th century, though nothing about his life is known. The relatively modern mausoleum covering his grave is a cuboid structure with a white dome, and it's the centrepiece of a larger cemetery with a small orchard offering shade. There's no entrance fee, but do put a small donation in the green box by the entrance to help pay for the upkeep of the site.

Museum of the Aral Sea
(Muynak Harbour; ⊕ 09.00–18.00 daily; UZS30,000) This small museum on the north side of Muynak tells the tragic story of the Aral Sea and the fishing community who lived in the town. The exhibitions include paintings of the local area before the sea disappeared, model boats, and also vintage cans of fish processed in the factories here. There are some similarities in terms of subject matter with the Ecological Museum (page 125), which is larger so, if you are short of time, then just visit the ships here and skip the museum.

While in the area of the museum, you should also see the **Aral Sea Monument**, a pyramid structure in the square between the museum and the Ship Graveyard, and also **Muynak Lighthouse**, which was painted a couple of years ago in a funky black-and-white design by artists at Stihia Festival (page 128). The lighthouse is opposite the museum and if the gates are open you can climb to the top for views across the absent sea.

* Ship Graveyard
(Below Muynak Harbour; ▦ stumbles.bettered.gleam) Immediately below the Museum of the Aral Sea is Muynak's most famous attraction. Lined up on the sand in what used to be the harbour are the remains of the town's fishing fleet, a dozen or so rusting skeleton ships that look like something from an apocalypse movie. The ships to the left have been arranged somewhat unsatisfactorily in a very orderly and unnatural line with a footpath around them, but if you walk further to the right there are some larger ships that were probably more difficult to move and thus remain where they last docked before being marooned on the sand. The graffiti on their sides only adds to the dystopian feel. It is possible and permitted to climb on the ships but be careful where you put your feet as rust has made the metal brittle and in many places it has already corroded away. You don't want to fall through or cut yourself.

Use the ships as the start and end point for a walk out into the desert: you can walk for an hour or two and as the land is so flat you will still be able to see Muynak Lighthouse on the cliffs to get back where you started. Pay attention to the seashells in the sand, the new vegetation, and the trickles and puddles of water which allow

1 Muynak Lighthouse. 2 Museum of the Aral Sea. 3 Muynak's Ship Graveyard. ▶

Stihia Festival (w stihia.org) was founded in Muynak in 2017 by an eclectic group of electronic music lovers from across Uzbekistan. Their intention was to raise awareness of the Aral Sea environmental disaster and to help the surrounding region, in particular to bring sustainable development to the town of Muynak. The festival's name means 'force of nature', which is particularly apt in a landscape severely afflicted by climate change.

First and foremost, Stihia is an electronic music festival that has steadily grown and gained international attention and acclaim. The combination of its out-of-the-way desert location, performances by international artists, and the presence of hippies, steampunks and cyberpunks from around the world among the festival goers has earned Stihia comparisons with Nevada's Burning Man in the US, but the organisers prefer to describe it as 'Everest for DJs' because of the physical challenge and determination it takes to get there. The 2022 line-up included the Russian electronic music producer Vladimir Dubyshkin; Japanese DJ Wata Igarashi, who explores the more psychedelic elements of techno; Sicilian DJ Toto Chiavetta, who has recorded on multiple international labels but now runs his own label, Borders of Light; and Andro Gogibedashvili, the Georgian multimedia artist better known Saphileaum. But you can hear homegrown talent from Karakalpakstan and Uzbekistan, too: Tashkent-based singer-songwriter Nikina and techno, trance and acid DJ Mari Breslavets have both performed fabulous sets.

There's more to Stihia than the music, however. The organisers are building a community with the residents of Muynak and the surrounding area. That reach is expanding, as from 2023 onwards the festival is going on tour, with a new location every year. The Stihia+1 forum invites local and international experts to discuss the region's challenges and propose solutions, addressing critical topics such as models for rural development, desert ecosystems, including water usage, and the critical impact of tourism. Local families open up their houses and apartments during the festival to host guests, though it is also possible to bring a tent or stay in the festival's yurt camp; and local entrepreneurs make the most of the opportunity to sell their handicrafts, food and drink, as well as to provide taxi and

plants and occasional small beetles and flying insects to survive in this otherwise inhospitable landscape. Muynak is a town where you should take time to reflect on local history and what mankind has done to nature and to itself, and this is the ideal place to walk meditatively. Just check the weather forecast in advance, as you don't want to get caught out here when a dust storm blows through!

SOUTH OF MUYNAK

The main road from Nukus to Muynak comes via Kungrad (page 103) and then branches off as the P173 through the southern part of Muynak District. It is a reasonably fast road and if you are driving or travelling by public transport you are unlikely to need to stay overnight en route, but there are three sites of historic interest along the way where it is worth stopping to stretch your legs and have a look around.

HAKIM ATA (Doslik; ⅲ clipping.merger.meerkats; ⊕ 24hrs) This large memorial complex is dedicated to the Sufi saint and scholar Sulaymon Bakirgani; Hakim Ata is his honorific. He was born in Bakirgan, close to the Aral Sea, in 1122 and

guiding services. Stihia also funds **STIHI AGEN** (w stihiagen.org), a non-profit educational project encouraging Muynak's youth to develop their skills in IT, art, design and more.

Though the festival dates and location for Stihia now change annually, they are publicised well in advance on the official website. Co-organisers **PeopleTravel** (w people-travels.com) sells official festival packages, including transport and accommodation, as well as pre- and post-festival tours. If you are able to make your trip dates coincide with those of the festival, you will be part of an initiative that is inspiring not only economic development but cultural development in an otherwise deprived area of the republic.

Festival goers at Stihia.

Muynak and the Aral Sea   SOUTH OF MUYNAK

became a disciple of Khoja Ahmed Yasawi, who is still revered across Central Asia and is buried at Turkestan in Kazakhstan. Inspired by and learning from Yasawi, Hakim Ata established himself as a Sufi mystic and a poet. His collection of poems, *Bakirgan Kitabi* (*The Book of Bakirgan*), explores how love can release a person from his ego and find spiritual perfection. Hakim Ata's other surviving literary works include *Akhirzam Kitabi* (*The Book of the End of the World*), *Maryam Ana Kitabi* (*The Book of Mother Mary*) and *Ismaghil Qissasi* (*The Story of Ismail*), all of which are known throughout the Turkic world.

Hakim Ata died in 1180 and his tomb, which is the centrepiece of this memorial complex, remains an important pilgrimage centre for Sufis. Many pilgrims want to be buried near the saint, too, which is why there's an extensive graveyard here. The mosque and supporting buildings at the front of the site are completely new, and Hakim Ata's mausoleum (which is located to the rear of the complex, past the graveyard) has recently been rebuilt, seemingly on a grander scale than the original building. Nevertheless, the architecture is very attractive and the construction work and decoration is of a high standard. Look out in particular for the hand-carved wooden pillars and the beautifully painted green and blue dome inside the mausoleum. The saint's white marble tomb is simple yet elegant, carved with an Arabic inscription.

To get to Hakim Ata you need to drive north from Kungrad towards Muynak on the P173 for approximately 25km, and then turn west on to the 4N-1 and drive for a further 6km to reach the village of Doslik. The shrine complex is clearly marked.

JANTEMIR ISHAN MAUSOLEUM (hacker.numbered.eases; 24hrs; free)

Continuing another 5km north along the P173 after the turn-off to Hakim Ata brings you to this mausoleum, about 200m west of the main road along a track. This small, curiously shaped white building, which dates from the 18th to the 19th century, has a dome panelled in such a way that it almost looks as if it has scales. It's a simple structure, unrenovated but attractive, and somehow feels a more authentic and spiritual place than the overly polished Hakim Ata. Jantemir Khan was a local hero who protected his people against Turkmen raiders.

MAUSOLEUM OF AJINIYAZ (cowhide.emancipated.reassure; 24hrs; free) This

attractive 19th-century brick structure topped with two blue domes is about 45km south of Muynak on the western side of the road. Ajiniyaz (1824–78; page 98), known by his pen name of Ziwar, was a celebrated Karakalpak intellectual and poet. Around 100 of his poems survive. This is officially his burial place, though some local people believe he was actually interred in the village of Kamis Boget where he was born.

SUDOCHYE-AKPETKI STATE RESERVE

The area southwest of Muynak is one of the most scenic and biodiverse in all of Karakalpakstan, an oasis in the desert and a refreshing sight after hours of driving through dry and often quite barren landscapes. Established in 2021, the Sudochye-Akpetki State Reserve covers an area of 280,507ha. It incorporates the wetlands commonly known as **Sudochye Lakes**, the lake and surrounding tugai forest in Akpetki, desert ecosystems and Ustyurt chinks. Sudochye Lakes is not one single body of water but rather a succession of large, shallow freshwater and saltwater lakes, dense swampy areas, reed beds and thickets. Combined with the cliffs above, it is an ideal environment for birds. If you want to experience a yurt stay but are unable or unwilling to drive all the way to the BesQala Yurt Camp beside the Aral Sea (page 110), the small yurt camp overlooking the lake at Old Urga will be a good alternative. The location isn't as impressive, but it is tranquil.

GETTING THERE AND AWAY It takes approximately 2 hours to drive from Muynak

to Old Urga. You will need your own vehicle as there is no public transport, but the road condition is reasonable, even where it is unsurfaced, and so a 4x4 is optional. It is an attractive drive, part of which is along the top of a low dam created to manage the water levels in Sudochye Lakes. You can even see sand dunes en route at mixes.starbursts.knotting.

WHERE TO STAY *Map, page 140*

A small **yurt camp** (rodeo.chunked.demolishes; $$) with two yurts has been constructed at Old Urga and will open for guests in summer 2023. The camp

---

1 Sudochye Lakes. 2 Mausoleum of Ajiniyaz. 3 Hakim Ata. 4 Glossy ibis are one of many species to be found at Sudochye Lakes. ▶

belongs to the State Committee for Ecology and Environment Protection and is situated in a scenic spot between the ruins and the lake with views across the water. It is not possible to book the yurt camp directly; ask a local tour operator (page 46) to enquire on your behalf. You will need to bring food with you as there are no cafés or shops.

WHAT TO SEE AND DO The primary reason for coming to Sudochye-Akpetki is for the **birdwatching**. Some 117 different species have been recorded at Sudochye, and the area serves as an important nesting and migration site for globally threatened bird species. Remarkably, this includes 50% of the global population of white-headed duck, as well as White and Dalmatian pelicans, little egret, glossy ibis, flamingo, mute swan and white-eyed pochard. Looking up to the cliffs it is possible to see steppe kestrel, saker falcon, houbara bustard, roller and Turkestan barbel. In addition to those species you can see at Sudochye, Akpetki also has four kinds of eagle (white-tailed, imperial, golden and short-toed snake eagle) and pin-tailed sandgrouse. You will need your own binoculars and a good field guide (page 200) as there are not yet any local guides specialising in birding.

Akpetki is also home to 18 globally endangered species of vertebrates, among them well-camouflaged desert monitor (a carnivorous type of monitor lizard), Central Asian tortoise and goitered gazelle. You might also see foxes and smaller mammals here and along the bottom of the cliffs at Sudochye.

The abandoned fishing village of **Old Urga** sits at the bottom of the cliffs looking out across Sudochye. In ancient times there was a citadel here, but all that remains of this is the **watchtower** (⊞ likening.relational.inflated) on the cliff top. The exact date of the tower is unknown but archaeological excavations suggest the area was already populated by the 10th century. The commanding views – essentially for spotting approaching raiders – affirm why this location was chosen, but please don't climb on the walls as it is very fragile.

Closer to the lakeshore are more substantial ruins, including the former school, hospital and **fish factory** (⊞ almost.herb.fetchingly), as well as residential buildings. These buildings mostly date from the late 19th and early 20th century, when the islands of the Aral Sea were a place of exile. The first community banished here were Old Believers, mostly Ural Cossacks, who rejected reforms made by the Russian Orthodox Church and continued to worship in their old ways. Tsar Nicholas I (1796–1855) viewed the Old Believers as a threat to the imperial Russian state, and having been advised by the Russian Geographical Society that Sudochye Lakes was well suited to fishing, he deported them here at the very edge of the Russian Empire.

There was a second wave of deportations to Old Urga under Stalin. Nominally these people were evacuees from World War II, but they seem to have mostly been ethnic Poles and Ukrainians forcefully relocated here from the fringes of the USSR. Some 997 Poles arrived in the village in late November 1941, in freezing weather, and many of them lacked adequate clothing and footwear. The existing community of Karakalpaks and Kazakhs, whose numbers the new arrivals were intended to boost, rallied round to help them survive the winter. The fish factory, which produced smoked, dried and salted fish, seems to have been relatively productive, but after Stalin's death and the admittedly relative reduction in state repression, Urga's inhabitants left as soon as they could, leaving the village empty. The buildings soon fell into disrepair, but the ruins and the **Orthodox cemetery** (⊞ queens. realness.chemists) are a poignant reminder of those who were forced to live and die here against their will.

ARALKUM NATIONAL NATURE PARK

Had you come to Muynak in 1960 and walked or driven north out of the town, you would have got wet. But now there is a huge expanse of desert, the Aralkum, between you and the Aral Sea, which you must cross if you want to reach the water. With only tracks across the seabed and no real infrastructure to speak of, it is a tough and unforgiving journey, but it is possible to drive through the new Aralkum National Nature Park to reach Resurrection Island and to gain sight of the sea. This is the less common alternative to visiting the Aral Sea from the western side in the Saigachy Reserve (page 108).

HISTORY Resurrection Island, the dominant feature of the Aralkum National Nature Park, (Vozrozhdeniya in Russian) sounds harmless enough, and for most of its history, it was. Geologists believe that this island in the Aral Sea was created at

BIOLOGICAL WEAPONS TESTING AT ARALSK 7

From the late 1930s onwards, the Red Army began using Resurrection Island for biological weapons testing. The leader of the programme, Ivan Mikhailovich Velikanov of the Biotechnical Institute, was purged after the first round of tests, but his programme continued. A top secret laboratory was built here in 1948 to test agents including anthrax, bubonic plague and smallpox, and in 1954 the Ministry of Defence established Aralsk 7 at Kantubek on the island's northeast coast. This infamous bioweapons facility, belonging to the Microbiological Warfare Group, was used to develop and test a wide range of fatal diseases, including on monkeys, sheep and horses. Resurrection Island became an open-air test site, strictly off limits to foreigners and protected by patrol boats. Although the USA and USSR signed the Biological Weapons Convention (BWC) after it opened for signatures in 1972, agreeing to stop bioweapons development and destroy existing stocks, work continued on the island after the BWC came into force in 1975, with testing done at night to avoid US satellite detection.

Following Uzbekistan's independence in 1991, President Karimov recognised the political and environmental need to clean up the Chemical Research Institute in Nukus (page 79) and Aralsk 7 and other contaminated areas on Resurrection Island. Under pressure, in 1995 Russia handed over some documents about the research sites, and four years later a bilateral agreement was signed between Uzbekistan and the US to decontaminate the island, including burial pits containing anthrax. The work was done by the Pentagon's Threat Reduction Agency, who in 2002 made the sites safe. The buildings at Aralsk 7 were subsequently demolished, so little physical evidence of this notorious period of history remains.

In 1992, Kanatjan (Ken) Alibekov, who had been the First Deputy Director of Biopreparat (the Soviet agency responsible for the biological weapons programme), emigrated to the USA and in a CIA debriefing provided a detailed account of the work undertaken at Aralsk 7. He also testified before Congress, and in 1999 published *Biohazard: The Chilling True Story of the Largest Covert Biological Weapons Program in the World – Told from Inside by the Man Who Ran It*. Bleak as it is, this is the best book to read if you are interested in learning more about what happened here.

the same time as the Ustyurt Plateau. It was identified by Russian explorers on board the schooner *Konstantin* in the mid 19th century, at which time the island measured around 200km². As the Aral Sea shrank, however, Resurrection Island grew to more than ten times this size. By the early 2000s it was no longer an island at all but a peninsula, and now there is so little water that it has joined up with the mainland.

It's not just this aspect of Resurrection Island's history that is dark and depressing, however. Its isolated location made it ideal for a prison camp and so in the 1930s Stalin exiled large numbers of *kulaks* (wealthy peasants) here to live in terrible conditions. These prisoners sarcastically nicknamed the island Vozrozhdeniya, meaning 'resurrection' or 'rebirth', and the name stuck. But it gets worse. This desolate, hard to reach place caught the eye of the Red Army. It was the ideal place to build what becomes the infamous Aralsk 7 (page 133).

GETTING THERE AND AWAY There is not, and is not expected to be, any public transport to Aralkum National Nature Park, so you will need to hire a car and driver from Nukus (page 81) or Muynak (page 123) and allow a full day for the drive. There is a helipad within the park, which could in theory be used for a private helicopter charter, but as Uzbekistan's commercial helicopter fleet is based in Tashkent, the cost of this would be unreasonable for the time saved.

WHERE TO STAY AND EAT As the park is a work in progress, there is not yet much discernible tourism infrastructure. A tourism base camp, including a **yurt camp** [map, page 120] (33 089 3327), has recently been built at Sulama on the eastern shore of the Aral Sea. It has five simple but clean yurts right on the water's edge so you can have a paddle. You can further enjoy the view from the picnic benches or by driving a quad bike along the gravelly shore. There's a volleyball pitch, too, for when you are feeling especially energetic. The camp will ultimately complement the local homestays that are also being developed in villages between Muynak and the island.

WHAT TO SEE AND DO Aralkum National Nature Park was created by presidential decree in 2022 and is being developed for tourism. Part of the 'Resurrection Island: enterprise, conservation and development around the Aral Sea' project (page 136), the park covers approximately 1 million hectares, though its exact boundaries and zoning are still under discussion; Resurrection Island sits at its heart.

The appeal of the Aralkum National Nature Park, and particularly Resurrection Island is in its landscapes (including geomorphological objects, the rocky features of the Earth's surface) and its biodiversity. The varied ecosystems include gypsum semi-desert with elements of sandy and rocky deserts, cliffs of chinks, fragments of tugai vegetation, and reed beds. Scientists have identified 123 species of higher vascular plants, including saxaul (page 8); and 128 species of vertebrates here, many of which have unique relict features because they developed in conditions of severe isolation. Of particular interest to wildlife lovers are the park's endangered species: Central Asian tortoise, Tatar sand boa, blotched snake, flamingo, osprey, golden eagle, lesser kestrel, pin-tailed sandgrouse, Brandt's hedgehog, corsac fox, caracal and saiga antelope.

Seeing these species is not guaranteed, but the saiga population in particular is growing, and the animals are regularly photographed with camera traps. Given the

5

◀ 1 Aralkum National Nature Park. 2 The watchtower, Old Urga. 3 The fish factory, Old Urga. 4 Central Asian tortoises can be seen at Aralkum National Nature Park.

RESURRECTION ISLAND: ENTERPRISE, CONSERVATION AND DEVELOPMENT AROUND THE ARAL SEA

With Joseph Bull, Elena Bykova, Alexander Esipov and E J Milner-Gulland
(darwininitiative.org.uk/project/DAR28003/)

The virtually disappeared Aral Sea is synonymous with ecological and socio-economic collapse, but carries the seeds of its own recovery. In the heart of the former sea, Resurrection Island's unusually pristine biodiversity flourished as the island was cut off for 400 years. The recent drying of the sea and decommissioning of the abandoned Aralsk 7 military base (page 133) allowed access to scientists, poachers and looters, revealing its conservation and cultural importance, but also its vulnerability.

The Aral Sea is transboundary (Uzbekistan/Kazakhstan), situated in the Ustyurt desert ecosystem. Regional biodiversity is rapidly declining due to environmental change, poaching (particularly of mammals, birds and reptiles), and large-scale industrial activity linked to resource extraction. Unemployment rates in the Aral Sea region are at 40%, incentivising poaching and looting, but there is also enormous untapped potential for adventure, ecological and cultural tourism. Developing nature-based tourism can help conserve biodiversity as it attaches an economic value to the landscapes and wildlife, incentivising local communities to protect them.

Pilot surveys of Ustyurt residents in 2020 – including discussions with civil servants, residents and businesses – demonstrated a strong desire for sustainable livelihoods (particularly tourism-based), responsible development and biodiversity conservation. These findings align closely with regional and national government priorities: dramatic expansion in tourist revenue combined with increased natural resource extraction and transport construction are seen as key to growing Uzbekistan's economy. The 'Resurrection Island: enterprise, conservation and development around the Aral Sea' project, funded by the Darwin Initiative (a UK government grants scheme that helps to protect biodiversity and the natural environment) is supporting stakeholders in building the skills, market structures and policy environment to realise these ambitions. It is focused on two key settlements with direct access to Resurrection Island: the town of Muynak (a potential tourism gateway) and the village of Kyr-Kyz (an industrial development hot spot).

The project:

- addresses drivers of unemployment and poaching through piloting new tourism-linked income streams (crafts, homestays, guiding) linked to Resurrection Island;
- addresses potential damage from industrial infrastructure around Kyr-Kyz through technical support for effective biodiversity impact mitigation;
- addresses poaching and lays the foundation for tourism through supporting protected area designation for Resurrection Island.

The aim is for the approach to all these issues to be replicable and support the development of sustainable economies throughout the country.

Sunrise at the South Aral Sea ▶

SAXON BOSWORTH

large distances involved you will need to drive across the park, keeping binoculars at the ready in case you see something move in the distance that deserves a closer look; and then hike, as it is on foot that you are most likely to see the smaller creatures.

SOUTHEAST OF MUYNAK

As discussed on page 4, the Amu Darya no longer reaches the Aral Sea and instead comes to an ignominious end at **Kok Su**, an admittedly scenic reservoir in the desert. As the crow flies, Kok Su is about 30km southeast of Muynak, but Makpaikul Lake is between the two so you need to drive two sides of a square. Head south 20km from Muynak along the P173 to Shagirlik, and then east through a succession of small villages on the 4R-175, which runs parallel to the northern shore of the lake. You will need your own vehicle, but the road service is not too bad so you will manage without a 4x4.

There is a conveniently located **viewpoint** (⧉ emotionally.considering. hyacinths) close to the village of Porlitov, from where you can appreciate the beauty of Kok Su but also note the falling water levels. If you want to linger longer, though, then it is better to go to the **Kok Su yurt camp** (⧉ destitution.capricious.tongs; ☎99 114 7168; $), which is about 2km west of the viewpoint, back towards the village of Shege. Here among the trees is a single yurt, though owner Mirzabay is planning to erect more. It is possible to stay here between April and September, and it is a wonderfully relaxing place to sit reading and drinking tea on one of the *tapchans*, watch the cows grazing, or take the wooden rowing boat out on to the water to go fishing.

In the extreme southeastern part of Muynak District but best accessed by car from neighbouring Kegeyli District (page 143) and visited at the same time as the Karakum Ishan Necropolis (page 152) is the **Mausoleum of Ernazar Alakoz** (⧉ outdoes.spendthrift.recalling). You will find it 6km east of the village of Kazakhdarya. Ernazar Biy (Alakoz was his nickname) was Karakalpakstan's answer to Robin Hood, and this was his ancestral homeland. Born in 1805, he lived at a time when the Karakalpak people were ruled by the Khan of Khiva, who demanded crippling taxes from his subjects. After a rebellion in which multiple tax collectors were killed, Ernazar took over tax collection but distributed the proceeds to local people. His reputation grew not only among the Karakalpaks but among the Kazakhs too, and in the 1850s he became the leader of the Karakalpak revolt against Khiva (page 19). Ernazar's independent khanate was short-lived, however. The Khan of Khiva allied with the Turkmen, and after losing a battle at Khujayli, Ernazar was forced to retreat to the shore of the Aral Sea. Here he was besieged for three months, and then killed in 1856. His tall, yellow-brick mausoleum, open sided with a simply painted pale blue dome on top, rises high above the otherwise flat landscape. It is much less ornate than many mausolea you will see in Karakalpakstan, but is a proud tribute to an important Karakalpak hero.

5

◄ 1 Kok Su reservoir. 2 Mausoleum of Ernazar Alakoz. 3 Kok Su yurt camp.

6

Central Karakalpakstan

The districts of central Karakalpakstan, Kanlikul, Kegeyli, Chimbay, Karauzyak, Shumanay, and Takhtakopir, spread to the north and east of Nukus. They are typically rural and sparsely populated, and the agricultural activity that does take place there, including extensive cotton production, is facilitated only by a complex

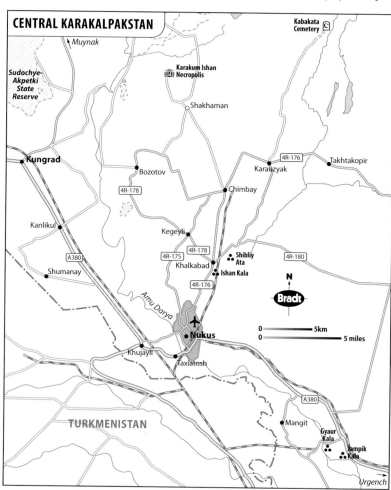

CENTRAL KARAKALPAKSTAN

Kabakata Cemetery

Muynak

Sudochye-Akpetki State Reserve

Karakum Ishan Necropolis

Shakhaman

Kungrad

Bozotov

4R-176

Takhtakopir

Karauzyak

4R-178

Chimbay

Kanlikul

Kegeyli

4R-175 4R-178

Khalkabad

Shibliy Ata

4R-180

Shumanay

A380

Ishan Kala

4R-176

Amu Darya

N

Bradt

0 ———— 5km
0 ———— 5 miles

Nukus

Khujayli

Taxiatosh

A380

TURKMENISTAN

Mangit

Gyaur Kala

Jampik Kala

Urgench

network of irrigation canals. For the most part, the region's attractions are within a couple of hours' drive of the capital, so you can stay in comfort in Nukus and visit them on a day trip. The main appeal of this area from a tourism perspective is the crafts workshops – including yurt building workshops – in Chimbay, where you can learn about traditional handicrafts and meet the artisans in person. There is also an assortment of cemeteries, including elaborately constructed necropolises connected with Sufi saints and the Karakalpak poet Berdaq; and the impressive ancient fortresses of Gyaur Kala and Jampik Kala.

KANLIKUL DISTRICT

You will pass through Kanlikul District when driving from Nukus and Khujayli towards Kungrad on the A380. Kanlikul town is 80km by road northwest of Nukus, just off the main road, and the drive takes around 90 minutes as the road surface is in good condition. There is a train station in the town but currently no regular passenger service, so you will need to travel by road.

Kanlikul is not a destination in its own right, but a convenient stop for a cup of tea and a snack on your drive to the Ustyurt Plateau (page 103). **Café Arba** (cranberries.cutest.abounding; 10.00–22.00 daily; $) is on the western side of the A380 about 1km south of the junction for Kanlikul. It is named after a traditional large-wheeled cart, a replica of which is on show in the grounds. Besides the main building there are two yurts for private dining, plus several *tapchans* in the shade under the trees. The *shashlik* here are particularly good.

Of all the things we expected to find in Karakalpakstan, a museum dedicated to the 1990s was not one of them. But right on the A380 at the junction where you turn off for Kanlikul is the **90s Museum** (Amir Temur 3; 09.00–22.00 daily; free), a small shrine to nostalgia, complete with early mobile phones, cameras, computers and typewriters, cassette players and more. You will almost certainly see something you used to have in your home and be forced to exclaim with an unexpected level of enthusiasm: 'I had one of those!'. There is a small **café** ($) here, too, serving basic meals and cold drinks. The staff don't speak English but are friendly, and there is free Wi-Fi.

SHUMANAY DISTRICT

Shumanay is a small district of 780km² immediately to the west of Kanlikul. More than a quarter of the district's population of 57,000 people live in the only city, which is also called Shumanay; the rest live in rural communities.

The reason you may want to come to Shumanay is to visit the **Felt Workshop** (Uzbekistan; 905 76 1657; free entry), one of very few open craft workshops outside Chimbay (page 146). There is a large population of sheep and camels in central Karakalpakstan, and Altinai Naubetova collects their fleece to use in her workshop. Naubetova and her apprentices wash each fleece gently by hand to remove any dirt and oil, and then dye it with natural pigments from berries and leaves foraged during local walks. Yellow comes from elaeagnus bark, liquorice root, or the mulberry tree; red is from glasswort; and blue is indigo, which isn't grown locally and has to be imported. The techniques may be timeless, and everything is still done by hand, but the products are carefully designed to suit modern lifestyles and modern homes. In the workshop you can watch both felt making and carpet weaving: the carpets are also made from wool. The yarn is spun on a spindle or hand wheel and then woven into a patterned carpet on an *ormek*, a narrow beam weaving machine. You can buy felt slippers and lace-up boots in

gorgeous earthy shades, purses and handbags, and also children's toys and small felt figurines that would look super hanging from the Christmas tree.

KEGEYLI DISTRICT

Kegeyli is the district immediately to the north of Nukus, between the capital and Muynak District. It is a predominantly agricultural area producing cotton, and takes its name from the canal that runs through the district and provides water to irrigate the crops. There are two towns of a reasonable size here: the regional centre of Khalkabad, which is on the 4R-176 between Nukus and Chimbay, around 40 minutes' drive from Nukus; and slightly smaller Kegeyli, 10km northwest of Khalkabad on the 4R-178. Of the two towns, Khalkabad has more useful facilities but neither has any tourist attractions; those are in the rural parts of the district.

GETTING THERE AND AWAY Both Khalkabad and Kegeyli are accessible by bus or shared taxi. Buses between Nukus and Chimbay stop at Khalkabad bus station (from Nukus: 20mins; UZS2,400; from Chimbay: 25mins; UZS3,324), which is on the main road, Dustlik, immediately outside the Khalkabad Sports Complex. If you do have a need to go on to Kegeyli (which is unlikely), you can change here for Kegeyli bus station (15mins; UZS1,752).

PRACTICALITIES You are unlikely to want to stop for long in either of these towns, but should you need it, Khalkabad's **Central Bazaar** (Dustlik 74) is on the highway between the junctions with Uzbekistan and Sh Tokseytova. There are plenty of stalls within the market selling snacks like *samsas* and *laghman*, as well as bread, fruit and nuts, so you can quickly rustle up enough for a meal. At the same address, facing on to the road, there is a mini branch of **Alokabank** (09.00–13.00 & 14.00–18.00 Mon–Fri) and an **ATM** that accepts Visa. Just to the north of the bazaar there is a small **pharmacy** (Cnr of Dustlik & Sh Tokseytova), and on the next city block is the **post office** (Dustlik; 09.00–18.00 Mon–Sat), immediately opposite Khalkabad's modern Friday Mosque. It is worth noting that the **District Hospital** (Kegeyli Guzar; 24hrs) is in Kegeyli, not in Khalkabad, but in the case of an emergency you would be better driving back to Nukus and going to the emergency hospital there (page 89) as it has more doctors and better facilities.

WHAT TO SEE AND DO There are three historic sites of interest in Kegeyli District, two of which are easily accessible from Khalkabad; the third, Karakum Ishan Necropolis (page 152), is best reached from Chimbay.

Ishan Kala (rosary.condense.chills; 24hrs; free) On the southeastern side of Khalkabad, accessed via Najim Daukaraeva, this archaeological complex, mosque and graveyard – its name means 'Fortress of the Elders' – was 150 years ago a separate village, though Khalkabad has now expanded and enveloped it. Imam Ata Ula Ishan was a Sufi elder, and the complex was built by his son in the mid 19th century. The walls of the original citadel are still standing, in places 10m high; you can visit Imam Ishan's tomb; and there's a mosque, which is still in use and is liveliest on Fridays. Many of the people who come here to pray are ethnically Turkmen and their traditional clothing is particularly colourful. In an act of service volunteers

◀ 1 Shibliy Ata necropolis, Kegeyli. 2 & 3 Exhibits at Kanlikul's 90s Museum. 4 Yurt-building workshop in Chimbay.

Irrigation in the Aral Sea Basin and upstream along the Amu Darya is nothing new. The inhabitants of cities like Termez have proactively managed the river, diverting water into canals to irrigate crops, for millennia. Indeed, the growth of such population centres in largely desert environments would not have been possible without effective manipulation of natural resources.

The position of the Amu Darya Delta moved naturally multiple times during its history but deliberate attempts to change the course of the river and harness its water didn't begin on an industrial scale until the 20th century. The rapid growth in the number, scale and intensity of water management projects in Central Asia during the Soviet period transformed the landscape and the economy beyond all recognition, but at an environmental cost many people in Karakalpakstan – the area worst affected by such schemes – would now question was worth paying.

When the Soviets seized power they nationalised both land and water resources. Modernising agriculture and increasing productivity were priorities for the new government, but they ignored traditional water management practices and introduced water-intensive crops such as cotton and melons that had not previously been farmed in this region on a commercial scale. The only way to make this possible was to significantly increase the volume of water available for irrigation, diverting the Amu Darya, Syr Darya and other rivers into a succession of canals, channels and reservoirs. Major engineering projects ensued, including the construction of the Great Fergana Canal in 1939 and the Karakum Canal (1954–88), which opened up vast new areas of land for agriculture, but significantly decreased the volume of water flowing into the Aral Sea (page 4).

One of the major problems with the irrigation canals was the construction quality: they weren't watertight, and even more water was lost to evaporation. In fact, it is estimated that somewhere between 30% and 75% of the water that enters the Karakum Canal, the largest in Central Asia, is lost. Poor management of such canals also results in waterlogging, increased salinity, and other issues which further exacerbate the environmental problems. Reconstructing and improving ageing irrigation infrastructure, including canals and hydraulic structures, is a priority for modern economic development and environmental restoration in Karakalpakstan, financed by donors such as the Asia Development Bank and the World Bank as well as from the state budget.

If this fact box has piqued your interest and you want to learn more about the history and impact of irrigation in Karakalpakstan, the definitive and very readable book on the topic is Maya K Peterson's *Pipe Dreams: Water and Empire in Central Asia's Aral Sea Basin* (page 200). The Museum of the Aral Sea and the Ecological Museum of Muynak Region (page 125), both of which are in Muynak, have small but insightful displays.

at the mosque also prepare large quantities of *plov* to feed devotees after Friday prayers, and they are happy to extend this generous hospitality to curious (and hungry) tourists. Eating together is a delightful way to feel part of the community, immersing yourself in local culture.

Shibliy Ata (⬛ nostrils.loaf.athlete; ◔ 24hrs; free) Also confusingly sometimes transliterated as Shimiliy Ata, this well-kept necropolis is 4km northeast of Khalkabad, just off the 4R-180. The drive will take you around 15 minutes and if you don't have your own vehicle you can pick up a taxi (approx. UZS20,000) from the bus station in Khalkabad (page 143).

This memorial complex is named after Sheikh Abubakr Shibliy, a Sufi saint who lived from the 9th to 10th centuries. Born in Samarra in Iraq to a family that was originally from Central Asia, he traced his spiritual lineage back to the Prophet Muhammad through his teacher, the mystic Junaid Baghdadi. During his lifetime, Shibliy Ata was thought to be mad, was imprisoned, and may even have been sent to a medieval mental asylum. However, his unconventional behaviour, which included burying himself in a small hole, rubbing salt into his eyes, and beating himself with a stick, was later recognised as part of his search for divinity and spiritual engagement with god.

The physical deprivations he subjected himself to took their toll and Shibliy Ata died in Baghdad in 946. This means that although there is a mausoleum here with his name on it, the saint's body is not inside. Instead, the attractive baked brick structure, which is a modern building constructed on the foundations of something older, is a memorial, a reminder that these were his ancestral lands. The pastel-coloured tiles on the roof are in a poor state of repair, in spite of not being old, so the mausoleum may well be given a facelift in the lifespan of this guide. This necropolis is a place where those who consider themselves as belonging to his Sufi chain can come to reflect on his sacrifices and teachings. It is a sacred site for local Muslims and a popular place of pilgrimage, as is attested to by the signs affixed to the building reminding pilgrims (probably ineffectually) not to venerate saints and buildings but rather to direct their prayers to God and to put some cash in the official donation box to help pay for the upkeep of the site. Devotees like to be buried close to the saint they revere, which is why there are plenty of other mausoleums on the site, including one that looks like a twin of the Shibliy Ata's.

CHIMBAY DISTRICT

Chimbay is by quite some way the most populous district in central Karakalpakstan, with a population of around 115,000 people, and the eponymous district centre is the largest and liveliest town in the area. Importantly for tourists, it is a hub for traditional crafts, which can otherwise be rather hard to see in Karakalpakstan. A number of community-based tourism initiatives, including those by the German development agency GIZ, have supported local artisans to open up their workshops to visitors, showing off their skills, sharing their knowledge and passion, and also selling their products directly to customers. It is therefore probably the best place in Karakalpakstan for souvenir and gift shopping. Although technically in neighbouring Kegeyli District, you can more easily reach the Karakum Ishan Necropolis from Chimbay, and hence it is listed here.

GETTING THERE AND AWAY The town of Chimbay is 60km north of Nukus on the 4R-176. The road surface is in reasonable condition, and by car the journey will take just over an hour, more than half of which is the section from Khalkabad to Chimbay. If you are travelling by public transport rather than in a car, you can catch a bus from Nukus (1hr 40mins; UZS5,724). Chimbay's **bus station** is on Temir Jol, about 200m west of the junction with the 4R-176.

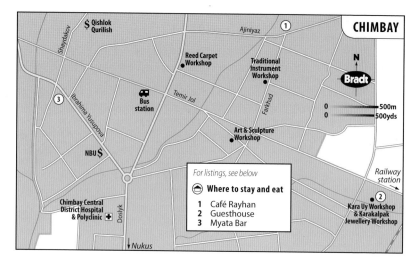

For listings, see below
🛏 **Where to stay and eat**
1 Café Rayhan
2 Guesthouse
3 Myata Bar

If you plan to visit Chimbay on a day trip from Nukus, our recommendation is that you book a private or small group tour. There are several local companies who will arrange the transport, guide and workshop visits for you, making the logistics of getting there and around effortless and also ensuring that you will have a guide who can translate what the artisans are saying. The best of these itineraries is with **Ayim Tour** (page 46), whose standard programme includes the yurt- and carpet-making workshops, plus a delicious, memorable lunch with a charming local family in their home. There is no minimum number of guests for the trip, but the cost varies depending on the group size, from US$90 per person if you are on your own, down to US$35 per person if there are four or more participants. **Muynak Oazis** has a similarly priced day trip, which includes the Ishan Kala in Khalkabad (page 143) and a yurt workshop in the morning, stops in Nukus for lunch, and then goes to Mizdakhan (page 162) in the afternoon.

For those travelling independently and perhaps staying at the new guesthouse (see below), you can still visit the workshops. You should call ahead where possible to make sure they're open and able to host you, but you should note that little English is spoken. This is why the guided tours are a preferential option.

🏠 **WHERE TO STAY AND EAT** *Map, page 158*

Accommodation options in Chimbay are limited, which is why it is best to visit the town on a day trip from Nukus. However, a two-storey guesthouse has been constructed at the **Kara Uy Workshop** (see opposite) and is due to open in summer 2023, which will at least give you a choice to stay overnight.

For something to eat and drink, you currently have the following options. It is also possible to arrange to have lunch at the Kara Uy Workshop ($; call them in advance to request it) – for most visitors to Chimbay this will be the best option as the food is home cooked and tasty.

Café Rayhan Jct Ajiniyaz & Farkhad; 🕐 10.00–22.00 daily. On the northeast side of Chimbay, this large modern building is easy to spot from the road because of the artificial grass laid outside. The restaurant is on the 1st floor. It Is clean & well organised, & serves *shashlik*, salads, *laghman* & *pelmeni*, as well as cold drinks & beers. $$
Myata Bar Ibrahima Yusupova; 🕐 11.00–midnight. Located near the Chimbay Bazaar, this is a very simple café & worth considering only

as a back-up if Café Rayhan is closed. Although there are a lot of dishes listed on the menu, on our visit only a couple were actually available, such as kebabs, salads & *laghman*. The inside of the building is quite dark, & not particularly inviting. The waiting staff don't speak English or Russian, so be prepared to point & take a gamble on what you're going to eat unless you're with a local person who can translate. $

OTHER PRACTICALITIES To withdraw or change money, go to **Qishlok Qurilish Bank** (Shaydakov 36) or the **NBU** (Yusupova 70). Both branches are open 09.00–17.00 Monday–Friday and have ATMs. In a medical emergency you can go to the **Chimbay Central District Hospital** (Doslyk 43) and neighbouring **polyclinic**, which are open 24 hours. There are also multiple pharmacies on Doslyk and the surrounding streets that sell basic medications.

WHAT TO SEE AND DO Karakalpakstan has a rich and varied handicrafts tradition, as attested to by the collections in the Savitsky Museum (page 89) and the State Museum of History and Culture of Karakalpakstan in Nukus (page 93), but it can be difficult to find places to see contemporary artisans at work and learn about their crafts. This is the reason why everyone with an interest in Karakalpak applied arts should come to Chimbay: numerous workshops are open to the public free of charge, and the craftspeople who work there are keen to welcome tourists and to share their knowledge and skills. It is also possible to buy many of the creations they produce, so you can go on a shopping spree confident that every som you spend on a souvenir or gift goes directly into the pocket of the person who made it.

Kara Uy Workshop (🌐 renewing.sulk.amber; Atajurt 82; 📞 90 650 4585) The Kara Uy Workshop is without doubt the most popular craft workshop for tourists to visit in Chimbay. Azamat Turekeev is a third-generation yurt maker, having been engaged in the craft since he was six years old. He is already teaching his own son the skills he needs to continue the family business. Yurts have a critical place in Karakalpak culture (page 150), and as there has been renewed interest in recent years, Turekeev not only has a full order book, but has also begun teaching yurt-making masterclasses, ensuring the future of this craft.

Getting the materials he needs to construct a top-quality yurt is not easy, so Turekeev plants his own willow and poplar trees. He cuts them while they are still flexible saplings, soaking them in water so he can bend them to the requisite shape. Once bent, the wood is then dried in a clay oven, fixing the curve, before the bark is stripped off and the wood underneath is painted. The traditional colour of the frame is red. This process is a labour of love but it ensures that the frame of the yurt is not only light and strong but also a work of art. Each yurt is made to order (and yes, you can order one: a mid-sized yurt with all the decorations costs US$1,800); Turekeev and his team produce a variety of styles, including traditional Karakalpak, Kazakh, Kyrgyz and Turkmen designs. You can even buy a miniature play yurt for children, which is the perfect compromise if you don't have space for a full-size yurt in your home. After your workshop tour you can have lunch with the family (independent visitors can also organise this in advance), and there is also a small gift shop inside their home selling various souvenirs such as mini yurts, wood statuettes and traditional clothing.

Karakalpak Jewellery Workshop (Atajurt 82; 📞 995 92 3840) Adilbay Tadjimuratov, son of Daribay Tadjimuratov (page 149), is following in his father's

6

creative footsteps and proudly reviving traditional styles and techniques at his Karakalpak Jewellery Workshop. If you see a silver Karakalpak necklace, pendant earrings, or a bracelet in a museum in Nukus and think 'I'd love to wear something like that!', Tadjimuratov's cooperative is the place to come.

Tadjimuratov specialises in silver jewellery which is hammered and engraved by hand. Some of the pieces are embedded with coloured stones or glass. He is a sought-after speaker and teacher as well as a craftsman, and travels extensively in Uzbekistan and abroad to participate in exhibitions and conferences. If he isn't at home when you visit, another member of the cooperative (who will likely be one of his students) will show you around and explain about the design and manufacturing processes. The jewellery is also on sale.

Art and Sculpture Workshop (▨ adverts.imagines.undergoing; ☎ 992 83 5505) Daribay Tadjimuratov, recognised as one of Karakalpakstan's greatest living artists, has exhibited his work across Uzbekistan and abroad. Inspired by the natural world and the materials it offers, he began drawing as a child but was forced to do military service and then study architecture before he could concentrate on making art.

Tadjimuratov's most dramatic sculptures are made from carved wood. His human figures are often totem-like and seem to be growing out of the timber. They can be as much as 4–5m tall. His clay sculptures tend to be a little smaller, but still with an emphasis on shape and texture. Understandably you may not have space in your luggage (or home) for a substantial piece of statuary, in which case you might be more interested in browsing and buying one of Tadjimuratov's watercolours, most of which are of Karakalpak landscapes, or his monochrome graphics.

Traditional Instrument Workshop (▨ lightest.angry.abilities; ☎ 97 348 8314) You can learn all about Karakalpak instrument making, and hear the instruments played, at Azat Pirniyazov's Traditional Instrument Workshop. The workshop specialises in three types of stringed instrument – *dutar*, *rubab* and *kobuz* – and every one is marked with the maker's stamp so it can be identified and credited to them.

Early in his career Pirniyazov spent nine years studying physics and acoustics. He considers this essential training for anyone wanting to make traditional musical instruments as the quality of the sound is paramount. Preparation of the wood, which often comes from a mulberry or apricot tree, is key. It needs to be dried for two years, boiled in water, and dried out again. Only once this process is finished will the craftsperson start bending the wood into the desired form. Cutting corners will result in a substandard instrument and sound.

The most popular instrument Pirniyazov makes is the *dutar*, a Karakalpak instrument that is common, with minor variations, across Central Asia. You will find one in almost every Karakalpak home, because it is believed that possessing a *dutar* will protect the family against evil spirits. In appearance a *dutar* is similar to a lute, with two strings and a long neck. The instrument is usually made from apricot wood but across this wooden body Pirniyazov stretches camel skin, which vibrates to create the sound. The *kobuz* is another two-stringed instrument, but with a differently shaped body and sound board. The strings are thicker and made from horse hair. Pirniyazov finds it difficult these days to get hair of the right length as farmers tend to cut the horse's mane and tail too short. He is also concerned about who will carry on his work after he retires: he doesn't have a student to pass his skills on to and he

6

◀ Workshops at Chimbay: 1 Weaving decorative items. 2 You can see *kobuz* and other instruments at Traditional Instrument Workshop. 3 A craftsperson at the Karakalpak Jewellery Workshop.

'Yurt' is a Turkic word that refers to a portable, round tent common across Central Asia. The word came into English via Russian, but Karakalpaks have their own term for this essential domestic structure – *qara u'y*, meaning 'black house' – because the animal skins they traditionally used to cover the roof and make it watertight became darker over time. Simple and light to build and transport, it is probably one of the earliest forms of dwelling, and yurts were already commonplace across Eurasia 3,000 years ago. The Greek historian Herodotus (484–425BC) described the nomadic Scythians (page 15) as living in yurt-like tents, and you will still occasionally see such homes today, though most are used for entertaining. Yurts are also used for special occasions: an *otaw* (a secondary yurt separate from the main living quarters), for example, may be erected by Karakalpak families at the time of a wedding, when it is used for receiving guests and to give the newly married couple some privacy on their wedding night.

The frame of a yurt is built from a lightweight lattice of wood that can be easily collapsed to transport it on the backs of camels or horses (or, latterly, by truck) from one site to another. In Karakalpakstan, the wood is usually poplar or willow, as both these species of trees grow locally. The wooden strips are bound together with strong bands woven from goat hair or cotton, and the wall and the roof are covered with an insulating felt which is also water-resistant due to natural oils in the fleece. Historically the Karakalpaks didn't tend to raise sheep and goats themselves as the marshy land around the Aral Sea wasn't suitable for herding, so they purchased the wool from Kazakh and Turkmen nomads who grazed their flocks on drier pastureland on the fringe of the desert. Often, an additional layer of animal pelt was added to the roof.

There are several features that set Karakalpak yurts apart from those of other groups in the region. Firstly, the roof is shaped like a cone rather than a dome, and thus the overall structure tends to be slightly higher. Woven white tent bands criss-cross the roof. The wooden frame is much lighter than those used in Uzbek yurts as the Karakalpaks would move their yurts more often as they took their livestock to different pastures; the Uzbeks tended to leave the frames in situ in the winter months, simply removing the felt covering. Karakalpaks often also stained the lattice frame a vibrant red.

The doorway of a yurt is its focal point. In a traditional Karakalpak design there are two hinged wooden doors that open inwards, attached to upright struts with a bar across the top. In the past the wood was undecorated, but carved patterns started to become popular in the early 20th century; you can see examples of these in the museums in Nukus and Muynak. In front of the wooden door is a reed screen, an *esik*, which is not only ornamental but also acts as a draft excluder and is rolled up to allow people to come and go. Often you will see a triangular patchwork ornament hanging on or close to the door, with tassels on each corner:

worries that his craft will die out as it takes so much time, effort and materials to make each instrument. Sadly, few customers recognise the value of such work and are prepared to pay for it.

Reed Carpet Workshop (🌐 obviously.casually.sharpens; 📞 944 54 0954) Kunduz Kurbanova, who weaves decorative panels from locally grown reeds, is a master craftswoman: not only does she make products herself, but she has also set up a

it may have evolved from the *tumar*, a protective amulet, and it is supposed to shield the inhabitants from evil spirits or bad luck.

The decoration of a yurt has always been very much a local affair. Until the early 20th century, before a young woman was married, she was expected to make reed carpets and screens for her future home, a yurt which would be made – or at least refurbished and decorated – for her and her husband. Her mother, sisters, and other older women in the community would help, and the techniques and designs were very similar to those still made by Kunduz Kurbanova in her Reed Carpet Workshop (see opposite) today. One of the most common motifs in Karakalpak weaving is the symbol of rams' horns, which are usually visible on the textile panels either side of the door, and have had sacred connotations across Central Asia since ancient times.

There are plenty of places in Karakalpakstan where you can still see and learn about traditional yurts, their construction and their decoration. Azamat Turekeev and his colleagues make yurts in time-honoured fashion at the Kara Uy Workshop in Chimbay (page 147); there are excellent historic examples in the State Museum of the History and Culture of Karakalpakstan (page 93), the House Museum of Amet and Ayimkhan Shamuratov (page 93) in Nukus and in the Ecological Museum of Muynak Region (page 125) in Muynak; and you can sleep soundly in a Karakalpak yurt in multiple places, including the BesQala Yurt Camp (page 110) and the Ayaz Qala Yurt Camp (page 181).

MAXIMUM EXPOSURE PR/S

crafts school teaching girls and young women from Chimbay the skills they need to weave reeds, sew and play traditional musical instruments. In this way she is guaranteeing the future of Karakalpak crafts and creating economic opportunities for those who would otherwise have few job prospects.

Reed carpets are used to decorate Karakalpak yurts, and you find them hanging on the walls of the yurt as well as lying on the floor. Reeds are readily available in the marshy areas of the Amu Darya Basin (though as water levels fall, the quantity of reeds is declining) and can easily be decorated in different colours. Red is perennially popular, but there are other bright colours, too. Kurbaonva's carpets are typically woven from two types of reed: the most commonly used is *shiy*, but there is also *jezshiy*, which is harder to work with. There are hidden messages in the designs of the carpets if you know how to read them, for example information about how many children a family has, and how many of those children are married. Kurbaonva is very knowledgeable about Karakalpak domestic culture and will explain to visitors in detail, but you will need a guide to translate as she doesn't speak English or Russian.

As well as the reed carpets, Kurbanova and her students also produce embroidery work. They have a good selection of items on sale, including attractive purses, bags, hats and other easily portable souvenirs with Karakalpak motifs such as horns, diamonds and octagons.

Karakum Ishan Necropolis (incumbents.soften.experienced; 24hrs; free) This extensive complex is quite difficult to reach, and although it is in Kegeyli District it is in better accessed from Chimbay (page 145) than Khalkabad. You will need your own vehicle to get there as there is no public transport. Drive 40km northwest from Chimbay to the village of Shakhaman and on the northern side of the village take the left fork in the road. It is a further 15km on to the graveyard, which is at the dead end of the road.

The Karakum Ishan Necropolis dates from the 18th to 20th centuries. It is a sprawling site with many graves, the most important of which are helpfully highlighted on a map on the outside wall of the white pilgrims' rest house by the car park. The most prominent figure buried in the complex is the Karakalpak poet Berdaq (page 98), the style of whose recently restored mausoleum is reminiscent of that of the Samanid Mausoleum in Bukhara, the oldest surviving monument in Central Asia. It is an attractive cubic structure topped with a dome, with multiple bands of differently patterned decorative brickwork and a carved wooden door; inside, literature lovers have laid colourful artificial flowers on the grave.

KARAUZYAK DISTRICT

Driving through parts of Karauzyak, which is due east of Nukus, Kegeyli, and Chimbay, the landscape is noticeably greener than many other areas of Karakalpakstan. Irrigation canals bring water to productive fields of cotton and other crops, and between them are reed beds and trees. Thanks to the water and availability of food, there is a noticeable increase in the number of birds, which are few and far between in the more arid parts of Karakalpakstan.

The district's main attraction is the Kabakata Cemetery (page 156), and there are also two impressive fortresses in the far south of Karauzyak District. However, the fortresses are best visited on a day trip from Nukus or while travelling through the southern part of Karakalpakstan, rather than coming from Karauzyak town.

GETTING THERE AND AWAY Karauzyak is the eponymous town of the district. It is midway between Chimbay and Takhtakopir on the 4R-176, and you can get here from either of those towns by bus (from Chimbay: 25mins; UZS3,420; from Takhtakopir: 20mins; UZS2,880). The direct route from Nukus to Karauzyak is

1 Jampik Kala. 2 Karakum Ishan Necropolis. 3, 4 & 5 Scenes from Kabakata Cemetery, including 4 the triple-domed mausoleum of Zholbaris Tunegan Ush Sheikh Baba. ▶

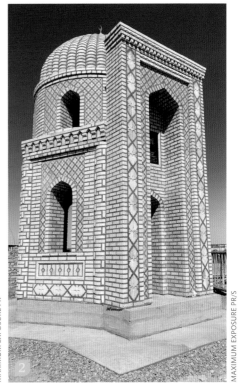

80km but it is faster to drive via Chimbay; although the distance is about 30km longer, the road is in better condition. In total it will take you just over 2 hours, the last 30–40 minutes of which is the section from Chimbay. Given the significant distance to the cemetery (60km) you are unlikely to be able to get a taxi to take you out there. You would therefore need your own vehicle or to find a family going there to pray.

PRACTICALITIES Almost everything you might need in Karauzyak is on or very close to the main road, Garezsizlik. The **bus stand** and **bazaar** are side by side on Ajiniyaz and around the corner is **Agrobank** (Cnr Berdaq & Garezsizlik; ⏰ 09.00–13.00 & 14.00–18.00 Mon–Fri), which has an ATM accepting Visa and UnionPay cards. Continuing further east along Garezsizlik brings you to **Jayhun** (Cnr Garezsizlik & Karakalpakstan; ⏰ 09.00–23.00 daily; **$$**), a pleasant enough restaurant with a menu of eclectically named dishes such as Titanic and Genghis Khan. Most of them are kebabs and grilled meats, so less exciting than the names might suggest, but tasty enough. The one thing you might want to take a photo of while in Karauzyak is the **clock tower** (Karakalpakstan), which seems to have been vaguely inspired by Big Ben, but built on a much smaller scale.

WHAT TO SEE AND DO
Kabakata Cemetery (▦ progenitors.shun.stubble; ⏰ 24hrs; free) Reaching the Kabakata Cemetery, which is 60km north of Karauzyak town, requires a rough and uncomfortable drive along mostly unmade roads. The journey takes about 2½ hours. There is no public transport and taxis are unlikely to agree to come out this far, unless you were to hire one for the full day, so you will need your own vehicle to visit. The cemetery may feel like it is in the middle of nowhere, but until a generation or two ago there was a lake here and a village. It is still in use; people still come and say prayers at the graves of their ancestors, and want to be buried in plots alongside them. There are small buildings near the parking area where families can sacrifice a chicken or sheep and cook it. Such rites are an intriguing insight into local customs, even if they would be considered heretical by many orthodox Muslims. The mausoleum of Kabakli Ata, the local saint after whom the complex is named, was built only in 1997, though the underlying grave is much older. More interesting are the unrenovated mud-brick mausoleum of a Kazakh, Sina bi Telek Uli (1830–1900), which has an archway similar in style to those seen around Khiva; and the triple-domed mausoleum of a local man named Zholbaris Tunegan Ush Sheikh Baba, which is towards the back of the site. There are name plaques on the mausolea so you will be able to identify them. Wandering between the graves you can see a variety of vernacular styles, all of which have been made by local artisans from assorted building materials. Some are decorated with tiles or even painted ceramic plates that have been embedded in the façades.

Gyaur Kala (▦ silent.defensible.supervised; ⏰ 24hrs; free) Not to be confused with the smaller, less significant fortress of the same name in Khujayli (page 166), Gyaur Kala is on the southern side of the village of Karatau in a position overlooking the river. *Gyaur* means 'fire worshipper' and there was indeed a Zoroastrian fire temple here, a sanctuary in the heart of the fortress. This is probably why the Arabs later called it the Fortress of Infidels. Gyaur Kala was founded in the 4th century BC and expanded and redeveloped over the next 700 years. Although only the southern and western walls survive, you can still clearly see the original trapezoid shape and how impregnable the 10m-high, double-layered walls would have been. These walls consisted of two storeyed galleries for archers, which are still immediately identifiable, plus substantial towers and battlements. There is no doubt that this would have been a formidable military installation.

Inside, one monumental building survives, the halls of which would have originally been decorated with columns, wall paintings and niches for statues. During the Arab Conquest of Central Asia (page 16), Gyaur Kala was besieged for more than a year, and when the fortress did finally fall, the inhabitants were forced to convert to Islam. Those who refused were killed. People continued living at Gyaur Kala until the 13th century when Jochi, a Mongol commander and the eldest son of Genghis Khan, ordered that it be destroyed. The fortress was never rebuilt and those people who did survive the attack moved elsewhere.

Jampik Kala (■ acquainted.erase.townsfolk; ⊕ 24hrs; free) Some 7km southeast of Gyaur Kala as the crow flies but necessitating driving three sides of a square back on to the A380 to get there, Jampik Kala is bigger than its neighbour and has even more of a wow factor. This rectangular city was founded in the 4th century BC, though the extant walls are later, mostly dating from the 9th and 10th centuries. The fortress occupied a strategic location between the Sultan Uvays Dag mountain range in the east and the floodplain of the Amu Darya in the west. Jampik Kala was an important river port, and archaeological excavations here have identified bronze discs, jewellery, glass, ceramics and metalwork from as far away as India, China and Egypt. Such products would have travelled here along the Silk Road.

Great lengths of Jampik Kala's exterior walls survive, demarcating a floor plan of around 1.1km². In the northeast corner are the remains of a smaller royal citadel with dramatic columned buildings, all made from mud bricks. In places you can still see the wooden poles inserted into the brickwork to give it additional strength and support, as well as decorative motifs that are typical of medieval Khorezm (page 16). Coins found here help date the periods of occupation; the settlement seems to have recovered from the destruction wrought by the Mongols in 1220 and been inhabited for another hundred years. Anywhere else in the world there would be queues of tour buses lined up outside, but this being Karakalpakstan you are likely to have the wonder that is Jampik Kala to yourself.

TAKHTAKOPIR DISTRICT

The town of Takhtakopir, the administrative centre of the district of the same name, lacks much which might qualify it as a tourist destination, but if you are driving or cycling through, there are a few useful bits of infrastructure. These include a branch of **Agrobank** (Doslyk 62; ⊕ 09.00–13.00 & 14.00–18.00 Mon–Fri) with an ATM that accepts Visa and UnionPay, **UZ Post** (Berdaq 9; ⊕ 09.00–13.00 & 14.00–17.00 Mon–Fri), and a small nameless **café** next door to the agricultural college towards the northern end of Doslyk. The new **Khalkh Mosque** (Karakalpakstan) was under construction at the time of our visit but has an attractive green dome, and there's a small **Russian cemetery** a few minutes' walk away on Kudyarova.

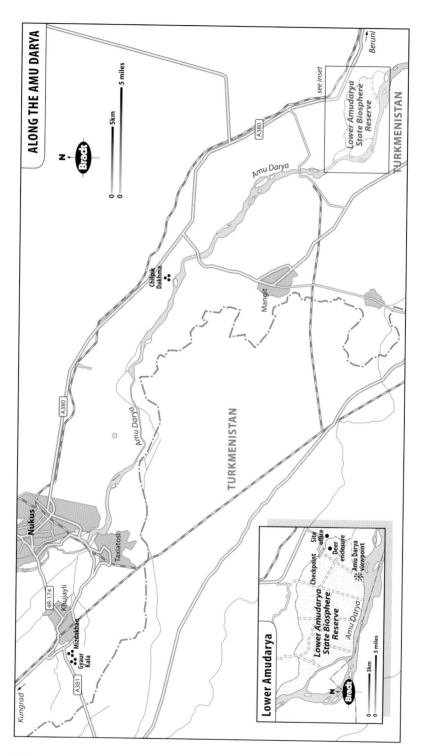

ALONG THE AMU DARYA

N

5km

5 miles

Beruni

see inset

A380

Lower Amudarya
State Biosphere
Reserve

Amu Darya

TURKMENISTAN

Chilpik
Dakhma

Mangit

Amu Darya

TURKMENISTAN

Nukus

A380

Amu Darya

Taxiatosh

Khujayli

4R-174

Kungrad

Mizdakhan

Gyaur
Kala

A381

Lower Amudarya

Checkpoint

Site
office

Deer
enclosure

Amu Darya
viewpoint

Lower Amudarya
State Biosphere
Reserve

Amu Darya

N

3km

3 miles

7

Along the Amu Darya

The Amu Darya is the lifeblood of Karakalpakstan. Without this river there would be no water for people or animals to drink, or to irrigate the crops. The two districts covered by this chapter, Amu Darya and Khujayli, lie along the riverbank to the south and southeast of Nukus, and their western edges form the international border with Turkmenistan. They are easily accessed from the capital and when driving through southern Karakalpakstan to or from neighbouring Khorezm.

The must-see site in this region is Mizdakhan (page 162), one of the most extensive and sacred archaeological sites in Karakalpakstan. Nature lovers should also plan to visit the Lower Amudarya State Biosphere Reserve (page 169), which is home to a flourishing wild population of Bukhara deer, a species that just 20 years ago was on the brink of extinction. The reserve straddles Amu Darya and neighbouring Beruni District but it is included in this chapter due to the importance of the river in its geography.

KHUJAYLI DISTRICT

In 2017 Khujayli District, which lay south of Nukus, was subdivided into two: Khujayli to the southwest and Taxiatosh in the south. The sites of interest are concentrated in Khujayli; you may pass through Taxiatosh but there's no reason to stop there. In Khujayli there is one reasonably sized town of the same name, with a population of 125,500. The Khujayli–Konya Urgench border post (page 53) is also here, on the international border with Turkmenistan, but the main tourist attraction in the district is the important archaeological site of Mizdakhan.

GETTING THERE AND AWAY The town of Khujayli lies just 15km west of Nukus. The easy drive along the 4R-174 takes about 20 minutes by car, but a bit longer if there is rush hour traffic getting out of the city. In town, **taxis** and **minibuses** heading for Nukus depart from the parking area next to the main bazaar on Kubra, on the northern side of the centre (15mins; UZS1,440) and Kungrad (90mins; UZS12,360).

WHERE TO STAY AND EAT *Map, page 161*
Given how close Khujayli is to Nukus, few tourists opt to stay here. If you do need local accommodation, however, you could try **Hotel Xojeli** (Garezsizlik; ☏ 90 714 2065; $$), which is basic but centrally located. There are several simple places in Khujayli to get a meal, but all of them are unremarkable; the following two are your best bet.

Restaurant Caravan (Cnr Garezsizlik & Kubra; ① 10.00–22.00 daily). This restaurant has an attractive outdoor seating area & serves a mixture of local & European foods, ice cream & beers. It

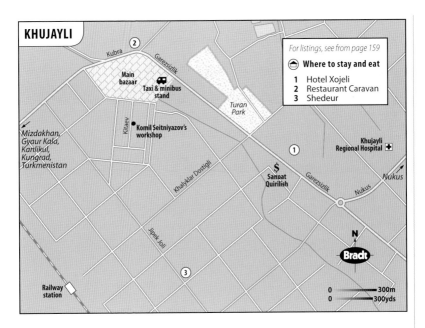

KHUJAYLI

Kubra

Garezsizlik

Main bazaar

Taxi & minibus stand

Turan Park

Kitaev

Komil Seitniyazov's workshop

Mizdakhan, Gyaur Kala, Kanlikul, Kungrad, Turkmenistan

Khalyklar Dostigli

Sanoat Quirilish

Garezsizlik

Nukus

Nukus

Khujayli Regional Hospital

Jipek Joli

Railway station

N

Bradt

For listings, see from page 159

Where to stay and eat
1 Hotel Xojeli
2 Restaurant Caravan
3 Shedeur

0   300m
0   300yds

---

also offers AC, which is welcome on a sweltering hot day. $
Shedeur (Jipek Joli; ⏲ 10.00–22.00 daily. In most ways this is pretty similar to Caravan, but it has the added advantage of having *tapchans* to relax on in the garden. $

SHOPPING Khujayli's **main bazaar** is on the northern side of town, on Kubra. It is smaller and less well stocked than the bazaar in Nukus, but nevertheless has a reasonable selection of fresh fruits and vegetables, bread and other basic foodstuffs you might want for a picnic or road trip.

OTHER PRACTICALITIES **Sanoat Quirilish Bank** is on Garezsizlik, immediately opposite Hotel Xojeli. Its ATM is accessible 24/7 and accepts MasterCard, Visa and UnionPay. The **Khujayli Regional Hospital** (↘ 61 556 2795; ⏲ 24hrs) is on Nukus in the centre of Khujayli. There are **pharmacies** within the hospital grounds and immediately opposite on the other side of the street.

WHAT TO SEE AND DO In the centre of Khujayli, very close to the bazaar, is **Komil Seitniyazov's Workshop** (Kitaev 9). This is the family home of patriarch and accomplished craftsman Komil, who along with his four sons makes *besiks*, traditional wooden cradles for babies, from black willow. This style of cradle is still popular across Karakalpakstan, especially in rural areas, and the *besik* is handed down through the generations as a family heirloom. Komil is happy to invite visitors into his home, share a cup of tea, and show off each step of the manufacturing process in his workshop, which is in the garden at the back of his house. But, if you do want to buy a cradle, he will point you in the direction of a trader in the bazaar as he doesn't keep finished cradles at home. They retail for UZS120,000 to 500,000 depending on the complexity of the design.

Along the Amu Darya   **KHUJAYLI DISTRICT**

7

◀ The Amu Darya flowing through the Lower Amudarya State Biosphere Reserve

Turan Park (Cnr Garezsizlik & Khalyklar Dostigli) is a large, green space with a Ferris wheel, and while it is not going to be the main reason for your visit to Khujayli, it is a convenient, pleasant location for a picnic.

✳ Mizdakhan (A381; ▦ skirting.carefully.issue; ◷ 24hrs; free) The greatest attraction of Khujayli lies 3km west of the town centre on the south side of the road to the Turkmen border. Mizdakhan is arguably the most important complex of archaeological sites in Karakalpakstan, covering 300ha spread across three low hills. Academics believe that Mizdakhan may be the location of Mazda, a city mentioned in the Zoroastrian holy book Avesta, in which case it was already occupied by the 4th century BC. It would have been the second largest city in ancient Khorezm, only exceeded in size by Konye Urgench in what is now Turkmenistan. Included within Mizdakhan are four main areas: Gyaur Kala (page 166); the ruins of an 80ha city with clearly visible neighbourhoods, streets and residential buildings; an extensive irrigation network, which served urban areas as well as agricultural purposes; and a 100ha necropolis, one of the oldest and most sacred in Central Asia.

In July 2022 it was announced by Tigran Mkrtychev, Director of the Savitsky Museum (page 89), that Mizdakhan is to be designated as a History and Archaeology Park. The details are still to be finalised, but once implemented this will give the site vital legal protection, conserving the ancient layers which archaeologists are yet to have time and resources to study, and also protecting the above- and below-ground structures that are otherwise vulnerable to collapse or damage from poor quality reconstruction work.

Local myths have it that Mizdakhan is the burial place of Adam, of Adam and Eve fame. His supposed grave is marked by an **apocalypse clock** in the necropolis. Every year more and more bricks fall from the mausoleum, and it is said that when the last brick falls, the world will end. In order to postpone the apocalypse for as long as possible, pilgrims – mostly local Muslims, but in theory any followers of Abrahamic faiths who accept the Creation story – visiting this site make a point of putting fallen bricks back on to the structure, just in case.

Also in the necropolis, the **Mausoleum of Mazlumkhan Sulu** tops a large subterranean complex dating from the 12th to the 14th centuries. Initially there were two burials here, plus a portal, but after the portal was destroyed the structure was redeveloped and more bodies were interred. Access to the crypt is via a staircase that leads inside a domed underground room with adjoining chambers with vaulted ceilings; in places there are decorative stalactites fashioned from terracotta. On the walls and arches, yellow mud bricks alternate with majolica tiles with a turquoise glaze, creating a geometric pattern, and there are also some finely drawn floral motifs.

We do not know exactly who is buried here, but it is thought that at least one of the graves belonged to a woman. It is inscribed with the epitaph 'Do not think that I am unhappy in the cell of ashes: Know that I am the closest sanctuary of holiness and consider that I am one of the hermits of paradise.' A second inscription reads, 'Life is beautiful. What a pity that it is not eternal.' Such romantic, evocative words seem to have inspired a legend. It is said that the master craftsman who built the mausoleum fell in love with the daughter of his patron, and when he finished work on the dome he proposed to her. Her name was Mazlum. She replied that she would love him if he rushed to her. He did, but tripped and fell, dashing his brains out on

1 Gyaur Kala. 2 Tomb interior at Mizdakhan. ▶

the stone floor. In horror, the girl committed suicide. The couple, so they say, were buried here together, so perhaps they are Mizdakhan's answer to Romeo and Juliet.

As a pilgrimage site it is unsurprising that there are a number of mosques among the graves at Mizdakhan. Perhaps most interesting of these lie within the **Sulaiman Khaddadiya complex** (12th–14th centuries), where there is a summer and winter mosque, facilities for ablutions, and another underground mausoleum. The summer mosque is particularly attractive, with a multicoloured hall and, unusually, two mihrabs, both of which are decorated with stalactites and Kufic calligraphy.

Jumard Kassab Hill, in the central part of the necropolis, may be named after Jumard, patron saint of pastoralists, a 12th-century butcher who won the hearts of local people by distributing free meat when times were tough. Academics have also hypothesised that the name could be a corruption of Gavmard, an ancient Iranian hero who is associated with the bull and in Zoroastrian cosmology may have been the first man. At times when livestock were sick or suffering from hunger, their herders would drive them in a circle around this hill seven times. It was hoped that this would bring good luck, ensuring the good health and survival of the animals and, by extension, their owners. Archaeological evidence suggests that there was a Zoroastrian sanctuary in this part of the site: quite a few ossuaries dating from the 2nd to 3rd centuries have been excavated here, some of which are now in the Savitsky Museum (page 89).

Gyaur Kala (A381; ▥ frantic.blossom.treaty) One kilometre beyond the main entrance to Mizdakhan, also on the south side of the road, and overlooking the Amu Darya, is Gyaur Kala. Archaeologists believe that this fortress was built in the 4th century BC, most likely by the Achaemenids, but that it was destroyed by fire within 200 years and had to be rebuilt. Gyaur Kala remained inhabited until the 4th century. It is only a small site and much less impressive than many other fortresses in Karakalpakstan, including the Gyaur Kala in Karauzyak District (page 156) with which it shares a name, but if you are planning to visit Mizdakhan anyway and have time, you might as well take a look around.

AMU DARYA DISTRICT

Amu Darya District spreading southeast of Nukus covers an area of 1,020km² and is home to a population of about 205,000 people. The largest town, Mangit, is on the Turkmen border though it is not possible for foreigners to cross here: you need to go north to Khujayli (page 159). Mangit was the site of an important battle during the Khivan Conquest (page 19) in 1873, when the Russians were attacked by Yomut, Turkmen tribesmen. There was already a small settlement in this location, but it wasn't until the second half of the 20th century that modern Mangit was formally founded. The local economy is based on growing and processing cotton, including a small amount of textile manufacturing; and the Mangit hydroelectric power plant, which takes its water from the Amu Darya. The two most important tourist attractions in the district, both of which are well worth your time, are Chilpik Dakhma, a Zoroastrian tower of silence (page 167); and the Lower Amudarya State Biosphere Reserve (page 169).

GETTING THERE AND AWAY Mangit is 65km southeast of Nukus and the drive, most of which is along the A380, takes around an hour. The town's **bus station** is at the junction of Shifokorlar and Buyuk Turon and there are frequent departures

Zoroastrianism was the dominant religion in Karakalpakstan until the arrival of Islam (page 28). Zoroastrians believe that a person's soul is made by Ahura Mazda (the creator god) and is immortal. At the moment of death the soul must pass over a narrow bridge guarded by the *daenā*, which represents conscience. Good souls will see the *daenā* as a beautiful woman and be led by angels into the House of Songs, the Zoroastrian version of paradise; those who have lived an evil life will see a witch and fall through a dark, cold ravine to the House of Lies (Hell). At the time of the Great Renewal, evil will finally be destroyed but good souls will be reunited with their bodies and will be resurrected.

The death of the body is the work of Angra Mainyu, who is the antithesis of Ahura Mazda. The corpse is contaminated by Nasu (a female demon) and must be disposed of as quickly as possible, ideally without the rotting flesh coming into contact with the sacred elements of fire, water and earth. It is placed on top of a *dakhma* (tower of silence), a circular, raised structure. In the first millennium BC, the *dakhma* would just have been a hill outside a settlement, the same sort of location you'd use for a cemetery, but later on towers were built on top. There are modern versions in India, serving the country's Parsi (Zoroastrian) community, which are in or close to cities, but usually separated from other buildings by gardens or forest. At the *dakhma*, the body is exposed to the air and sunlight and accessible to birds of prey. The birds, vultures in particular, will pick the flesh from the bones, leaving them clean. This can take up to a year.

In some areas, the bones are then moved into a pit within the *dakhma* and covered with a layer of lime to help them decompose. More commonly in Karakalpakstan, though, they were removed from the *dakhma* and placed into an ossuary, a box which is often richly decorated. The family of the deceased could then bury the ossuary close to home or at another site of religious significance. Some incredibly beautiful ossuaries have been excavated from Toprak Kala (page 182) and Mizdakhan (page 162), and some of the finest examples – including one with a relief carving of a realistic lion stood between two stylised pomegranate trees – is on display in the Savitsky Museum in Nukus (page 89).

to Nukus (UZS9,000) and Urgench (UZS8,000). You can get shared taxis from the same locations.

PRACTICALITIES There are few places of interest to tourists in Mangit but it may be helpful to know the location of the **Amu Darya District Hospital** (Shifokorlar 21; ⊕ 24hrs), **Halyk Bank** (Berdaq 1; ⊕ 08.00–17.00 Mon–Fri), and **Agro Bank** (Berdaq 11; ⊕ 09.00–13.00 & 14.00–16.00 Mon–Fri). Mangit's **main bazaar**, on the southeastern side of Khalklar Dostigli, one block south of the banks, sells the usual selection of basic foodstuffs, including fresh fruit and bread.

WHAT TO SEE AND DO

Chilpik Dakhma (smuggled.dollhouses.remainder) Chilpik Dakhma, also known as Chilpik Kala (which is incorrect, as it was never a fortress), is a Zoroastrian tower of silence, or burial place (see above). Entering Amu Darya District on the

A380 from Khujayli, you cannot miss the dramatic stone and loosely compacted mud structure; you will inevitably spot it from quite some distance away as it rises high above the otherwise flat desert, and although the low hill at its base may be natural, the huge round construction on top is clearly manmade. A depiction of it appears in the centre of Karakalpakstan's official coat of arms.

Archaeologists, who first noted the site in the late 19th century but did not formally survey it until 1940, believe that Chilpik Dakhma was built in the 1st century BC and was used for around 800 years until the Arab Conquest in the early 7th century. Sitting on top of a conical hill 40m high, the imperfect circular structure measures almost 80m in diameter and 15m in height. A local legend suggests that some elderly people may have been brought to the site to die, but in general their families would wait until they died of natural causes and then just deliver the corpse here. It is thought that most bodies would have been brought by boat on the Amu Darya, which is feasible as the river bank would have been much closer to the *dakhma* than it is today.

Only a very small number of ossuaries have been found at Chilpik Dakhma, leading some archaeologists to hypothesise that the site was reserved for the ruling elite, who would have lived in the summer months at Toprak Kala (page 182) about 70km away. In this case, access to the *dakhma* would have been limited to the priestly class. Another interpretation is that the ossuaries were simply buried elsewhere, which is supported by the discovery of many of them in the foothills of the Sultan Uvays Dag Mountains, which aren't too far from the *dakhma*. Access from the bottom of the hill to the top of the *dakhma* was via a ramp and then a staircase. There was probably once an additional, tower-like structure on top of what you see today, but this seems to have been demolished in the Soviet period to make way for a trig point and then a telecoms tower.

☀ Lower Amudarya State Biosphere Reserve (Oltinsoy; ☎ 99 606 0425; w tugai.uz; ⏰ 24hrs; UZS15,000) The Lower Amudarya State Biosphere Reserve, a UNESCO Biosphere Reserve, covers an area of nearly 69,000ha and though it was only established in 2011, it includes at its heart the older Badai Tugai Nature Reserve. The reason you should visit LABR is that it is much more accessible and developed for tourism than any other protected area in Karakalpakstan. This does not mean that it is overrun with tour buses – far from it! Tourists are still few and far between, but the site office provides basic information and your chance of seeing wildlife, including Bukhara deer (page 170) is high.

The drive to the reserve from Nukus takes 1½ hours. There are buses (from Nukus: 1hr 15mins; UZS10,512; from Beruni: 45mins; UZS5,808) but you will need to disembark on the main road by the turn-off to the reserve and then walk 30 minutes to the **site office** (⊞ snob.prosthetic.organ). All visitors must sign in here on arrival, pay the entrance fee, and collect a ranger who will accompany you into the reserve and unlock the barrier at the **checkpoint** (⊞ backfire.invitees.repute). It is not permitted to enter the reserve on your own. A small, dusty museum at the office provides basic information about the reserve and the species found here; more useful are the illustrated information boards outside, which are bilingual in Uzbek and English.

LABR was created to conserve and restore the landscapes, flora and fauna of Karakalpakstan's tugai forests. Tugai is a type of riparian forest which grows in floodplains, and as their growth depends on the seasonal flooding of a river (in this

◀ 1 Chilpik Dakhma. 2 The view from Chilpik Dakhma.

The Bukhara or Bactrian deer (*Cervus hanglu bactrianus*) is a red deer native to Central Asia. In Karakalpakstan they are called *khangul*, which means 'royal flower', and they are indeed the royalty of the tugai ecosystem.

Historically Bukhara deer occupied a territory from the Amu Dayra Basin to the lower reaches of the Syr Darya. However, by the 1970s they had almost completely disappeared from the wild, hunted to the brink of extinction and suffering from the destruction of their forest habitat. There were no deer left at all in the area now covered by LABR: those you see today are the descendants of three deer brought here in 1976 from the Romit Nature Reserve in Tajikistan, plus a further nine who were added to the herd three years later. Initially these deer were kept within an enclosure for monitoring and security, but as they reproduced and the herd grew, many were released into the LABR's forest beyond the enclosure. The deer have now populated the tugai on both sides of the riverbank and it is estimated that there are in excess of 1,600 of them. It's a remarkable success story for conservation.

The deer in LABR rut in late August and September. This is the time when the males' antlers are at their hardest and most impressive: they need them to fight with other males and to win the attention of the ladies. At this time of the year you will hear them bellowing loudly, all night and sometimes even in the day. The sound can be heard several kilometres away! One male will usually impregnate several females, which is why the deer breed so rapidly, and the pregnancy lasts eight months with the calves born in May and June. The tiny newborn deer have a spotted coat and are well camouflaged in the dappled light of the forest, which helps protect them from predators, and within a week they are already up on their feet and running around.

An adult male deer is rarely more than 120cm tall, excluding his antlers, but can weigh as much as 250kg. He grows a new set of antlers each year, which can almost double his height, and you can tell the approximate age of the deer by the colour of the horn (which changes from light grey to dark brown) and the number of branches the antlers have: usually the more branches there are and the darker the colour, the older the deer. The female deer are smaller than the males and don't grow horns.

The deers' diet changes throughout the year, depending on what is growing. In springtime there's a short period when plants grow in the desert, and the animals will seek these out; and there is plenty of grass in summer, even if it is dry. The winter months are the most difficult period, but then they will eat bark and fallen leaves from the trees and the seeds of the liquorice, camel-thorn, saxaul and calligonum plants. The nutritional value of such plants is quite low, so the deer have to graze for most of the day. At dusk and dawn they will go to watering holes to drink, and they use the same slightly salty water to cool down and get rid of blood-sucking insects on hot days. When the water freezes in winter, the deer can get enough hydration from eating the hoarfrost and snow.

case the Amu Darya) rather than on rainfall, you find them in semi-arid and desert areas. The reduction of water in the Amu Darya and the associated climate change threatens the tugai and all the other species which depend on it, which is why the preservation of the forests within LARB is so vital. The reserve also protects two other types of ecosystem, scrubland and reeds, the latter of which grow as much as 6m high.

At LABR you will find the world's largest population of Bukhara deer, plus significant numbers of red fox, jungle and steppe cat, tolai hare, wild boar, Asian badger and golden jackal. In fact, the golden jackal is the most prevalent predatory mammal in the reserve, and you will often hear them howling (and occasionally screaming) to one another at dusk. They look like slightly small, fluffy wolves and will hunt and eat anything from birds and snakes to tortoises and frogs. They also like fruits from the oleaster tree.

Although there is now a large population of wild Bukhara deer in the park, the easiest place to see the Bukhara deer is within the **deer enclosure** (🏮 stark.surf. quarterfinals). These deer are certainly not tame and won't approach you, but there is a sufficient number of them, of all ages, that you are guaranteed a clear sighting unimpeded by the undergrowth of the forest. You are not allowed to go inside the enclosure but can watch through the wire fence. It is then worth walking or driving down to the **Amu Darya viewpoint** (🏮 leaky.scale.ultramodern) as you will see wild deer moving in the thickets on either side of the road. Try to move slowly and quietly so as not to startle them; frightened deer run deeper into the woodland, where you are quite rightly not allowed to pursue them. Once on the riverbank be prepared to sit and wait. You will hear the calls of the stags and, if you are lucky, be able to watch one or more of the deer coming down into the river for a swim. It is an unforgettable experience and a real honour to be so close to these majestic animals.

The richness of the bird life in LARB makes it an ideal spot for birding, too. There are more than 200 species here, including the protected Khiva pheasant. These endemic pheasants, which mostly live in grassland near the water, are quite similar to their British brethren in colour and shape, but they have a remarkable turn of speed and according to the info boards at the site office can apparently run and jump at up to 90km per hour! You can also expect to see white-winged woodpecker, shikra and white-crowned penduline tit, and you may hear the distinctive screech of the pallid scops owl, especially in the early evening.

◀ 1 Golden jackal. 2 Lower Amudarya Biosphere Reserve. 3 Shikra. 4 Tolai hare.

8

Southeast Karakalpakstan

Forts, forts, forts! Southeast Karakalpakstan has always been frontier territory, and just like the Scottish Borders or the northern fringe of Imperial China, its location historically necessitated the construction of dozens of fortifications to defend the land and the people living here from attack – often, but not always, from the west. There are more than 50 of what UNESCO calls the Desert Castles of Ancient Khorezm, the earliest of which date from the 1st millennium BC, and although you will find such fortresses elsewhere in Karakalpakstan, too, the greatest concentration of them is in this part of the republic. They are on UNESCO's Tentative List to become World Heritage Sites, and if the application is granted they would be the first sites in Karakalpakstan to be awarded that status. What is remarkable about these fortresses is the sheer number of them, their age and scale, and, in some cases, their state of preservation.

This region of Karakalpakstan comprises three districts, Beruni, Ellik Kala and Tortkul, with a combined population of around 585,000 people. There are three fair-sized towns in the area – industrial Beruni, Buston and Tortkul – which was for

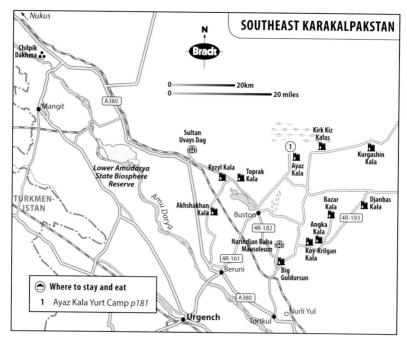

Abu Rayhan Muhammad ibn Ahmad al-Biruni (973–c.1050) is regarded of one of the great scholars of the Islamic Golden Age. Only Ibn Sina, known in the West as Avicenna, can rival him, and the two men corresponded at length on topics such as the eternality of the universe.

Al-Biruni was born in Kath and spent the first 25 years of his life studying in Khorezm. He mastered the so-called Arab sciences of grammar, jurisprudence and theology, but also astronomy, medicine and mathematics. He obtained the patronage of the Samanid ruler Mansur II, relocating to the court at Bukhara, and then worked in succession for the Ziyarid court in Tabaristan (Iran) and the Ghaznavid court in Ghazni (Afghanistan). He also travelled throughout India.

As a writer, al-Biruni was prolific: he authored 146 books, 95 of which were about astronomy, maths and related subjects. He wrote mostly in Arabic because he considered it to be the most suitable language for scientific topics, but he was fluent in more than half a dozen languages, including Greek, Persian and Sanskrit, and so could draw upon a wide range of source materials. Al-Biruni's first major work, produced while he was still in his 20s, was *Kitab al-athar al-baqiyah an al-qurun al-khaliyah (The Remaining Signs of Past Centuries)*, a comparative study of different calendars with supporting commentary on the history, cultures and religions of the civilisations that created them.

a short while in the 1930s the capital of Karakalpakstan before the administration moved to Nukus. As elsewhere in the republic, growing and processing cotton is an important part of the economy here, but there are also factories making concrete, asphalt, bricks and shoes. While in southeast Karakalpakstan you should also make time to visit the shrine of Sultan Uvays Dag, a lively regional pilgrimage centre that has recently been restored.

BERUNI

Named after the medieval polymath al-Biruni, Beruni is a substantial modern town on the northern bank of the Amu Darya, close to the border with Turkmenistan. Today it is an industrial centre with a lot of factories, but its history dates back further than almost any other still-inhabited settlement in Karakalpakstan.

More than 1,700 years ago, this was the city of Kath. It replaced Toprak Kala (page 182) as the capital of the Afrigids (page 16), a dynasty which ruled Khorezm, albeit as a tributary state to larger and more powerful empires, for nearly seven centuries. Silt deposit from the Amu Darya made the agricultural land in this area fertile, but the river's movements were a double-edged sword as the same land (and anything built upon it) was also at risk of flooding. The 10th-century Arab geographer Al-Maqdisi describes Kath as rivalling the Iranian city of Nishapur in size, suggesting it covered an area equivalent to about 36km². In addition to the citadel, there was a congregational mosque, a prison and a large market. Al-Maqdisi also noted that streets of Kath were very dirty, with overflowing drains, which seems to have been the result of the high water table and vagaries of the river.

Interestingly, although Zoroastrian was the dominant faith in pre-Islamic Karakalpakstan, in the 8th century Kath also seems to have been the seat of

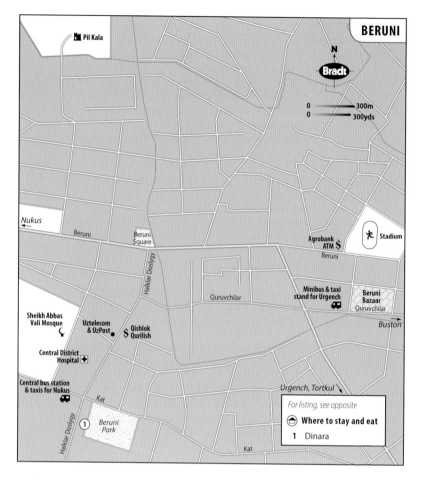

BERUNI

Pil Kala

N

0   300m
0   300yds

Nukus

Beruni

Beruni
Square

Halkiar Doslygy

Quruvchilar

Agrobank
ATM $

Beruni

Stadium

Minibus & taxi
stand for Urgench

Beruni
Bazaar
Quruvchilar

Buston

Sheikh Abbas
Vali Mosque

Uztelecom
& UzPost

Qishlok
Qurilish

Central District
Hospital

Central bus station
& taxis for Nukus

Kat

Halkiar Doslygy

1   Beruni
Park

Urgench, Tortkul

For listing, see opposite

Where to stay and eat

1   Dinara

Kat

a Christian bishopric. A century later, the Christian scholar Isa bin Yahya
Masihi Jorjani was born in the suburbs of Kath, applying himself to the study
of astronomy, mathematics, medicine and philosophy. Little is known about
his life for certain, but contextual evidence suggests that he may have been one
of Avicenna's teachers in Bukhara. Avicenna (locally known as Ibn Sina) was
an 11th-century Persian polymath and is considered to be the father of early
modern medicine.

GETTING THERE AND AROUND Beruni is 145km southeast of Nukus and 25km
northeast of Urgench, with major highways linking the town to each of these two
cities. Assuming there's not too much traffic, the driving times are 1½hrs and
30mins respectively.

Beruni's **Central Bus Station** (Kat 2) is the terminus for buses to Nukus (07.00;
UZS18,00), but also further-afield destinations such as Tashkent and Almaty. To
check the times for the long-haul routes and pre-book tickets, you need to call **SQT
Bus Co** (93 714 9494).

Shared taxis for Nukus (UZS50,000) depart from the **taxi stand** next to the
Central Bus Station, on the corner of Kat and Sheikh Abbas Vali. For Urgench there

is a separate **minibus and taxi stand** on the corner of Quruvchilar and Istiqlol, next to the bazaar. A seat in a minibus costs UZS4,000 and in a shared taxi UZS10,000. Both options depart when full.

WHERE TO STAY AND EAT   *Map, opposite*

Despite its reasonable size, there are very few places to stay in Beruni. The most convenient option, albeit a basic one, is **Dinara Hotel** (8 rooms; 99 584 3983; $). The hotel doesn't serve breakfast but there are a couple of **cafés** $ around the corner, opposite the bus station on Kat. There are also plenty of small cafés and places to buy bread and fresh produce within **Beruni Bazaar** (Quruvchilar).

OTHER PRACTICALITIES You won't have difficulty withdrawing and exchanging money in Beruni. Most conveniently located are **Qishlok Qurilish Bank** (Halklar Doslygy 10; 09.00–17.00 Mon–Fri), which is close to the hospital; and the **Agrobank ATM** (Beruni; 24hrs) next door to the Gorodskoy Stadium.

In an emergency, visit the **Central District Hospital** (Halklar Doslygy; 24hrs), that can provide basic treatment. There are several **pharmacies** nearby, several of which back on to the hospital on Semashko.

Uztelecom and **Uz Post** (Halklar Doslygy; 09.00–17.00 Mon–Fri) share the same building, which is next to the hospital.

WHAT TO SEE AND DO   Pil Kala (slopes.buying.someone; 24hrs; free) is within the limits of the modern town, at the northern end of Fir Kala (an alternative transliteration of the fortress' name). It is thought that the fortress was named after its founder, Firg, and was built sometime in the 4th century BC, though there was a second phase of construction between the 5th and 7th centuries.

Pil Kala has been subject to some less than sensitive conservation work in recent years. A lot of the walls have been rebuilt, but thankfully in such a way that you can immediately spot which parts are original and which are new. During excavations archaeologists discovered a burial site in the southwest corner, with the body of a man interred with his head pointing northwest. There were arrowheads in the grave, suggesting he may have been a soldier.

In terms of smaller sites around the town, it is pleasant to stroll through **Beruni Square** (Beruni), a small but attractive park with a monument to al-Biruni. This is not to be confused with the larger **Beruni Park** (Cnr Kat & Halklar Doslygy), which is a nice enough picnic spot, especially if you have got time to kill while waiting for a bus from the nearby bus station (see opposite). The **Sheikh Abbas Vali Mosque** (Sheikh Abbas Vali 9) is a modern building, but has an interestingly designed striped minaret.

AROUND BERUNI

Akhshakhan Kala (clearings.endangers.privileges; 24hrs; free) About 20km north of Beruni, close to the village of Kanyap, this site was discovered in 1956 and since 1995 has been the subject of an archaeological expedition led by the University of Sydney, Australia. Officially the excavations were supposed to end in 2022, but the local archaeologists are keen to continue so it is likely they will be on site at least in 2023 and possibly beyond that. Visiting while the archaeologists are working gives you the opportunity to talk to them about their latest finds and you will see rather more of the site. This is because at the end of the excavation season they fill in their trenches in order to protect the most fragile structures from the elements.

This fortress, which is thought to have been one of the largest and wealthiest in Ancient Khorezm, was founded in the 3rd century BC and occupied for around 500 years. It covers 42ha and was built on a rectangular plan. Almost a third of the site was the citadel, which was surrounded by fortified walls and a moat. The complex also included a religious sanctuary centred on a mausoleum, which may have been the burial place of the first king of Khorezm; and a royal temple, which would have been decorated with clay sculptures and wall paintings of the royal family. Some of these paintings were also accentuated with gold leaf, though they have been removed to museums elsewhere.

✴ **Sultan Uvays Dag** (▨ biography.chimneys.chops; ⏱ 06.30–18.00 daily; ⏱ 24hrs; free) This shrine is one of the most sacred places in Karakalpakstan. Sultan Uvays Dag, whose full name was Sayyidinaa Uways bin 'Amir al-Qarani, was a humble camel herder from the village of Qaran in Yemen. As a young man, he was determined to travel to Mecca to meet the Prophet Muhammad, but his blind mother gave him permission to go only if he would come home as soon as he reached the prophet's house. The journey took Sultan Uvays three months, and when he arrived Muhammad wasn't at home. Sultan Uvays kept the promise he made to his mother and returned to Yemen, and so the two men never met. In spite of this, there was a deep spiritual connection between them: Muhammad spoke often of Sultan Uvays, and shortly before his death he ordered two of his closest followers, including his son-in-law Ali, to deliver his cloak to him. As Sultan Uvays was initiated into Islam without physical teaching, he was pronounced as a saint, and indeed many Sufi Muslims consider him to be the founder of Sufism.

It is debatable whether Sultan Uvays ever came here, and even less likely that he is buried in the nearby mountains named after him. The mountains aren't especially high or scenic, but on their slopes grow many rare and endemic plants, including *Allium rinae* and *Astragalus centralis*. There are three sites in Yemen and Syria that claim to have his tomb, plus a fourth memorial complex in Namangan, Uzbekistan. However, this does not negate the historical and spiritual significance of this shrine, which was well established within a century of the arrival of Sufism in Central Asia in the 9th century. It remained an important pilgrimage centre until the 1960s, when it was closed by Soviet authorities as part of their clampdown on religious institutions, but it has experienced a glorious revival in recent years.

The first thing you will see when you arrive at Sultan Uvays Dag is the fish pond. From here it is a short walk up the hill to a rock marked with what is said to be the footprint and knee print of the saint. To the left of the pond is the yellow brick mausoleum, mostly dating from the 17th to 19th centuries and recently restored. Its whitewashed courtyard has some finely carved wooden pillars reminiscent of those in Khiva's Ichan Qala, and the indoor room in front of the grave is beautifully painted with intricate patterns in pale greens, blues and pinks, and with an impressive chandelier hanging from the ceiling. Devotees sit here and pray, and consequently it is requested that you dress respectfully (cover your head, shoulders and legs) and stay quiet. Smoking, eating and drinking are prohibited in the shrine.

It is a 40km drive north along the A380 from Beruni to Sultan Uvays Dag, so if you are coming to Beruni from Nukus it is best to stop at the shrine en route rather than having to retrace your steps.

◀ 1 A gateway in Ellik Kala. 2 Akhshakhan Kala.

BUSTON

Buston (population c. 15,000) is the district capital of Ellik Kala. Ellik means 50, so Ellik Kala is the place of 50 fortresses. It is an oddly shaped, mostly rural district, and Buston is the only town of notable size. Although not yet viewed as a tourism centre, it's fairly well connected from a transport perspective and is a convenient hub for visiting the fortresses. If you have time, the SP Tolstov Museum of Archaeology and History (page 182) in the town centre provides some helpful context to the archaeological sites.

GETTING THERE AND AROUND Buston lies 140km southeast of Nukus and the majority of the drive is along the A380. Driving from Beruni, which is 26km to the southwest of Buston on the 4R-161, takes around 40 minutes. The **Central Bus Station** stands on the corner of Beruni and Nukus Tortkul. There is a daily bus to Nukus (2hrs; UZS18,000); you can expect to pay about twice that price for a seat in a shared taxi, but the journey time is slightly shorter.

WHERE TO STAY AND EAT

Ayaz Kala Yurt Camp [map, page 174] (10 yurts) Ayaz Kala 3 ☏ 94 140 0070. There are a couple of options in Buston itself, but if the purpose of your trip is to visit the desert fortresses, it is a much more exciting experience to stay at this camp. Located at the bottom of Ayaz Kala 3, it is entirely surrounded by desert, with not a single modern building as far as the eye can see. The location lends itself to memorable sunsets & as there's absolutely no light pollution, it's the perfect choice for those who love the night sky. The yurts are comfortable with plenty of warm blankets for cooler nights, & the basic but clean toilets & showers are in an outhouse. The family that manages the yurt camp provides home-cooked dinners & breakfasts. $$$

Xumo Hotel (12 rooms) Nukus; ☏ 97 353 7608. Simpler & with fewer amenities than Buston City,

Xumo is nevertheless a satisfactory place to stay. The hotel is clean, with slightly outdated décor. Staff are friendly, & each room has AC. There's a dining room serving a budget-friendly menu of traditional & local dishes. $$

Buston City (28 rooms) Tortkul; ☏ 99 956 1570; e Buston_city@mail.ru. For a budget hotel, Buston City is remarkably well equipped, with a restaurant, conference facilities, sauna, & even a swimming pool, although there didn't seem to be access to the sauna & swimming pool when we visited. The restaurant has a reasonable selection of dishes on the menu, with private dining rooms if you don't feel like eating with other guests. Every room has AC & in theory there is Wi-Fi, though it wasn't working when we visited. B/fast not included but can be added for UZS20,000. $

OTHER PRACTICALITIES Several banks have branches in Buston. The most useful are **Agro Bank** (Sh Rashidov 24; ⏰ 09.00–16.00 Mon–Fri) and **Halyk Bank** (Sh Rashidov 18; ⏰ 08.00–18.00 Mon–Fri).

Ellik Kala District Hospital (Nukus Tortkul 19; ⏰ 24hrs) can provide basic healthcare in an emergency, and there's a **pharmacy** at the same address.

WHAT TO SEE AND DO

Amir Temur Botanical Garden (⏢ faltering.splinter.stretcher; ⏰ 24hrs; free) Situated just to the north of the town centre, this is one of only two botanical gardens in Uzbekistan, the other being in Tashkent, though a third garden is planned in Urgench. There are more than 200 types of trees and bushes here, and 70 types of flowers. The botanical garden has a nursery nurturing seedlings of plant species not

◀ The interior of Sultan Uvays Dag.

Southeast Karakalpakstan   BUSTON

8

common in Karakalpakstan, which are being adapted to the local climate and sent to other districts to be planted. It is mostly visited by university students on field trips, but it is open to everyone.

SP Tolstov Museum of Archaeology and History (Nukus Tortkul; ☏ 61 585 2564; ⊙ 09.00–16.00 Mon–Sat; UZS30,000) Set within J Manguberdi Park in the centre of Buston, this diminutive museum houses a small number of exhibits, mostly pottery, excavated from the desert fortresses, plus photos, plans and models to help visitors understand how they looked when they were new. Sergei Tolstov was the Soviet archaeologist who rediscovered many of the fortresses, including Ayaz Kalas and Toprak Kala, in the late 1930s and spent decades carefully excavating the sites.

AROUND BUSTON
* Toprak Kala (🎦 earlobes.wildcats.flow; ⊕ 24hrs; free) Some 16km northwest of Buston, to the east of Kyzyl Kala, Toprak Kala was founded in the 3rd to 2nd centuries BC and became the capital of the Afrigid kings. It was rediscovered by Sergei Tolstov in 1938 and Soviet archaeologists then spent almost 30 years

SERGEI TOLSTOV

Sergei Pavlovich Tolstov was a Soviet archaeologist and ethnographer born in Saint Petersburg in 1907. His father was a military officer, and the young Tolstov was able to gain a first-class education at Moscow State University, where he studied in both the faculties of physics and mathematics, and history and ethnography. His first job was as a researcher at the Museum of the Peoples of the USSR in Moscow, whose collections are today held by the Russian Museum of Ethnography in Saint Petersburg.

Tolstov's passion, however, was field work. He founded and was the first director of the Chorasmian Expedition which would go on to excavate more than 1,000 archaeological sites in Uzbekistan, Turkmenistan and Kazakhstan between 1937 and 1991. The earliest of these sites dated from the middle of the first millennium BC. It was the largest and longest-running expedition in the Soviet Union. His initial focus was ethnography but his discovery of ancient sites in the Karakum and Kyzylkum prompted him to switch to archaeology. He brought together experts on topics as different as religious cults, pottery and numismatics, pioneering multidisciplinary works.

Some of Tolstov's most important discoveries were made in the late 1930s, but it would not be until after World War II that he had the resources to excavate them. The highlights of his career included the excavations of Toprak Kala and Djanbas Kala, both of which are in southeast Karakalpakstan, as well as the medieval town of Konye Urgench in what is now Turkmenistan.

Tolstov's achievements were recognised from the very top. He was appointed the Director of the Ethnography Institute of the Academy of Sciences, making him the highest ranked ethnographer in the Soviet Union. He was elected as a corresponding member of the Academy of Sciences in 1953 and remained in charge of the Chorasmian Expedition until his death in 1976. Tolstov's archive, including field diaries, topographic maps and plans, drawings of finds, and photographs are preserved by the Institute of Ethnology and Anthropology of the Russian Academy of Sciences in Moscow.

painstakingly excavating this important site. It is a vast and very well-preserved fortified town measuring 500m by 350m (17ha) and surrounded by walls, some of which are still 8–9m tall. The walls were strengthened with four-sided towers with round corners, and had a deep ditch in front of them to make it even harder to attack. You can still see these marked on the landscape. Although the fortress is now without a water supply, it was originally connected to the Amu Darya via an ancient canal called the Gavkhor.

In the northern part of the complex was a palace citadel, raised on a platform. It is thought to have had a floor area of 80m^2 and been built in the shape of a truncated pyramid about 14m high. The mud-brick walls were covered in alabaster to give a smooth finish and then painted, and the vaulted ceilings were supported on columns. These decorative features are no longer visible, but around 100 ground floor rooms survive in this part of the fort, including sanctuaries with altars, storerooms for weapons, and multiple ceremonial halls. Of particular importance are the Hall of Kings, a dynastic sanctuary with an altar and niches that would have housed the statues of kings and possibly members of the Zoroastrian pantheon; the Throne Room, which had a central open courtyard flanked by two porticos supported by wooden columns on stone pedestals; and the Hall of Warriors, a smaller chamber with life-sized reliefs of men in armour. The Hall of Deer was decorated with paintings of animals, suggesting that two millennia ago this would have been good hunting ground. These rooms are not signposted and long ago lost their decoration, but the walls survive to a reasonable height and you get a strong sense of the scale of the complex walking between them or surveying them from one of the many vantage points.

The archaeological finds excavated from Toprak Kala are split between multiple museums, including the State Hermitage Museum in Saint Petersburg, but thankfully some of the wall paintings, coins and sculptures are on public display at the Savitsky Museum (page 89) in Nukus. This means that you can explore the fortress and see its treasures on a single trip.

Kyzyl Kala (🔲 instant.downplay.lighter; 🕐 24hrs; free) Meaning Red Fortress, though the colour is not noticeably different to other fortresses, Kyzyl Kala lies on the southern side of the village of the same name, 17km northwest of Buston. There is some debate as to its original use: archaeologists are divided as to whether it was a fortified manor house or a garrison for troops. In any case, its close position to the larger and more important Toprak Kala (see opposite), just over a kilometre away, suggests that there would have been regular movement of people between the two sites.

The earliest parts of Kyzyl Kala date from the 1st to 4th centuries and were built on a square plan, but the fortress was abandoned, fell into disrepair, and was almost completely rebuilt in the 12th century, shortly before the Mongol invasion (page 17). In a bid to conserve the ruins and show what the fortress might originally have looked like, a new external wall has been added, but it is debatable as to whether this adds or detracts from the aesthetics of the site.

As the fortress walls no longer reach their original height and the surrounding ground level has risen in the centuries since its construction, visitors today enter at what was the building's first floor. It is said that local people used to dig through the floor hoping to find gold, but they encountered only snakes sheltering from the heat of the desert sun. This has given rise to a legend that Kyzyl Kala does house hidden treasure, but that it is fiercely guarded by a snake demon who resists any attempt to steal it. In any case, the artefacts of greatest scientific interest – including frescoes,

bronze dishes, lamps and ceremonial dishes, were excavated by archaeologists from the fortress citadel, Zoroastrian temple and residential quarters from 1938 onwards and are now preserved in museum collections.

* **Ayaz Kala** (24hrs; free) Twenty-five kilometres northeast of Buston by road and close to the Ayazkol salt lake, this is probably the most-visited archaeological site in Karakalpakstan – it's an easy diversion from the drive between Urgench and Nukus. It also occupies an impressive location: from the top of the site you can see for miles. There are, in fact, three fortresses here – Ayaz Kala 1, 2 and 3 – and although they are technically divided between two different districts, Beruni and Ellik Kala, they are all on one huge site and you can drive or walk between them. Ayaz, after whom they were named, was a Turkic folk hero, a slave warrior who fell in love with a princess.

Ayaz Kala 1 (detained.homeruns.bookmaking) is the oldest of the fortresses. Construction began on this hilltop in the late 4th century BC, with additional mud-brick watchtowers added a hundred years later. Most of it was built by the Kushans. It is a rectangular structure with a footprint measuring 182m by 152m. There were two layers of walls, accessed via a gateway, and the fort could be defended by archers shooting through two storeys of slits. The structure is in remarkable condition given its age, with the walls and towers still standing, albeit not to their original height. Although Ayaz Kala 1 was abandoned in the 1st century AD, it is thought that local people still sought refuge among the ruins well into the medieval period.

Ayaz Kala 2 (respecting.anonymously.insolently) is to the southwest of Ayaz Kala 1, on top of a conical hill. The early parts were built by the Kushans, but it was then reconstructed by the Afrigids in the 6th to 8th centuries, as attested to by the discovery of coins showing the image of King Bravik or Fravik. Unlike the earlier fortress, Ayaz Kala 2 was oval in shape, with an entrance on the southwest side. Inside the complex was a columned hall and residential quarters, and also a 4th-century fire temple, which predates the construction of the fortress. Due to the changing ground level, these structures are actually now beneath your feet: when you visit you are walking on the roof and in some places where the roof has eroded away you can see down into the rooms. It goes without saying that they are very fragile and you need to be careful where you tread.

Ayaz Kala 3 (varnished.fickle.slumps) dates from the 1st and 2nd centuries AD and may have been a garrison to Ayaz Kala 1, protecting farmsteads and homes. There is also some evidence that Kushan rulers may have lived here at one time, though the poor state of this site compared to the other two makes it difficult to study. Little is left now beyond the rubble, so it is better to concentrate your attention and time on Ayaz Kala 1 and 2.

Kirk-Kiz Kalas There are two Kirk-Kiz Kalas, situated near to each other and to the village of Kyrykkyz, which is named after them, 35km northeast of Bustan. The drive takes around an hour. Kirk-Kiz, meaning '40 girls', is a reference to a Karakalpak legend known in variations across Central Asia (page 40). It is the story of Gulaim, a fierce 16-year-old warrior who defended her homeland from invaders with the help of 40 other young women.

Big Kirk-Kiz Kala (caking.excites.mysteries; 24hrs; free) is a double-walled fortress founded in the 4th or 3rd century BC and occupied until the 8th century. In the Afrigid period it was a regional centre of ceramics production and there

◀ Kyzyl Kala

Once upon a time, Guldursun was called Gulistan, the garden of roses. It was a wealthy city, with plenty of water, and surrounded by fertile fields and gardens. The king had a beautiful daughter, whose name was Guldursun.

Tragically, Gulistan was attacked by Kalmyks, who destroyed the fields and everything else they found, and laid siege to the city for many months. There was nothing left to eat, and both the attackers and the inhabitants of Gulistan were starving. The king had a cunning plan: he sent out his last fat bull to the Kalmyks, who killed it and had a feast. But it also confused them, just as the king hoped. It made them think that there was still plenty of food left inside the city, and that the Kalmyks would die of hunger long before the people of Gulistan surrendered. They started packing up in preparation to leave.

This could have been a happy ending for the Gulistanis, but it wasn't. Unbeknown to her father, Guldursun had fallen in love with a Kalmyk knight and couldn't bear the thought of never seeing him again. She wrote him a letter, declaring her love and revealing that the Gulistanis were starving, too. The Kalmyks waited, and a day later the Gulistanis surrendered. The Kalmyks plundered the city, killing or enslaving its people.

Guldursun was brought before the knight. If she expected her love to be reciprocated, she would have been sorely disappointed. He despised her treachery, and punished her in the most brutal way. Her body was tied to wild horses, torn apart and scattered in pieces across the fields. From then on the fortress was known by the cursed name of Guldursun.

---

are still large quantities of potsherds scattered across the site. You can pick them up and look at them, but please do not take them home with you. The site isn't in as good condition as some others in the area, but what remains of the walls is still impressive in scale.

Small Kirk-Kiz Kala (dilates.whipped.submariner; 24hrs; free) was built at the same time as its larger neighbour but was only inhabited for about 700 years, so has been in an abandoned state for longer. It has two parts, east and west, and the western section was more heavily defended, with circular fortifications and double walls. Archers could shoot from two levels on the walls at once. The fortress also seems to have been used to send smoke signals to other settlements, warning of enemy attack, and as a secure place for trade. Sections of the walls are still standing several storeys high, and you can see the slots used by archers.

Narindjan Baba Mausoleum (etched.filmstrips.bellyful; 24hrs; free)

Situated 20km southeast of Buston by road, about 1km north of Big Guldursun, this is one of the most sacred places in Karakalpakstan. The mausoleum is the final resting place of the Sufi saint Muhammad ibn Musa ibn Daud Abu Abdallah an Narindjani, known as Narindjan Baba (13th–14th century). The mausoleum, which was erected shortly after his death, is said to have been built by Saint Mukhtar Vali (who is himself buried in Khorezm), and the surrounding chambers are likely to have been used for Sufi *dhikr* (rituals comprising meditation and chanting as a form of prayer). Archaeologists identified the site in the 20th century, translated the inscriptions, and removed the saint's tombstone to what is now the State Museum

---

1 Toprak Kala. 2 View towards Ayaz Kala. ▶

MEHMETO/A

DAVID TRILLING

of History and Culture of Karakalpakstan (page 93) in Nukus. The complex was then substantially rebuilt in the 1990s, improving its appearance but perhaps losing something of its character. Today you'll see the baked brick portico and a short minaret, and a veranda with some colourful wall paintings in green and blue.

Big Guldursun (mods.inflated.reimbursed; 24hrs; free) In Angyt village, 20km south of Buston on the 4R-182, this fortress, set atop a small hill, was founded in the 4th century BC. It was one of the largest fortresses in Khorezm, measuring 350m by 230m. The entrance is on the eastern wall.

The walls, ramparts and towers of Guldursun are built of rammed clay, with baked mud bricks on the upper parts. In places the walls still reach 15m in height, though these sections are largely of a later date, built by the Khorezm shahs in the 12th and 13th centuries. Guldursun was primarily a military facility rather than a residential settlement, but archaeologists working here in the late 1930s and 40s, and then again in the 1990s, did find a good selection of ancient and medieval coins, ceramics, bronze items and jewellery. The fortress seems to have been abandoned, like so many others in the region, after it was attacked by the Mongols in 1220.

TORTKUL

Tortkul, the eponymous district capital, was founded by the Russians in 1873 as a garrison town after the Khivan Conquest (page 19). For the first 50 years it was named Petro-Aleksandrovsk, and regionally speaking it was well developed and technologically advanced: as early as 1913 it had a telegraph station, and a decade later a radio station.

Tortkul (which can be translated as 'square') was given its present name in 1932 when it became the first capital of the newly created Autonomous Republic of Karakalpakstan. This prestige was short-lived, however, as Amu Darya was a vindictive neighbour, frequently flooding the city. Attempts were made to build flood defences, but they were seriously breached in 1942 and much of Tortkul was destroyed. The capital was therefore moved to Nukus in 1939.

Modern Tortkul is a small but pleasant enough place with a population of about 60,000 people. Factories processing cotton and producing concrete and asphalt are major local employers, and there is also a branch of Nukus Medical School.

GETTING THERE AND AROUND Tortkul lies 175km southeast of Nukus and as the crow flies less than 20km east of Urgench, though you have to route via the southern side of Beruni in order to cross the Amu Darya. A daily minibus from Tortkul to Nukus (07.30; UZS22,000) departs from the **bus station** at the junction of Gulistan and Beruni.

 WHERE TO STAY AND EAT

Hotel Royal Plaza (7 rooms) breath. salaried.optimists; 97 649 0363. Very nice hotel approaching international standards, with bright, recently decorated dbl, twin & trpl rooms & new bathrooms. An outdoor swimming pool was added to the hotel in summer 2023. Rooms have AC &

if it doesn't work staff will switch you to another room. $$
Hotel To'rtkol (12 rooms) presenter.upset. shunted; 88 500 3005. Spacious & clean dbl & trpl rooms, each with its own bathroom & AC unit. $

1 & 2 Big Guldursun. 3 Narindjan Baba Mausoleum.

8

Kafe Shirin Dunyo 🍽 corporations.bringing. woefully. Simple local cuisine. Most of the tables are in the main room, but you can also reserve a private dining room or take a table outside in the courtyard. In good weather sitting outdoors is the better option. The staff are really friendly & more than happy to help. $

SHOPPING Tortkul's **main bazaar** (⏰ 06.00–19.00 daily) is on Zavodskaya, next to the mosque. For food and consumer goods there is also the recently opened **Gipermarket** (Nukus; ⏰ 08.00–23.00 daily), which is just south of the hospital and is trying to model itself on a European hypermarket.

OTHER PRACTICALITIES In an emergency you can get basic medical care at **Tortkul Central District Hospital** (Nukus 36; ⏰ 24hrs). There are multiple **pharmacies** on Nukus on the same block as the hospital.

To exchange money or withdraw cash from an ATM, go to the **National Bank of Uzbekistan** (Tortkul 56; ⏰ 09.00–13.00 & 14.00–17.00 Mon–Fri) or **Savdogar Bank** (Tortkul 57; ⏰ 09.00–18.00 Mon–Fri).

WHAT TO SEE AND DO Tortkul's main place of worship, the **Friday Mosque**, is on Zavodskaya, next to the main bazaar. It has a tall and very attractive minaret decorated with bands of patterned tiles and calligraphy, and if you ask you can climb to the top for good views across the town.

AROUND TORTKUL

Koy-Krilgan Kala (🍽 graciously.reptiles.beckon) Some 40km northeast of Tortkul by road, near to the village of Taza-Kel'timinar and Angka Kala, Koy-Krilgan Kala is unique in Karakalpakstan. It was built in the 4th century BC as a religious complex rather than a residential fortress, and rediscovered by accident by Sergei Tolstov in 1938 when he was camped at Teshik Kala. The complex is technically octadecagonal in shape, though from the air that's pretty much indistinguishable from a circle. During excavations in the 1950s every part of the structure was exposed, clearly showing the concentric rings of the citadel and walls beyond it. Most of the site was then recovered to protect it, though sections of the walls and cylindrical buildings are still visible above ground.

In spite of the detailed studies, the exact purpose of Koy-Krilgan Kala remains unclear: a combination of fires, sacking and medieval squatters has destroyed much of the evidence. However, the Khorezmians had accurate calendars, monitored eclipses, and knew something of the movement of the stars, so it is possible that the central part of the complex was used as an astronomical observatory. Later inhabitants (2nd century BC to 4th century AD) seem to have used the same space to store and drink wine: archaeologists found large numbers of drinking vessels, rhytons and jugs, many of which were decorated with reliefs, and also wall paintings of people pouring wine and drinking. This space wasn't necessarily used for leisure purposes, however; the drinkers may have been members of a religious cult centred on viticulture. There were certainly plenty of vineyards in the vicinity, watered by a sophisticated irrigation system.

Perhaps the most marvellous things excavated from Koy-Krilgan Kala, though, are the statues. There are some fabulous ossuaries moulded into the shape of human figures, which are now in the State Hermitage Museum in Saint Petersburg; and also terracotta sculptures of gods and goddesses, human heads, horses and other animals, some of which are in the Savitsky Museum (page 89). The surviving walls at Koy-Krilgan Kala are much lower and less impressive than at some of the other fortresses, but enough remains to be able to pick out the unusual layout.

Angka Kala (■ reassure.vocational.delight) This square fortress lies 42km north of Tortkul town, 2km from Koy-Krilgan Kala and shortly beyond Bezirgen on the road to Djanbas Kala (see below). Preserved enough that there's something to see, even if it is not particularly impressive, Angka Kala had two distinct periods of construction, in the 1st to the 3rd and then the 10th to the 12th centuries. It is smaller than many of the other fortresses in this region but still well defended, and it may have been built to protect those travelling on the caravan route.

Visiting today, you can see that there was a corridor between the inner and outer walls; the lower parts of eight rectangular towers; and loopholes cut in the exterior wall for archers to shoot through. Interestingly, almost all the bricks surrounding the loopholes have the same *tamga*, a master craftsman's mark, suggesting they were made by the same person or at least in the same workshop. Note that the interior of the fortress was always open: it's not that buildings inside have been demolished or collapsed.

Bazar Kala (■ sonnet.churned.uncompleted) Located midway between Angka Kala and Djanbas Kala, 48km northeast of Tortkul, Bazar Kala is surrounded by fields. Even in ancient times this was productive farming land, on account of irrigation from the Bazarkalin Canal. The fortress itself was likely founded in the 6th century BC and remained in use until the early Kushan period, when it was abandoned in the 1st century AD. The square citadel in the northeast corner of the settlement is still in reasonable condition. It was protected by double walls and semi-oval towers. Evidence of pottery kilns and bloomeries for smelting iron suggest that Bazar Kala was an industrial centre with many craftsmen, as well as housing soldiers.

Djanbas Kala (■ unfurls.luscious.bendable) On the 4R-193 just to the east of the village of the same name, by road Djanbas Kala is 47km northeast of Tortkul. If it feels remote, don't be surprised: it always has been, as this was the last fortress in the ancient chain of fortifications. It sits on the side of a ridge looking down on the plain below. No-one knows quite why this position was chosen – it would have made more sense to erect it on the hilltop – but it earned the fortress its name: Djanbas means 'flank' or 'side'. This was one of the first sites excavated by Sergei Tolstov (page 182) during the Chorasmian Expedition in 1938, and some wonderful aerial photographs were taken here in the 1940s, which were subsequently published in Tolstov's book, *Following the Tracks of Ancient Khorezmian Civilization*.

It is thought that Djanbas Kala was built in the early 4th century BC, just after Khorezm gained independence from the Achaemenid Empire (page 16). The main part of the fortress measures 200m by 170m and the walls are still impressive, in places standing 20m high. Originally there would have been two tiers of covered galleries for archers, with possibly a third open-air storey above that. Had an attacker made it past the archers, they would have had to pass through a labyrinth gateway and a heavily defended courtyard in order to reach the citadel. Unusually, there are no towers, which made the lower parts of the walls vulnerable. Khorezm's architects and engineers must have come to realise this, as all the later fortresses they built have towers.

Inside Djanbas Kala were two city blocks divided by a central street. The total population could have been as many as 2,000 people, both men and women. At the

end of the street was a monumental building, probably a fire temple. Ossuaries found on the edge of the fortress in the 1960s suggest that there was a necropolis there.

The artefacts excavated at Djanbas Kala are incredibly varied and rich. They include ceramics and terracotta statues, metal jewellery, and glass beads that were imported from as far away as the Black Sea; some of these are on display in the Savitsky Museum (page 89). There were not any coins, however, which suggests that the fortress was already abandoned by the 2nd century AD. Tolstov hypothesised it was overrun by nomads who gained access by battering down the south wall; another theory is that the water supply failed, forcing the inhabitants to move elsewhere.

Kurgashin Kala (🔲 confer.kingpins.resettled) Some 88km northeast of Tortkul and 24km east of Ayaz Kala, Kurgashin Kala lies at the point where the Khorezm Oasis and Kyzylkum meet. It is the easternmost of the large desert fortresses, situated on the edge of a plateau with its corners oriented to face the four cardinal directions. It is thought that the name is derived from a local word for lead, which was already being mined nearby 2,500 years ago.

Kurgashin Kala was built in the 4th century BC and used at least until the Kushan period, but its good condition suggests that it may have been repaired and used as recently as 1,100 years ago. The fortress is rectangular and covers an area of 1.4ha. The west wall is positioned to take advantage of the slope of the hill, and the double walls are punctuated with a dozen round towers. These towers are relatively unusual, but the shape prevented attackers targeting the vulnerable corners. In places the walls are still 16m high. Entry to the complex was through a barbican, a gate between two sets of walls placed at right angles to one another to slow the advance of anyone passing through, giving defenders ample opportunity to rain arrows, rocks, and anything else they had to hand down on them if they needed to. The central part of Kurgashin Kala was filled with residential buildings; unlike in some of the other fortresses, there was no open space here at all. Outside the walls were farmhouses and store houses, and beyond them fields and vineyards irrigated with water from the canals, though there's no immediately obvious traces of these on the landscape today.

◀ 1 Angka Kala. 2 Djanbas Kala. 3 Kurgashin Kala.

8

Appendix 1

LANGUAGE

Karakalpak is the official language of Karakalpakstan (along with Uzbek; page 27); and after a number of script changes in the 20th century it is now written in Latin script, which makes it much easier for English speakers to read. However, Russian is also widely spoken and serves as a lingua franca between different communities, so we have included Russian words and phrases here, too. As Russian is written in Cyrillic script, we have transliterated it into Latin to make it easier to read.

WORDS AND PHRASES
Essentials

English	Karakalpak	Russian
Good morning	Qayırlı tan'/Assalam Aleykum or Sa'lem	S dobrim utrom
Good evening	Qayırlı kesh/Assalam Aleykum or Sa'lem	Dobriy vecher
Hello	Aleykum/ Sa'lem	Zdrastvuite
Goodbye	Xosh bol	Dosvidan'ye
My name is…	Menin' atım…	Menya zovut…
What is your name?	Sizin' atın'ız kim?	Kak vas zovut?
I am from …England/America/Australia	Men Angliyadan/ Amerikadan/ Avstraliyadan keldim	Ya iz …Anglii/Ameriki/Avstralii
How are you?	Qalaysız?	Kad dela?
Pleased to meet you	Tanısqanımnan quwanıshlıman	Priyatno poznakomitsya
Thank you	Raxmet	Spasibo
Please	Iltimas	Pojalusta
Cheers!	Qáne aldıq!	Na zdarov'ye!
Yes	Awa	Da
No	Yaq	Net
I don't understand	Men tu'sinbedim	Ya ne panimayu
Please would you speak more slowly	iltimas, ástenirek sóyleseñiz	Pojalusta, govorite medlee
Do you understand?	Túsindiñiz be?	Vi panimayete?

Questions

How?	Qalay?	Kak?
What?	Ne?	Shto?

194

English	Karakalpak	Russian
Where?	Qayerde/Qayjaqqa?	Gde?
What is that?	Bul ne?	Shto eto?
When?	Qashan?	Kogda?
Why?	Nege/Ne ushın?	Pochemu?
Who?	Kim?	Kto?
How much?	Qansha?	Skol'ko?

Numbers

1	Bir	Odin
2	Eki	Dva
3	U'sh	Tri
4	To'rt	Chetire
5	Bes	Pyat'
6	Alti	Shest'
7	Jeti	Sem'
8	Segiz	Vosem'
9	Tog'iz	Devyat'
10	On	Desyat'
11	On bir	Odinnnadsyat'
12	On eki	Dvinadsyat'
13	On u'sh	Trinadsyat'
14	On to'rt	Chetirnadsyat'
15	On bes	Pyatndsyat'
16	On altı	Shesnadsyat'
17	On jeti	Semnadsyat'
18	On segiz	Vosemnadsyat'
19	On tog'iz	Devyadnadsyat'
20	Jigirma	Dvadsyat'
30	Otiz	Tridsyat'
40	Qiriq	Sorok
50	Eliw	Pedisyat
60	Alpis	Shestidyat
70	Jetpis	Semdisyat
80	Seksen	Vosemdisyat
90	Toqsan	Devinosto
100	Ju'z	Sto
1,000	Min'	Tisyachya

Time

What time is it?	Saat neshe boldı?	Kotoriy Chas?
Today	Bu'gin	Sevodnya
Tomorrow	Erten'	Zavtra
Yesterday	Keshe	Vchera
Morning	Tan'	Utro
Evening	Kesh	Vecher

Days

Monday	Du'yshembi	Ponedel'nik
Tuesday	Siyshembi	Vtornik
Wednesday	Sa'rshembi	Sreda

English	Karakalpak	Russian
Thursday	Piyshembi	Chetverg
Friday	Juma	Pyatnitsya
Saturday	Shembi	Subota
Sunday	Yekshembi/Qala kuni	Voskresen'ye

Months

January	Yanvar	Yanvar'
February	Fevral	Fevral'
March	Mart	Mart
April	Aprel	Aprel'
May	Mai	Mai
June	Iyun	Iyun'
July	Iyul	Iyul'
August	Avgust	Avgust
September	Sentyabr	Sentyabr
October	Oktyabr	Oktyabr
November	Noyabr	Noyabr
December	Dekabr	Dekabr

Getting around
Public transport

I'd like…	Men… qa'leymen	Ya hotel bi
…a one-way ticket	Barıwǵa bilet	bilet v odnu storonu
…a return ticket	Qaytıwǵa hám barıwǵa bilet	obratniy bilet
I want to go to…	Men… ga/ge bariwdi qa'leymen	Ya hochu poity v…
How much is it?	Qansha?	Skol'ko?
What time does it leave?	Qashan ketedi ?	Vo skol'ko uyezjaet?
What time is it?	Saat neshe boldı?	Kotoriy chas?
The train has been…	Poyezd…	Poyezd…
…delayed	…keshiktirildi	…zaderjano
…cancelled	…biykar etildi	…otmenili
Platform	platforma	platforma
Ticket office	Kassa	Kassa
Timetable	keste	Raspisaniye
From	…dan	Ot
To	…shekem	Do
Bus stop	Ba'ndirgi	Avtobusnaya ostanovka
Railway station	Vokzal	Vokzal
Airport	Aeroport	Aeroport
Bus	Avtobus	Avtobus
Train	Poezd	Poezd
Plane	Samalyot	Samalyot
Car	Mashina	Mashina
Taxi	Taksi	Taksi
Minibus	Damas	Marshrutka
Bicycle	Velosiped	Velosiped

Directions

English	Karakalpak	Russian
Where is…?	…qayda?	Gde…?
Go straight ahead	Tuwrıg'a ju'rin'	Idi pryamo
Turn left	Shepke burılın'	Na levo
Turn right	On'g'a burılın'	Na pravo
…at the traffic lights	svetoforda	…na svetofore
North	Arqa	Sever
South	Qubla	Yug
East	Shig'is	Vostok
West	Batis	Zapad
Behind	Artında	Zadi
In front of	Aldında	V peredi
Near	qasında	Ryadom
Opposite	Qarama-qarsi	Na protiv

Street signs

Entrance	Kiriw	Vhod
Exit	Shig'iw	Vihod
Open	Ashıq	Otkrito
Closed	Jabıq	Zakrito
Toilets – men/women	Tualet – Er adam/Hayal	Tualet – Mujskoy/Jenskiy
Information	Maǵlıwmat	Informatsiya

Accommodation

Where is a cheap/ good hotel?	Arzan/Jaqsı miymanxana qayda?	Gde deshyoviy/ horoshiy otel'?
How much is it?	Qansha turadi?	Skol'ko?
Where is the toilet?	Tualet qayda?	Gde tualet?

Food and drink

Bread	Nan	Hleb
Butter	May	Maslo
Salt	Duz	Sol'
Sugar	Sheker/Qant	Sahar
Apples	Alma	Yabloko
Bananas	Banan	Banan
Oranges	Apelsin	Apel'sin
Carrots	Geshir	Markov'
Garlic	Chesnok	Chesnok
Onion	Piyaz	Luk
Potato	Kartoshka	Kartoshka
Beer	Pivo	Pivo
Coffee	Kofe	Kofe
Fruit juice	Shire	Sok
Milk	Su't	Moloko
Tea	Chai	Chai
Water	Suw	Voda
Wine	Vino	Vino

Shopping

English	Karakalpak	Russian
I'd like to buy…	Men…satıp alıwdı qa'leymen	Ya hotel/hotela kupit'…
How much is it?	Qansha turadi?	Skol'ko?
It's too expensive	Bul qimbat	Slishkom dorogo
Credit cards	Kredit karta	Kreditnaya karta
More	Ko'birek	Bol'she
Less	Azıraq	Men'she

Communications

English	Karakalpak	Russian
Bank	Bank	Bank
Post office	Pochta	Pochta
Church	cerkva	Tserkv
Embassy	Posol'stvo	Posol'stvo
Exchange office	Obmeni punkt	Obmen valyut
Tourist office	Turist ofis	Turisticheskiy ofis

Health

English	Karakalpak	Russian
Help!	Ja'rdem bering!	Pomogite!
Ambulance	Tez jardem	Skoraya pomosch
Hospital	Emlewxana	Bolnitsya
I am sick	Men awırıp turman	Ya zabolel/zabolela
Doctor	Shıpaker/Doktor	Doktor
Pharmacy	Da'rixana	Apteka
Asthmatic	Astma/Dem qıspa	Astma
Diabetic	Diabet	Diabet
Diarrhoea	Diareya	Diareya
Nausea	Kewil aynıw	Toshnota
Painkillers	Awırǵandı qoydıratuǵın dári	Obezbolivayuschiye
I'm allergic to…	Mende…g'a bar	U menya allergia na…
Penicillin	Penitsillin	Penitsillin
Nuts	G'oza	Orehi
Allergy	Allergiya	Allergiya
I was stung by a bee	Meni hárre shaǵıp aldı	Menya ujalila pchela

Appendix 2

FURTHER INFORMATION

In spite of the richness of its history and culture, there are very few books dedicated solely to Karakalpakstan; more often than not, the region is covered in combination with other parts of Uzbekistan and the Silk Road. The advent of digital publishing is giving more Karakalpaks the opportunity to write and publish about their history and culture, however, including in English, and consequently there are now some excellent online resources, which we've listed here in addition to printed books.

BOOKS
Archaeology and history

Boulnois, Luce *Silk Road: Monks, Warriors and Merchants* Odyssey Books & Guides, 2012. Detailed history of the people and ideas that spread along the Silk Road. Also available in French.

Cunliffe, Barry *The Scythians: Nomad Warriors of the Steppe* Oxford University Press, 2019. Authoritative book on the importance of the Scythians from one of Eurasia's greatest archaeologists.

Frankopan, Peter *The Silk Roads: A New History of the World* Bloomsbury, 2015. A superb reinterpretation of world history, with the Silk Road rather than Europe as its principal focus. Hiro, Dilip *Inside Central Asia: A Political and Cultural History of Uzbekistan, Turkmenistan, Kazakhstan, Kyrgyzstan, Tajikistan, Turkey, and Iran* Gerald Duckworth & Co Ltd, 2009. A straightforward introduction to the former Soviet Republics of Central Asia, and their immediate neighbours.

Morrison, Alexander *The Russian Conquest of Central Asia: A Study in Imperial Expansion, 1814–1914* Cambridge University Press, 2020. A deep dive into the history and historiography of Russia's southward expansion.

Thomas, Alun *Nomads and Soviet Rule: Central Asia under Lenin and Stalin* Bloomsbury, 2019. A harrowing portrayal of the impact of Soviet repression on the lives of nomadic peoples.

Tolstov, Sergei *Following the Tracks of Ancient Khorezmian Civilization* UNESCO, 2005. Republished account of the original excavations of the Khorezmian desert fortresses. Translated from Russian.

Culture and traditions

Friends of Nukus Museum *Homage to Savitsky: Collecting 20th-Century Russian and Uzbek Art* Arnoldsche Verlagsanstalt, 2015. Large-format gallery book of the Savitsky Museum in English and German.

Harvey, Janet *Traditional Textiles of Central Asia* Thames & Hudson, 1997. Informative introduction to the textiles of the region, including Karakalpakstan.

Kemery, Becky *Yurts: Architecture in the Round* Gibbs M. Smith Inc, 2006. A complete introduction to yurts, their history, evolution and construction methods.

Khakimov, Akbar (ed) *Atlas of Central Asian Artistic Crafts and Trades* Sharq, 1999. The first volume of this series covers Uzbekistan and has short essays on each craft written by anthropologists and curators.

Knobloch, Edgar *Monuments of Central Asia: A Guide to the Archaeology, Art and Architecture of Turkestan* I B Tauris, 2001. Scholarly overview of artistic styles and influences.

Levin, Theodore, Daukeyeva, Saida & Köchümkulova, Elmira (eds) *The Music of Central Asia* Indiana University Press, 2017. Informative and beautifully illustrated book with an accompanying CD.

Lukonin, Vladimir & Ivanov, Anatoly *Central Asian Art* Parkstone International, 2012. Architectural tour of Central Asia focusing primarily on the influence of Persia and China, Buddhism and Islam. Includes well-produced photographs.

Mkrtychev, Tigran *I.V Savitsky Karakalpakstan State Museum of Art: Collection Highlights* Scala Arts & Heritage Publishers, 2022. Latest international publication about the Savitsky Museum, written by its director.

Richardson, David & Richardson, Sue *The Qaraqalpaqs of the Aral Delta* Prestel Verlag, 2012. The first comprehensive description of the Karakalpaks and their folk art published in English. Richly illustrated.

Rouland, Michael, Abikeyeva, Gulnara & Beumers, Birgit *Cinema in Central Asia: Rewriting Cultural Histories* IB Tauris, 2013. Comprehensive introduction from a historian and the artistic director of the International Eurasia Film Festival.

Literature

Reichl, Karl *Edige: A Karakalpak Oral Epic as performed by Jumabay Bazarov* Academia Scientiarum Fennica, 2007. Translation and discussion of the most famous Karakalpak oral epic, as performed by its most famous singer.

Seisenbayev, Rollan *The Dead Wander in the Desert* Amazon Crossing, 2019. English translation of a novel inspired by the shrinking of the Aral Sea, written by Kazakhstan's best selling author.

Staniland, Andrew, Izentaeva, Gulbahor, Jadigerova, Gulnaz, Urazimbetova, Nargiza, Abdullaeva, Nilufar & Tursinbaeva, Shaxnoza (trans) *Three Karakalpak Poets* Independently published, 2023. New English translation of works by two historic Karakalpak poets, Ajiniyaz and Berdaq, and one contemporary poet, Ibrayim Yusupov.

Utegenov, Quatbay *Karakalpak Folk Tales* Trafford Publishing, 2006. English translation of traditional Karakalpak, Kazakh and Uzbek folk tales.

Nature and environment

Ayé, R, Schweizer, M & Roth, T *The Birds of Central Asia* Christopher Helm, Bloomsbury, 2012. A useful field guide for birders.

Peterson, Maya K *Pipe Dreams: Water and Empire in Central Asia's Aral Sea Basin* Cambridge University Press, 2021. A superb contribution to Central Asian and environmental history, focusing on irrigation, the Amu Darya and the Aral Sea.

Xenarios, Stefanos et al *The Aral Sea Basin: Water for Sustainable Development in Central Asia* Routledge, 2021. Multidisciplinary overview of water resources issues and management in the Amu Darya and Syr Darya basins.

Travel writing

Maillart, Ella *Turkestan Solo: A Journey through Central Asia* Bloomsbury, 2005. Journey across Russian Turkestan in the 1930s by a Swiss athlete, writer and photographer.

Metcalfe, Daniel *Out of Steppe* Arrow, 2009. Metcalfe traverses Central Asia in pursuit of distinct ethnic communities – including the Karakalpaks – who are disappearing as modernity impinges on their way of life.

Thubron, Colin *The Lost Heart of Asia* Heinemann, 1994. The celebrated travel writer journeys through Central Asia soon after the emergence of the independent republics.

Other Central Asia guides

For a full list of Bradt's guides, visit w bradtguides.com/shop.

Brummell, Paul *Kazakhstan* Bradt, 2018
Ibbotson, Sophie *Tajikistan* Bradt, 2019
Ibbotson, Sophie *Uzbekistan* Bradt, 2020
Mitchell, Laurence *Kyrgyzstan* Bradt, 2019

WEBSITES
Official government sites

w **e-visa.gov.uz** Electronic visa portal for nationals ineligible for visa-free entry to Uzbekistan.

w **gov.uk/foreign-travel-advice/uzbekistan** British Foreign Office travel advice for Uzbekistan.

w **gov.uk/world/organisations/british-embassy-tashkent** British Embassy in Tashkent.

w **karakalpakstan.travel** Tourist information site developed with the support of UNESCO.

w **karakalpakstan.uz/** Government portal of the Republic of Karakalpakstan, including contact details and official statistics.

w **tugai.uz** Information about the Lower Amudarya State Biosphere Reserve.

w **uzbekistan.travel/en** National tourism website of Uzbekistan, including Karakalpakstan. It is more up to date but less detailed than karakalpakstan.travel (see above) and is useful if you are planning to combine Karakalpakstan with other parts of Uzbekistan.

w **uzembassy.uk** Uzbek Embassy in London.

w **uznature.uz** The Ministry of Natural Resources has wide-ranging responsibilities, including for ecology and environment protection, and issuing permits for national parks and other protected areas.

News and political analysis

w **bbc.co.uk/uzbek** Home of the BBC Uzbek news service (in Uzbek).

w **eurasianet.org** Independent news and analysis covering Central Asian on a site funded by donors including the UK Foreign Office, Google & the Open Society Foundations.

w **novastan.org/en** A wide range of news from Central Asia, available in English, French and German, published by the non-profit association Novastan France.

w **thebulletin.news** Independent news site covering Central Asia and the Caucasus, founded in 2010 by the *Daily Telegraph*'s former Central Asia correspondent.

Other interesting or useful sites

w **beyondcatastrophe.com** Articles and resources exploring a positive future for the Aral Sea region, created by a small team of independent film makers and researchers.

w **caravanistan.com** The most comprehensive online guide to travelling in Central Asia, published by husband and wife team Steven and Saul Hermans. The site's primary use is for information resources but they can also arrange bespoke tours.

w **karakalpak.com** An online companion to the superb *The Qaraqalpaqs of the Aral Delta* (page 200), this website is an encyclopedia on the history and culture of the Karakalpaks.

w **orientalarchitecture.com** Detailed and authoritative guide to historical monuments including many of Karakalpakstan's fortresses, with plenty of photographs.

w **oxussociety.org** Washington-based non-profit dedicated to fostering academic exchange between Central Asia and the rest of the world, with well-researched and informative articles on contemporary issues

w **rsaa.org.uk** Royal Society for Asian Affairs, founded as the Central Asia Society in 1901. Regular events & articles about Central Asia, as well as an extensive library and archive of historic photos, maps, etc.

w **stihia.org** Official website of the Stihia festival.

Index

Page numbers in **bold** indicate major entries; those in *italics* indicate maps.

INDEX OF ADVERTISERS

Central Asia
Unlocked

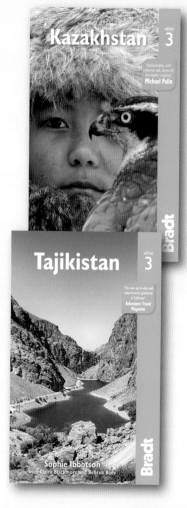

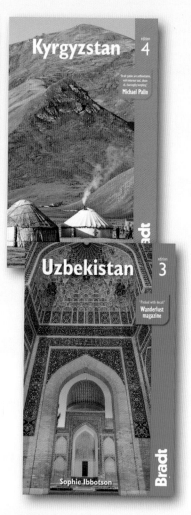

Bradt GUIDES

TRAVEL TAKEN SERIOUSLY